**W9-AOY-837**

# CREATURES IN THE MIST

# CREATURES IN THE MIST

## Little People, Wild Men and Spirit Beings around the World

### A Study in Comparative Mythology

Gary R. Varner

Algora Publishing
New York

ISBN-13: 978-0-87586-545-4 (trade paper)
ISBN-13: 978-0-87586-546-1 (hard cover)
ISBN-13: 978-0-87586-547-8 (ebook)

Library of Congress Cataloging-in-Publication Data —

Varner, Gary R.
  Creatures in the mist: little people, wild men and spirit beings around the world : a
study in comparative mythology / Gary R. Varner.
      p. cm.
  Includes bibliographical references and index.
      ISBN 978-0-87586-545-4 (trade paper: alk. paper) — ISBN 978-0-87586-546-1 (hard
cover: alk. paper) — ISBN 978-0-87586-547-8 (ebook) 1.  Mythology—Comparative
studies.  I. Title.

  BL312.V27 2007
  398.4—dc22

                         2006102141

Front Cover: © Layne Kennedy/Corbis
Howling Wolf on Mountain Peak © Corbis

Printed in the United States

For Tim and Brenna

# Other Books by Gary R. Varner

*Essays in Contemporary Paganism,* 2000

*Sacred Wells: A Study in the History, Meaning, and Mythology of Holy Wells & Waters,* 2002

*Water of Life — Water of Death: The Folklore & Mythology of Sacred Waters,* 2004

*Menhirs, Dolmen and Circles of Stone: The Folklore & Magic of Sacred Stone,* Algora Publishing, 2004

*The Mythic Forest, the Green Man and the Spirit of Nature,* Algora Publishing, 2006

*Strangely Wrought Creatures of Life & Death: Ancient Symbolism in European and American Architecture,* 2006

*The Dark Wind: Witches and the Concept of Evil,* 2007

# Acknowledgements

This book could not have been written without the people who have been recording folklore around the world for the last two centuries. Lewis Spence, Alexander Porteous, Lady Wilde, Anne Ross, James Mooney, Joseph Campbell, Mircea Eliade, John Gregorson Campbell, Donald A. Mackenzie, Sir James Frazer, H.R. Ellis Davidson, Carl Jung and Jyoti Sahi are just a few of those scholars, living and dead, that have offered so much to the study of the rituals and beliefs of human beings around the world and throughout time. I offer my thanks and gratitude for their work.

Thanks to Dr. Brian Siegel, Anthropologist, Sociology Department at Furman University, Greenville, South Carolina for permission to quote from his paper "Water Spirits and Mermaids: The Copperbelt Case."[1] Thanks also to David Catherine, formerly of the University of Kwazulu-Natal, South Africa for his assistance in providing materials on the indigenous traditions of the people of South Africa in regards to water spirits and water in general.

The line drawing illustrations that appear in this book are in the public domain. The Wild Man appearing in Chapter 7 is taken from *The Sports and Pastimes of the English People* by Joseph Strutt, published 1801. The drawings of the mermaid, the Snake People of Hell and the illustration on the title page are taken from *Adventures of Telemachus*, published by D. Appleton & Company, New York, ca. 1889. The other line drawings are from *The Complete Encyclopedia of Illustration* by J. G. Heck, published by Gramercy Books, New York, 1979. This is a reproduction of two of the four volumes of *The Iconographic Encyclopaedia of Science, Literature, and Art* published in 1851 by R. Garrigue, New York. The photographs of the Native American snake petroglyph in Arizona, the antlered-man pub sign in Ashland, Oregon, the bat carving on the Chester Cathedral in Chester, England, the Harpy that resides in the British Museum and the photo of Bast were taken by the author.

Gary R. Varner
California

---

1 A paper given at the Spring 2000 Southeastern Regional Seminar in African Studies (SERSAS), Western Carolina University, Cullowhee, North Carolina on April 14 & 15, 2000.

# TABLE OF CONTENTS

# Introduction

Little People, Fairies, Giants, Mermaids, Werewolves and Wild Men. Do we simply regard them all as products of the universal unconscious mind — a mind that stretches between cultures, times and geographic location? On the other hand, do we assign a possibility that they may be based on reality, or at least a reality that co-exists within our own sense of reality?

This question is not a new one by any means. Douglas Hyde, President of the Gaelic League at the turn of the 20th century wrote, "the problem we have to deal with is a startling one...Are these beings of the spirit world real beings, having a veritable existence of their own, or are they only the creation of the imagination of...informants, and the tradition of bygone centuries?...Is not the Mermaid to be found in Greece, and is not the Lorelei as Germanic as the Kelpy is Caledonian. If we grant that all these are creatures of primitive folk-belief, then how they come to be so ceases to be a Celtic problem, it becomes a world problem."[1]

What we do know is that accounts of "Little People," Fairies, Wild Men and giants are common among Native American people as they are among the people of Europe, Africa and Asia. Many of their stories and descriptions are for the most part, identical. Why is this? I am afraid that I do not have an answer to this question (only guesses) and can only provide more related folklore, theories and suppositions for consideration. I hope that by the end of this study you will be able to decide for yourself.

1. Hyde, Douglas. "Taking of Evidence in Ireland" in *The Fairy-Faith in Celtic Countries.* Mineola: Dover Publications Inc. 2002, pgs 25, 28. A reprint of the 1911 edition published by Henry Frowde, London.

The scope of this work is the folklore and mythology of Native American and the other indigenous people of the world. Part One is concerned primarily with the mystical creatures that are spoken of and written about for thousands of years in most every corner of the world. Part Two is about the spirit beings appearing in animal and insect form that have accompanied spiritual belief and traditions around the world. These spirit beings are universally recognized for many similar reasons. We will compare their accounts with similar tales from other times and places, and explore the commonality of these legends.

This book is admittedly one of a broad study. I have brought together many tales of a mythic and folkloric nature to illustrate how universal our beliefs truly are — not how different one culture is from the next, but how similar they are. Even though Victorian writers are no longer in favor these days, the Victorians were the best at collecting and relating folktales from many different cultures, so they cannot be left out. These references are based upon first hand knowledge of many indigenous people that no longer exist either physically or culturally. A book which deals with worldwide phenomena and oral histories must be approached in a way that allows a global comparison. Those who discount everything said by Victorian scholars such as Sir James Frazer because he made some assumptions that were later found to be incorrect do the rest of us a major disservice. A huge amount of knowledge would be lost without these works.

The subjects for this book were chosen because they are recognized the world over. Fairies and Wild Men, mermaids and giants have been important in many cultures throughout time. The twelve animal/insect spirits in Part Two were chosen for the same reason. By showing the similarities as well as the differences of these stories, we show the common mythic root that we all have. We also see that the importance of these subjects remains with all of us even today.

This book has been written with a broad readership in mind. It is written for individuals who are curious about history and ancient traditions and how these traditions are linked to the rest of humankind, regardless of geography or time. It is also written so that many of these ancient customs and traditions, superstitions and beliefs may be remembered, at least in book form. Anytime we lose facts, folklore, or other details of our history, we also lose much more that links all people together in our common experiences.

Finally, this book has been written to create questions and to challenge readers to conduct further exploratory research on their own so that other possibilities and realities may be experienced.

PART ONE

LITTLE PEOPLE AND GIANTS, WILD MEN,
MERMAIDS AND OTHER MYTHIC CREATURES

# Chapter 1. An Overview of the "Little People" in Native America

When we think of Fairy lore, many of us in the US naturally think of Ireland. However, Fairies appear in the folklore of most every culture and on every continent. The similarities are striking and some have suggested that a common source memory exists or existed widely among people at one time. John Rhys advanced this theory at the beginning of the 20th century. Rhys thought that the lore of the Fairy were ancient stories of the original inhabitants of Britain. They were called the "Corannians" in Wales, and Rhys believed that the name was derived from the word *cor*, which meant, "dwarf."

American 19th century ethnologist James Mooney, who studied American Indians in the minutest details, wrote: "The belief in fairies and kindred spirits, frequently appearing as diminutive beings in human form, is so universal among all races as to render citation of parallels unnecessary...usually benevolent and kindly when not disturbed, but often mischievous, and in rare cases malicious and revengeful."[1]

The Little People were thought to affect the minds of sane people. According to the Creek Indians in the 1800s, "Fairies or little people live in hollow trees and on rocky cliffs. They often decoy people from their homes and lose them in the woods. When a man's mind becomes bewildered — not crazy — this is caused by the little people."[2]

The Cherokee believed that the Falls of Tallulah, in northeastern Georgia, were occupied by a race of tiny people who lived in the rocks and grottos under the waterfalls. Known as the *Nûñnĕ'hĭ*, or the "immortals," they

---

1. Mooney, James. *Myths of the Cherokee.* New York: Dover Publications 1995, 475. A reprint of the 1900 publication "Nineteenth Annual Report of the Bureau of American Ethnology, 1897-98.
2. Mooney, op. cit., 476.

were thought to be no larger than children but were well formed with hair reaching to their feet. The tiny people exhibited a dual nature, being both helpful to humans as well as hostile — should anyone see the Immortals at their work, they would die. Because of this hostility, the Cherokee hunters and fishers avoided the falls. Mooney reported that just a few years prior to the turn of the 20th century, "two hunters from Raventown, going behind the high fall near the head of the Oconaluftee on the East Cherokee reservation, found there a cave with fresh footprints of the Little People all over the floor."[3] A belief in an inherent hostility on the part of the Fairy toward humans is not restricted to those in the Americas.

The Cherokee say that the *Yûñwĭ Tsunsdi'* or the "Little People," were known to help lost children, the ill and wounded, and would help the Indians with their work at night. Cherokee fishermen would pray to the Water-dwellers, a type of Fairy that lived in the water. Hunters also had Fairy people, called the *Tsăwa'sĭ*, to pray to for guidance. They were tiny, well-formed people with hair to the ground and had great power over game animals.

A similar being was familiar to the Iroquois. These Little People often dispensed wisdom and gifts of magic and it is said that a human in the company of one of these creatures does not age.[4]

The Yana Indians who lived along the Sacramento River adjacent to what is now Lassen National Park believed in a race of malignant little people, called *yo-yautsgi*, who appeared to be the size of small children but had the reputation of enticing travelers and eating them.

The Seri Indians who live on Tiburon Island in the Gulf of California, said at one time to be the "wildest and most primitive tribe surviving in North America",[5] speak of Abtiso'ma. It is said he is "the size of a child, has a beard, a golden staff, white clothes inside and black outside"; he lives in a cave and reportedly stole a young man "in order to dress him nicely."[6]

Little People also figured in the lore of the Maliseet-Passamquoddy tribes that occupied the area that is now Maine and New Brunswick. The Little People were thought to have "made concretions of sand and clay along the stream banks. Through the objects they leave behind one can divine the future. A small coffin-shaped object forewarned death."[7]

The "ruler of water" recognized by the Araucanians in the Tierra del Fuego region of South America sometimes appears as a "tiny manikin...with

3. Ibid., 329-330.
4. Blackman, W. Haden. *The Field Guide to North American Monsters*. New York: Three Rivers Press 1998, 123.
5. Kroeber, A. L. *The Seri*. Southwest Museum Papers Number Six. Los Angeles: Southwest Museum, April 1931, 3.
6. Ibid., 15.
7. Erickson, Vincent O. "Maliseet-Passamaquoddy" in *Handbook of North American Indians*, Vol. 15: Northeast. Edited by Bruce G. Trigger. Washington: Smithsonian Institution 1978, 133

dark skin and curly hair." Known as Sompallwe, he is, however, "more feared than reverenced."[8]

Among the Indian tribes of California, many of the Fairy were called "Water Babies" or "Rock Babies." Described as small, dwarf-like men in traditional Indian dress with long hair, the Water Babies were regarded as unusually potent spirit helpers, which lived along streams and water holes. The Water Baby was believed to enhance the power of the shaman. Archaeologist David S. Whitley remarked that "the sighting of Water Baby was believed to result in death — a metaphor, in fact, for entering or being in an altered state of consciousness."[9]

In the Owens Valley between California and Nevada is a large rock art complex known as Red Canyon. Here are found large rock outcroppings with unusual rock art. The stone is covered with small, engraved human-like footprints said to be those of the Water Baby. Next to the Water Baby tracks are engraved bear tracks, which appear to be walking in the same direction.

As noted above, Water Babies are an important aspect in the folklore of most Indian cultures in the Great Basin. The Kawaiisu mythology includes a story on the origin of these beings, which are called the *Pagazozi*. Ethnologist Maurice L. Zigmond noted that the term *Pagazozi* refers to a people who lived to the north of the Kawaiisu and also to "a queer people, i.e. mythological. They are 'water people'".[10] According to legend, the trickster god Coyote fell into the water at Owens Lake and as he floated to the surface "big worms" emerged from his hide and swam to shore, transforming into people as they transitioned from the water to the land.[11] This legend is a short but important one, tying the origin of the Water Babies directly from a god through the medium of water where they not only live but from where their powers are also generated.

There are hundreds of lakes in the Pacific Northwest between Mount Adams and Mount Rainier and a majority of them are reported to be inhabited by strange animals and spirits. Ella Clark noted in her book, *Indian Legends of the Pacific Northwest*, that these spirits were of little children "who had lived in the days of the ancient people. Their cries sometimes broke the silence of the nighttime. The next morning," according to Clark, "the prints of their little naked feet were found in the wet sand along the margin of the lake."[12] Are these spirits the same spirits of the Water Babies?

Among the Chinook Indians of Oregon and Washington, a race of little people known as the *Kwak-wa-etai-mewh* existed. These little people had

8. Krickeberg, Walter, et al. *Pre-Columbian American Religions.* New York: Holt, Rinehart and Winston 1968, 264.

9. Whitley, David S. *A Guide to Rock Art Sites: Southern California and Southern Nevada.* Missoula: Mountain Press Publishing Company 1996, 53.

10. Zigmond, Maurice L. *Kawaiisu Mythology: An Oral Tradition of South-Central California.* Ballena Press Anthropological Papers No. 18. Menlo Park: Ballena Press 1980, 55.

11. Ibid.

12. Clark, Ella E. *Indian Legends of the Pacific Northwest.* Berkeley: University of California Press 1953, 51.

beaks instead of mouths, ate shells and, according to legend, while their skin was protection enough against knives or arrows, the feathers of birds could inflict mortal injury. According to 19th century ethnologist George Gibbs, the *Kwak-wa-etai-mewh* "are not withstanding their size very strong, and one of them can paddle a great canoe by himself and catch it full of salmon, halibut and sturgeon."[13]

The Lakota believed in a race of "ugly" small men and women that they referred to as "tree dwellers." Similar to tales of other Fairy folk around the world, the tree dwellers, called *Can Otidan*, reportedly stayed in the woods and forests and "would lure hunters away and lose them or they would frighten them so that they would lose their senses."[14] The *Can Otidan* apparently were more than simple Fairy spirits as they were classed in a group referred to as "bad gods".

Little people[15] referred to as "travel-two" were among the forest spirits in the Nehalem Tillamook (Oregon) world. Called "travel-two" because they always traveled in pairs, these Fairy-like creatures were hunters and would often give a human they encountered on their travels the skills to become a good hunter — if the travel-two happened to speak with him.[16]

In New Brunswick, Canada, the Little People are called *Geow-lud-mo-sis-eg*. There are two types of these creatures, one Healers and the other Tricksters. The Healers are said to do "some super marvelous things for a person who may be stricken or inflicted with some kind of physical ailment." The Tricksters, as their name implies, play pranks and tricks on people that are more annoying than they are dangerous. Both types of Fairy are closely linked to water sites such as lake shores, rivers, brooks and marshes.[17]

Whitley believes that the belief in "little people" worldwide may be the effect of certain hallucinogens, used by shamans, which temporarily change the optic nerve. When this happens, according to Whitley, an unusual "Lilliputian hallucination" takes place that makes everything appear much smaller than it is in "reality." This is an interesting hypothesis; however, it is not convincing in itself. The thousands of legends from around the world of Fairy and Water Babies have not been sourced from shamans alone. It would also seem logical that if a hallucinogen were responsible, then stories of other diminutive creatures (deer, birds, etc) and landscapes would also be contained in the mythic literature — and they simply aren't. Such beliefs may stem from the effects of poor nutrition, as periodic food shortages and seasonal

13. Clark, Ella E., editor. "George Gibbs' Account of Indian Mythology of Oregon and Washington Territories" in *Oregon Historical Quarterly* Vol. LVI, Number 4, December 1955, 309.

14. Walker, James R. *Lakota Belief and Ritual*. Lincoln: University of Nebraska Press 1991, 107.

15. Other "little folk" in Tillamook lore are the dit'kátu who lived in lakes. He is described as "like a little brownie, about one and a half feet high."

16. Jacobs, Elizabeth D. *The Nehalem Tillamook: An Ethnography.* Corvallis: Oregon State University Press 2003, 182.

17. Paul, Pat. "Little People: Geow-Lud-Mo-Sis-Eg". ramseyc@nbnet.nb.ca.

shortages of fruit and vegetables would routinely cause vitamin deficiencies of the type that may be associated with signs of delirium.

Much of the rock art located in certain areas are said to be the work of Rock Babies who actually live within the rock surfaces — normally also near water sources. The Kawaiisu, living in the area around the southern Sierra Nevadas in California and Nevada, call the Rock Babies "uwani azi," derived from "uwa uwa," which is said to reflect the sound of a baby crying.

Ethnologist Maurice Zigmond reported that the Rock Baby are believed to be responsible for many of the pictographs in the Kawaiisu territory and they are never finished working on them — as indicated by the changing patterns of the rock art. The pictographs of the Rock Baby are character-ized by the use of at least five colors rather than the one or two colors used by humans. "Both the Rock Baby and his pictographs are 'out of bounds' for people," says Zigmond, "the paintings may be looked at without danger, but touching them will lead to quick disaster. One who puts his fingers on them and then rubs his eyes will not sleep again but will die in three days."[18] De-scribed as looking just like a baby, with short black hair, the Rock Baby is seldom seen but more commonly heard. To see one is to court disaster. Like the Fairy, the Rock Baby is also capable of stealing human babies and ex-changing them for non-human look-alikes.

Like the Kawaiisu, the Mono Indians living around the Mono Lake area also believed in a water-spirit similar to the Water or Rock Baby. Called Pauwiha, they live in springs and rivers and can cause illness. According to Mono Indian Gaylen D. Lee, "Pauwiha has long, very shiny hair, sometimes blond, sometimes black, but it is never seen, because it jumps back into the spring when someone approaches...if, by chance, Pauwiha is glimpsed, only its hair and body are seen, never its face. If the face is seen...the person be-comes 'sick, many different ways'."[19] Rock art sites were also out-of-bounds with the Mono as well. "Don't go near there," Gaylen Lee was told, "because they're places of power."[20]

A small race of mysterious beings called *Surem*, that some believe to be the ancestors of the Yaqui Indians in Mexico, live in the Sonoran Desert. These people, about three feet tall, are considered nomads who do not fall ill or know death and are able to communicate not only with animals but also with plants. "The little people moved about," says writers Carol and Dinah Mack, "and carried a lake with them, rolled up like a carpet, and whenever they needed water or fish, they would unroll the lake and fish in it."[21] Legend says that the Surem still live in the Sonoran Desert today but in a parallel universe where the world still exists in its wild state.

18. Zigmond, Op. cit.

19. Lee, Gaylen D. *Walking where we lived: Memoirs of a Mono Indian Family.* Norman: University of Oklahoma Press 1998, 36.

20. Ibid., 39.

21. Mack, Carol K. and Dinah Mack. *A Field Guide to Demons, Fairies, Fallen Angels, and Other Subversive Spirits.* New York: Owl Books 1998, 139.

Similar beings are those called *chaneques,* which have been part of Olmec culture since 1500 BCE. These creatures, similar to Water Babies, are still believed in today and are described as "old dwarfs with faces of children."[22] The chaneques live in waterfalls, dominate wild animals and fish, and are truly wild in nature. They can cause illnesses, foresee rain, and are said to eat the brains of humans. To buy their good behavior it is a practice to provide the chaneques with buckets of water, which is regarded as "the magic food."[23]

The Yupa Indians, located in the mountains between Columbia and Venezuela known as the Sierra de Perijá, also tell tales of a race of dwarfs known to them as the Pïpïntu. In a story similar to that told by the Kawaiisu in California, the Pïpïntu live in a world almost identical to our own and yet it is different. Entering a large cave of the dead and working yourself through a small opening in the rocks is the only way to find them. Yupa lore describes them as "sporting long beards, but without hair on their heads (which they lost because the waste of all humanity falls down upon their heads from the world above)." The Pïpïntu are said to be very friendly but obtain almost all of their nourishment by breathing in smoke from their fire; they are unable to eat food through their mouths because they have neither intestines nor anuses.[24]

It should be noted that the Yupa believe some of this race of pygmy Indians intermarried with them, and their abilities in warfare are legendary. Anthropologist Johannes Wilbert, who worked among the Yupa, wrote that according to the Yupa, "the white man is easy to kill because he can't see us with his blue eyes, but the Pïpïntu move quickly and sometimes we can't see them."[25]

The story is an interesting one in that a true race of pygmies exists with characteristics attributed to other "little people" around the world. The mythic Pïpïntu also live in a parallel world to our own, on the other side of a rock barrier inside a large cave used to bury the dead.

The Fairies were also a common theme in Polynesian mythology. Among the Maori the Fairy are described as fair-skinned with light or reddish hair; they eat only raw, uncooked food, never age, are fond of dancing and music (but dislike singing after dark), and traverse between our world and the spirit world through a magical fountain. The Fairy of Hawaii, it is said, are "so small and industrious (that) any task undertaken must be finished in a single night."[26] All of the characteristics noted for the Polynesian Fairy are commonly recorded throughout the world in other folklore accounts.

---

22. Berrnal, Ignacio. *The Olmec World.* Berkeley: University of California Press 1969, 100.

23. Ibid.

24. Wilbert, Johannes. *Yupa Folktales.* Latin American Studies Volume 24. Los Angeles: Latin American Center, University of California 1974, 87.

25. Ibid., 12-13.

26. Andersen, Johannes C. *Myths and Legends of the Polynesians.* Rutland: Charles E. Tuttle Company: Publishers 1969, 137.

Not only the Fairy but also "water cannibals" live at the bottom of rivers, springs and lakes. Some American Indian tribes called them "River Mermaids," spirits who lure unsuspecting individuals to the water's edge and then pull them down to their deaths. The Northern California Yana called these spirits *hat-en-*na or "water grizzlies" and described them as creatures with white and black spots. Cherokee mythology places this creature at the bottom of deep rivers where they await the chance to sneak out to find someone, preferably a child, asleep. They then "shoot him with their invisible arrows and carry the dead body down under water to feast upon it."[27] Like the elves, they leave a changeling or "shade" in the individual's place, which acts like a human but withers and dies within seven days.

According to Schoolcraft, the Fairy of the Algonquin "comprise two classes, into which they are divided according as the location of their haunts is either on the land, or in the water. The favorite residence of their land fairies is the vicinity of promontories and water-falls, and in solemn groves. Besides furnishing a habitation for its appropriate class of fairies, the water is supposed to be the residence of an animal called *nibau-auba*, which has its counterpart, except as to sex, in the mermaid. The Indian word indicates a male."[28]

The next chapter will discuss these mysterious water beings.

27. Mooney, op. cit. 349.
28. Schoolcraft, Henry Rowe. *History of the Indian Tribes of the United States: Their Present Condition and Prospects, and a Sketch of their Ancient Status.* Philadelphia: J. B. Lippincott & Co. 1857, 662.

# Chapter 2. Mermaids & Water Beings

Stories about mermen and mermaids can be traced back to ancient Babylonian mythology, from the Old Babylonian times onward through the history of Mesopotamia and into the modern world. In fact, as Richard Carrington
so aptly put it, "There is not an age, and hardly a country in the world, whose
folklore does not contain some reference to mermaids or to mermaid-like
creatures. They have been alleged to appear in a hundred different places,
ranging from the mist-covered shores of Norway and Newfoundland to the
palm-studded islands of the tropic seas."[1]

The Babylonian god Oannes, a half-man half-fish deity, has been depicted
on sculptures dating back at least to 2000 BCE. Like all mermen, he is shown
with the body of a man but from the waist down, he is in the form of a fish.
Oannes taught the Babylonians the arts, sciences and letters and possessed
vast knowledge.

"To the Assyrians," wrote Jeremy Black and Anthony Green, "the creature was known simply as kulullû, 'fish-man'...representations of these figures
were used in Neo-Assyrian art for the purpose of protective nature..."[2] This
"fish-man," wrote Black and Green, "is perhaps the prototype for the merman figure in Greek and medieval European art and literary tradition."[3] The
kulullû obviously was an important mystical symbol for the Babylonians as
priests were often garbed in the fish-man guise as part of healing rituals.

The ancient grain god of the Philistines, Dagon or Dagan, was half man
and half fish, although Black and Green dispute this. According to them, "A

---

1. Carrington, Richard. *Mermaids and Mastodons: A Book of Natural & Unnatural History.*
New York: Rinehart & Company, Inc. 1957, 5.
2. Black, Jeremy & Anthony Green. *Gods, Demons and Symbols of Ancient Mesopotamia.*
Austin: University of Texas Press 1992, 131-132.
3. Ibid., 131.

tradition dating back at least to the fourth century AD of Dagan as a fish deity is erroneous."[4] Dagon was worshipped in most of the Near East as an ancient grain god and inventor of the plough and it would seem implausible that he could be referred to as a fish-god at the same time.

Vishnu, one of the most venerated and sophisticated deities of the Hindu pantheon, known as the "preserver and restorer," is depicted at times as a man-fish. One of his forms is that of Matsya, the Fish, which saved humankind from the Flood. According to traditional lore, Vishnu, in the form of a fish, told King Manu that a flood would occur in seven days. He told the king to build a boat and to ensure that the seven sages, or hermits, were on board along with seeds of all plants and one animal of each species. When the boat was finished and loaded, the fish (Vishnu) told the king to tie the boat to the fish. The king used the royal serpent Vasuki as a rope and tied the boat to the back of the giant fish. The fish then towed the boat to Mt. Himavan until the flood waters receded. The world was then able to be repopulated with plants, animals and humankind. Matsya is Vishnu's first incarnation as a protector and preserver of the world.

*Shiva as Matsya, the Fish*

Folklorist Horace Beck wrote "it is my belief that what we are dealing with when discussing...mermaids is really a fractured mythology — beliefs so old as possibly to reach back to Neolithic times, beliefs long since vanished into limbo, with only fragments remaining."[5] Beck believes that the core myths of the mermaids have a northern European origin but I believe that they have a common origin that was "hard wired" in our minds as a species and not as geographical mythology. It would seem that a common religious and cultural tradition existed at one time in our ancient history; a tradition that still surfaces now and then in our mythology and folklore. Like the Fairy, the legend of the mermaids may also come from this tradition.

Mythic stories of mermaids, nymphs and water spirits may be survival tales of the sea goddesses. Through time, the original stories became more and more elaborate and took on a flavor of their own from the people who passed the stories on. Folklorist Shahrukh Husain, in her book *The Goddess*, wrote, "the sea goddess survives in a debased form as water-sprites, sirens or mermaids. Probably the first mermaids were images of the fish-tailed Aphro-

4. Black and Green, op. cit. 56.
5. Beck, Horace. *Folklore and the Sea.* Mystic: Mystic Seaport Museum Incorporated 1973, 266.

dite — they are famously able to seduce men away from the land, and draw them down to their underwater kingdom. A reminder of their lost divinity lies in the tales of a mermaid....receiving the souls of drowned men."[6]

Part of the fascination we have with Mermaids is not only their beauty, but also the danger associated with them. In fact, according to Joseph Campbell, the mermaid image reflects the life-threatening as well as the life-furthering aspects of water.[7] Legends of sailors capturing these creatures for a short time or living with them longer as husband and wife are interspersed with other stories with more dire results. Fiske noted, "it has been a common superstition among sailors, that the appearance of a mermaid, with her hair comb and looking-glass, foretokens shipwreck, with the loss of all on board."[8]

Native Americans possess many legends of River Mermaids. The ancient Greeks had Eurynome, who was said to be the daughter of the god Oceanus. Eurynome was "a woman down to the buttocks and below that like a fish".[9] Of Eurynome Brewster wrote she "was most probably a local river nymph with the body like a mermaid's."[10]

*19th century rendering of the mermaid*

In Nigeria, the Benin people also speak of mermaids. In Benin folklore the River goddess Igbaghon ruled the underworld, which was below the water. She was waited upon by mermaids who informed her of trespassers who went to the river to wash or to fetch water — they never returned from their tasks.[11]

South African anthropologist Penny Bernard, who has studied water spirit lore and traditions in that part of the world, has found that many of the traits of the Native American river mermaids also exist in South African tribal beliefs. These water spirits are re-

6. Husain, Shahrukh. *The Goddess.* Alexandria: Time-Life Books 1997, 51.

7. Campbell, Joseph. *The Masks of God: Primitive Mythology.* New York: The Viking Press 1959, 62.

8. Fiske, John. *Myths and Myth-Makers: Old Tales and Superstitions Interpreted by Comparative Mythology.* Boston: Houghton, Mifflin and Company 1881, 103.

9. Brewster, Harry. *The River Gods of Greece: Myths and Mountain Waters in the Hellenic World.* London: I.B. Tauris & Co. Ltd. 1997, 97.

10. Ibid.

11. Osoba, Funmi. *Benin Folklore: A Collection of Classic Folktales and Legends.* London: Hadada Books 1993, 40.

ferred to as the "River People" and are believed to live in certain deep pools of water, especially below waterfalls. Bernard notes, "some informants say they are fair skinned, with long dark hair, are naked and some have half-human, half-fish physical attributes (mermaid like)."[12] She also reports that these creatures only live in "living water" — that is, water that is flowing in rivers, the ocean or waterfalls. Some, however, are also reported to reside in wells in Zimbabwe. Normally this tradition is found only in the more arid areas of Africa.

Water spirits cannot simply be dismissed as metaphors. The almost universal application of human-like characteristics and supra-natural powers, like those of the Fairies, demands a broader approach. At least through the 19th century, the people of Norway left offerings to water spirits every Christmas Day. The following account appeared in the December 17, 1859 issue of the British journal, *Notes & Queries:*

> ...a fisherman wished on Christmas Day to give the Spirit of the Waters a cake; but when he came to the shore, lo! the waters were frozen over. Unwilling to leave his offering upon the ice, and so to give the Spirit the trouble of breaking the ice to obtain it, the fisherman took a pickaxe, and set to work to break a hole in the ice. In spite of all his labour he was only able to make a very small hole, not nearly large enough for him to put the cake through. Having laid the cake on the ice, while he thought what was best to be done, suddenly a very tiny little hand as white as snow was stretched through the hole, which seizing the cake and crumpling it up together, withdrew with it. Ever since that time the cakes have been so small that the Water Spirits have had no trouble with them.

In the folklore of Tobago, the mer-people are always male and live in the deep sea but they mate with "fairymaids" that live in the rivers and "secret mountain pools." These fairymaids are described as beautiful with long lush hair and one foot shaped like a deer's hoof. The fairymaid is said to live in caves behind waterfalls, near waterwheels and under bridges over deep rivers. The fairymaids of Tobago appear to have many similar traits to the river mermaids of American Indian lore.

According to Beck, mermaids and Fairies may have a common origin. Mermaids "seem to be related to the Celtic fairies through their coloring, the name — Marie Morgane — and their underwater cities, love of music and ability to grant gifts."[13]

Mysterious water creatures have been reported throughout the world's folklore for hundreds and thousands of years. Like the Fairy, these creatures also have almost universal characteristics and descriptions. California Miwok Indians called these creatures *He-Há-Pe*, or "River Mermaids" and described them as "beautiful fish-women [that] had long black hair and lived

---

12. Bernard, Penny. "Mermaids, Snakes and the Spirits of the Water in Southern Africa: Implications for River Health", lecture given in *Short Course on the Role and Use of Aquatic Biomonitoring.* Rhodes University, Grahamstown, South Africa, 2000.
13. Beck, Op. cit., 265.

in deep pools and rivers".[14] Other California tribes referred to these creatures as "Water Women" in their mythology. The "River Mermaids" reportedly pulled victims to their deaths in these deep waters.[15]

Nineteenth-century writer S. Baring-Gould reported several instances of the capture of supposed mer-people. One such instance was the capture of a "Marmennill" or merman off the Icelandic island of Grimsey in the early 14th century; one also reportedly washed up on the beaches of Suffolk in 1187.[16] Baring-Gould notes other cases as well of mermen not only being seen but caught in 1305 and 1329 off Iceland; 1430 in Holland; 1531 in the Baltic; 1560 on an island west of Ceylon; and 1714 in the West Indies.

According to Baring-Gould, the 1560 incident occurred near the island of Mandar. It was here that "some fishermen entrapped in their net seven mermen and mermaids, of which several Jesuits, and Father Henriques, and Bosquez, physician to the Viceroy of Goa, were witnesses. The physician examined them with a great deal of care, and dissected them. He asserts that the internal and external structure resembled that of human beings."[17] Baring-Gould gives several other accounts of mer-folk being captured and examined by sailors and other villagers from Ceylon, Holland and the Shetland Islands. Other reported sightings include one made by Henry Hudson's men on June 15, 1608; Captain Richard Whitbourne in 1620 at St. John's Harbor in Newfoundland; and Captain John Smith in 1614 in the West Indies. Even today, mermaids are reportedly commonly seen near the Isle of Man.

John C. Messenger, in his ethnography of a small Irish island he called Inis Beag, noted during his study that "At least one and maybe three mermaids are associated with particular locations along the coastline of the island. The spirit usually is found sitting on a rock with her tail in the water and combing her long hair, although she has been seen hovering over the surface of the sea in a 'robe of mist.'" [18]

Angelo Rappaport noted, "The sacred wells are a very favourite place with the fair children of the sea. Here, undisturbed by men, the green-haired beauties of the ocean lay aside their garb and revel in the clear moonlight."[19] There are very few sacred wells at the ocean however, and Rappaport does not say how they journey to these places.

---

14. Varner, Gary R. *Sacred Wells: A Study in the History, Meaning, and Mythology of Holy Wells & Waters.* Baltimore: Publish America 2002, 129.

15. Merriam, C. Hart. Editor. *The Dawn of the World: Myths and Tales of the Miwok Indians of California.* Lincoln: University of Nebraska Press 1993, pg. 228-230.

16. Baring-Gould, S. *Curious Myths of the Middle Ages.* New York: John B. Alden, Publishers 1885, 205.

17. Ibid., op. cit., 227.

18. Messenger, John C. *Inis Beag: Isle of Ireland.* Case Studies in Cultural Anthropology. New York: Holt, Rinehart and Winston 1969, 100.

19. Rappoport, Angelo. *The Sea: Myths and Legends.* London: Senate 1995, 184. A reprint of the 1928 edition published by Stanley Paul & Company, London. Originally titled *Superstitions of Sailors.*

In Zulu lore mermaids would, at times, possess mediums and give them healing powers. They were also believed to come out of the waters at night, causing humans to avoid rivers and the ocean after nightfall.

Among both American Indian and African beliefs is that the River Mermaids and the River People must be treated with respect and fear — for both of these creatures would often lure unsuspecting individuals to their deaths or to live the remainder of their lives under water. This fear is universal among the world's indigenous peoples. The Udmurt people of Estonia say water spirits would drown those humans who swam at the wrong time or swam without wearing a crucifix. [20]

Russia has its own tales of dangerous Water Spirits. "Water Grandfather," according to Joseph Campbell, "is an adroit shapeshifter and is said to drown people who swim at midnight or at noon."[21] Like the beautiful Mermaid, this shapeshifter likes to sit in the moonlight and comb his long green hair and beard. He is not above asking humans for help, however. He often seeks out a village midwife when one of his wives is about to deliver a baby and she is paid handsomely in gold and silver.

The "Mami Wata" (mother Water) is West Africa's mermaid deity. She is not the only one, however. Mamba Muntu and Chitapo are two other mermaid figures, which closely resemble the typical mermaid characteristics. However, anthropologist Brian Siegel of Furman University believes that these mermaids, while derived from an ancient lake spirit, are examples of cultural diffusion. While other scholars have claimed that the mermaid is perhaps one of the oldest and widespread symbols in Africa, Siegel responds that the African mermaid is "derive[d] from 'Der Schlangenbandinger' (The Snake Charmer), an 1880-87 chromolithograph of the exotic, long-haired, snake-charming wife of a Hamburg zookeeper. Moreover, it has since been determined that copies of this popular lithograph being sold in West Africa in the mid- to late 1950s originated in Bombay and England."[22]

There are, indeed, many similarities among the African water deities-mermaids and those of other parts of the world. All seem to possess beautiful long hair, combs, mirrors and very fair skin. In fact, Mamba Muntu is occasionally depicted with blond hair. However, in this particular case the reasons for the similarities are easy to explain. According to Dr. Siegel, "Until replaced by Old Testament scenes and portraits of Jesus in the 1980s, the Mamba Muntu mermaid...dominated the popular art of urban Shaba Province for twenty years. First introduced into Lumbumbashi by West African traders by the 1950s, she became the omnipresent subject of bar murals, sit-

---

20. Lintrop, Aado. "On the Udmurt Water Spirit and the Formation of the Concept 'Holy" Among Permian Peoples" in *Folklore*, Vol. 26, April 2004, 9. Published by the Folk Belief & Media Group of the Estonian Literary Museum, Tartu.

21. Campbell, Joseph. *The Hero With a Thousand Faces*. New York: MJF Books 1949, 80.

22. Siegel, Brian. "Water Spirits and Mermaids: The Copperbelt Case". Paper presented at the Spring 2000 Southeastern Regional Seminar in African Studies (SERSAS), Western Carolina University, Cullowhee, North Carolina April 14-15, 2000, 1.

ting room paintings, and record covers."[23] By the 1970s similar images had spread from Central Africa into Zambia. This is a perfect example of popular culture from one part of the world creating an important icon in another — an icon that eventually was regarded as an ancient one even though, in reality, it was only a few decades in the making.

Other explanations for such tales may be the sighting of unexpected but perfectly natural animals appearing in many of the eerie water locations around the world. Would the flash of a large fish in a "spooky" lake be misinterpreted as a mermaid? Perhaps. But can such an event explain the mermaid tales from other areas that did not have the same exposure to such primal cultural symbols?

The Pascagoula Indians of Louisiana not only respected the mermaid — they worshipped one. According to E. Randall Floyd, "legend has it that an entire...tribe — the Biloxi, also known as the Pascagoula — marched into a raging river at the command of a mermaid-like sea-goddess and drowned."[24] This happened, according to legend, in the 1500s. It was said that within a week after a white priest appeared to them, commanding them to "abandon their superstitions in an underwater goddess," they disappeared in the waters of the Pascagoula River.

Some Native American lore states that a merman actually was responsible for their arrival on American shores. According to Rappoport, such a creature led the ancestors of modern Indians from Asia to America when he took pity on them one day when they were suffering from hunger. "Following the fish-man," Rappoport wrote, "they ultimately reached the American coast."[25] The merman was described as having green hair and beard, a forked tail and a face shaped like a porpoise. This creature, according to Baring-Gould, appeared suddenly one day "in the season of opening buds." "The people of our nation," so says the legend, "were much terrified at seeing a strange creature, much resembling a man, riding upon the waves....But if our people were frightened at seeing a man who could live in the water like a fish or a duck, how much more were they frightened when they saw that from his breast down he was actually a fish, or rather two fishes, for each of his legs was a whole and distinct fish."[26] Contemporary accounts of mermaid sightings read like daily news reports. Explorer Henry Hudson, on one of his attempts to open the Northwest Passage, wrote of one such event:

> This evening [June 15] one of our company, looking overboard, saw a mermaid, and, calling up some of the company to see her, one more of the crew came up, and by that time she was come close to the ship's side, looking earnestly on the men. A little after a sea came and overturned her. From the navel upward, her back and breasts were like a woman's, as they say that saw her; her body as big as one of us. Her skin very white, and long hair

23. Ibid., 2.
24. Floyd, E. Randall. *Great Southern Mysteries.* Little Rock: August House Publishers 1989, 118.
25. Rappoport, op. cit., 165.
26. Baring-Gould, op. cit., 222.

hanging down behind, of colour black. In her going down they saw her tail, which was like the tail of a porpoise, speckled like a mackerel.[27]

Mermaids are also found in Medieval church architectural ornament. However, she does not appear to be regarded as simply "ornamental," on the contrary the mermaid is "a symbol of the lure for mankind" to sin.[28]

Some scientist believe that sightings of mermaids are the result of seals, sea-cows and manatees seen from afar. However, it is not that simple to explain these ancient tales through scientific analysis. Anthropologist Richard Carrington wrote "...the natural history of mermaids cannot be understood by the methods of natural science alone. These hauntingly beautiful goddesses of the sea, full of mystery and danger, were surely conjured from the chaos of the waters in answer to some primal human need. Their genus and species may not be carefully docketed in the *Nomenclator Zoologicus*, but their reality in terms of poetic truth is firmly established in the impassioned imagination of men."[29]

## WATER SPIRITS

Water spirits are one of the most widely recognized "otherworldly" creatures in the world. Reported in most every land throughout time, these nature beings are benign and mischievous, helpful and deadly.

As noted, American Indian legends are full of water-beings such as the Water Babies of the west, river mermaids and water dragons. In Mexico, creatures like the Water Babies were called "Wachoqs" and were described as little people who lived in streams and lakes and had the ability to walk underwater.

More nature spirits than "Little People", the Australian Aborigines have legends of water-spirits, also referred to as "Good Spirits," who reside in streams and other water sources. Smith reports that these water spirits "dwell in the form of tiny bubbles that cling closely together in the limpid pools and make the surface look as white as snow."[30]

In Mongolia, shamans often invoke water spirits, called *lus*, for the purpose of removing bad fortune and unseen dangers. According to shaman Sarangeral, during rituals to cure an ill person, water is mixed with milk, tea, and liquor. The *lus* dissolves the evil forces that surround the individual in this concoction and it is then thrown outside in a direction dictated by the spirit. Because many streams, rivers, lakes and other bodies of water contain these spirits, it is forbidden to throw anything into the water. The worst

---

27. As quoted by Richard Carrington in "The Natural History of the Mermaid", in *Horizon*, January, 1960, Vol. II, Number 3, 131.
28. Cave, C.J.P. *Medieval Carvings in Exeter Cathedral.* London: Penguin Books 1953, 21.
29. Carrington, 1957 op. cit. 19.
30. Smith, William Ramsay. *Aborigine Myths and Legends.* London: Senate 1996, 112. A reprint of the 1930 edition, *Myths & Legends of the Australian Aborigines* published by George G. Harrap, London.

offense, of course, is to urinate in the water.[31] This prohibition also occurs in other locations around the world. "In olden days," said Zulu leader Credo Mutwa, "Africans used to risk their lives in protecting water. In olden days our people used to severely punish anyone caught urinating into a stream or a river."[32]

Nature spirits, water spirits in particular, have played an important role in the cultures of most people. Many times the stories of these particular spirits are passed on from one generation to another as well as from one cultural system and tradition to another. An example of this cultural transference is the *simbi* spirits of West-Central Africa found in the South Carolina Lowcountry. Carried by the slave trade, this cultural diffusion was an important cultural attribute of the South Carolina slave population. According to Dillard University researcher Ras Michael Brown, "West-Central African nature deities, called *simbi* spirits in Kikongo, served the enslaved people of the early Lowcountry as spiritual benefactors around which captives of diverse African origins and those born in the Lowcountry built their communities."[33]

The simbi spirits were reportedly of human form, albeit "vaguely human," and they were fond of preying upon women who went to the springs to draw water, or children who attempted to swim in the springs. These spirits were greatly feared, and people would go to great lengths not to offend them as occasionally the springs would disappear suddenly which was "interpreted as a sign that the resident spirit had died or departed because of some human offense..."[34]

To the slaves and their African forebears the simbi represented "the permanence and potency of nature." These nature spirits provided for their human neighbors by giving abundant harvests and hunts as well as providing a healthy socio-economic environment for the villages that maintained simbi shrines and upheld the required rituals. This give and take relationship with the simbi is a common aspect of the nature-spirit/human coexistence around the world.

The simbi water spirits first showed up in the South Carolina Lowcountry in the early 1840s as the West-Central African slave population expanded. Brown writes, "Through the *simbi* spirits...enslaved people in the Lowcountry claimed their place on the landscape and...the presence of *simbi* spirits may have offered enslaved people powerful spiritual benefactors within the harsh realm of plantation slavery..."[35]

31. Sarangeral. *Riding Windhorses: A Journey into the Heart of Mongolian Shamanism.* Rochester: Destiny Books 2000, 56.
32. Mutwa, Credo. Keynote Address at the Living Lakes Conference, October 2, 1999, Lee Vining, California.
33. Brown, Ras Michael. "West-Central African Nature Spirits in the South Carolina Lowcountry." Paper given at the Southeastern Regional Seminar in African Studies (SERAS) Fall Meeting 27-28 October 2000, University of Tennessee, Knoxville, 1.
34. Ibid., 2.
35. Ibid., 4.

Water spirits are protectors, the guardians of bodies of water that give and renew life on earth. It is believed in Africa that the water spirits "live in pools and swamps that never dry out. It is said that their [water spirits] role is to protect water sources and keep them alive."[36] It is the water spirit that controls human behavior around the important water caches of the earth. Water spirits dictate the proper attitude to have with this life force. Their punishment is swift and dreadful if their laws are broken. This is the role of the nature spirit — to act as the supernatural protector of nature, to enforce her laws and to reward or punish those who are under a spirits influence. It is unfortunate that "modern" humans have turned their backs upon this ancient archetype and now are beginning to suffer for their refusal to acknowledge nature for what she is.

Nature spirits try to keep nature in balance, for when that balance is upset catastrophe is always nearby. In cultures where indigenous traditions can still be found those ancient traditions are put to use when the balance begins to tip. Bernard, in writing of the Natal Midlands in South Africa, noted, "certain rural communities have re-instituted the ancient day of rest for the heavenly princess, *iNkosazana.* This day was...regarded as the day when no-one was allowed to utilise the river or to tend their fields. The re-institution of this day of rest was in response to claims made by a number of individuals who say she has visited them and complained that she needs the rivers to be left alone completely so she can enjoy them and renew them without any disturbance."[37]

The power of water spirits is greatly feared. The Zulus believe that to look into pools of water could result in the loss of one's soul as the water spirits have the power to steal the human soul.

Water spirits were greatly feared as well by Native Americans who believed that they would steal children and take them into the water depths to live with them. Mooney reports one such legend:

> In "A Yanktown Legend," recorded by Dorsey,[38] a child falls into the water and is taken by the water people. The father hears the child crying under the water and employs two medicine men to bring it back. After preparing themselves properly, they go down into the deep water where they find the child sitting beside the water spirit, who, when they declare their message, tells them that if they had come before the child had eaten anything he might have lived, but now if taken away "he will desire the food which I eat; that being the cause of the trouble, he shall die." Similar prohibitions concerning the eating of the food of fairies are found in European cultures, especially Great Britain.

36. Bernard, Penny. "Water Spirits: Indigenous People's Knowledge Progamme: The relevance of indigenous beliefs for river health and wetland conservation in southern Africa", in *South African Wetlands*, No. 11, November, 2000, 15.

37. Ibid., 16.

38. Dorsey was another early ethnologist who recorded many Native American myths and legends.

## THE WATER HORSE

> There is scarcely a loch in the Highlands which has not its water-horse or water-bull, not graminivorous like its earthly prototype, but a carnivorous demon, whose taste in animal food is chiefly directed to innocent young maidens. The picturesque superstition of the water-kelpie is a general idealization of the whole class of watery monsters.[39]

The monstrous Water Horse, a Fairy being of Scotland and the Hebrides, Ireland, France and the east coast of the United States would lay in wait in the form of a beautiful horse, sometimes even with saddle and bridle, for unsuspecting pedestrians. Should a weary traveler come across the magnificent animal and mount it to finish his journey it may be finished in a way not to his expectations. For once in the saddle, the beast would run off and drag the hapless traveler to the depths of a lake or river where he would be devoured. The Water Horse was also known in Wales by the name *glashtyn*. The *glashtyn* was described as "a goblin of the shape and appearance of a small horse or yearling foal in his rough, unkempt coat."[40] The Water Horse was said to "beguile lonely travelers with his numberless tricks, one of which is to lure them to a stream, swamp, or water-hole. When he has succeeded he vanishes with a long outburst of mockery, half neigh, half human laughter."[41] The Water Horse could be killed if it was shot with a silver bullet much like the cinema version of the werewolf. Once killed, it "proved to be 'nothing but turf and a soft mass like jelly-fish.'"[42]

*The Water Horse*

Anthropologist John Messenger reported that the water horse appeared as a black steed with a tail of a giant fish. He wrote, "Until 40 years ago [around 1920 based on the date of Messenger's ethnographic study] it lived in the fresh water lake of Inis Beag, where it was seen on certain nights traveling abreast the surface with its head held high and mane waving in the wind. Now it is seen only at sea and infrequently at great distance."[43]

39. Anon. *Blackwoods Edinburgh Magazine*, Vol. 82 (504) Oct 1857, pg 452 ("Our Hagiology").
40. Rhys, John. *Celtic Folklore: Welsh and Manx*. New York: Gordon Press 1974, 324. A reprint of the 1901 edition published in Oxford. Lewis Spence agrees with Rhys' description of the water horse but also states that it "had the power of transforming its shape, and could appear as a young man or a boy, or even at times as an inanimate object." (*The Magic Arts in Celtic Britain*, 94. Published by Dover Publications, Mineola, New York.)
41. Ibid.
42. Spence, Lewis. *The Magic Arts in Celtic Britain*. Mineola: Dover Publications Inc., 1999, 95. A reprint of an undated edition published in London and New York by Rider & Co.
43. Messenger, op. cit. 100.

The kelpie was said also to appear as a black horse that resided in the lochs and pools of Scotland. It would rise swiftly and powerfully to the surface whenever a hapless human erroneously wandered nearby. Reportedly, "their neighing and whinnying could be heard from beneath the depths during thunderstorms."[44] One of the telltale proofs of the kelpie, should one happen to come across it, is that its hoofs are reversed. John Campbell disagrees with this, saying "the kelpie that swells torrents and devours women and children has no representative in Gaelic superstition....The water-horse haunts lochs, the kelpie streams and torrents."[45]

It is possible that the kelpie evolved into another mythic form — that of the mermaid. According to folklorist Horace Beck, "It may be that this particular animal is the most ancient and primitive type of all the mermaid's northern ancestors."[46] In fact, according to Beck, the folktales of the kelpie may be some of the most ancient in the Old World.[47] The kelpie, like Pan before him, became part of Christian folklore as well. While the kelpie may assume the form of a handsome young man, its hoofed feet were still part of its physical characteristics seen by those who would look. The pagan mythic creature became another aspect of the Christian devil.

MacCulloch describes the dreaded water horse of the Scottish Highlands somewhat differently than Rhys: "a horse with staring eyes, webbed feet, and a slimy coat."[48] This *Each Uisge* ("Water Horse"), according to MacCulloch, "assumes different forms and lures the unwary to destruction, or he makes love in human shape to women, some of whom discover his true nature by seeing a piece of water-weed in his hair and only escape with difficulty."[49]

The Water Horse, or something like it, is part of Central American folklore also. "There is [a] ...fierce monster called the *Wihwin*," wrote Alexander Porteous, "resembling a horse, which, although its native place is the sea, takes up its residence for the summer in the mountains, and roams through the forests at night in search of victims."[50]

The various tales of these Water Horses and water monsters claiming the lives of humans or of the annual drownings that occur in rivers may, in reality, reflect the human sacrifices that were made each year in the rivers and lakes to appease the gods of water, or the accidental deaths of those who venture unwarily into the forbidding mountains. The obviously close association of horses with water may also reflect the horse-sacrifices made in the

44. Andrews, Tamra. *A Dictionary of Nature Myths*. Oxford: Oxford University Press 1998, 221.
45. Campbell, John Gregorson. *The Gaelic Otherworld*, edited by Ronald Black. Edinburgh: Birlinn Limited 2005, 115.
46. Beck, Horace. *Folklore and the Sea*. Mystic: Mystic Seaport Museum 1973, 269.
47. Ibid., 270.
48. MacCulloch, J.A. *The Religion of the Ancient Celts*. Mineola: Dover Publications, Inc. 2003, 188. A reprint of the 1911 edition published by T. & T. Clark, Edinburgh.
49. Ibid.
50. Porteous, Alexander. *The Lore of the Forest: Myths and Legends*. London: Senate 1996, 146.

Norse countries that may have reverberated in the nature of the folklore surrounding the Water Horse. There are no explanations as to how such similar stories reached around the world however among peoples with little or no contact such as the Celts and the Central American Indians.

## MONSTERS OF THE SEAS

Perhaps no creature in the long history of the world has inspired so many tales of terror and awe as the sea monster, more commonly referred to as a sea serpent. "When Enlil [an ancient Babylonian god] began to rule," wrote E.A. Wallis Budge, "the earth was in the possession of a monster called Labbu, which came up from the sea....Both Babylonian and Egyptian texts tell of a monster serpent which finds its equivalent in modern times in the 'Seaserpent'".[51] While the Loch Ness monster has captured most of the headlines in recent times, there are countless other creatures appearing in the folklore and mythology of the world that also defy explanation. The earliest mention of the sea serpent in historical records can be found in Aristotle's *Historia Animalium* written in the 4th century BCE. "In Libya," Aristotle wrote, "the serpents are very large. Mariners sailing along that coast have told how they have seen the bones of many oxen which, it was apparent to them, had been devoured by the serpents. And as their ships sailed on, the serpents came to attack them, some of them throwing themselves on a trireme and capsizing it."[52]

Mysterious and dangerous beasts are commonly associated with water and are universal throughout the world's folklore. American Indian mythology is full of accounts of "enchanted lakes," "water monsters" and "water gods." Many of these myths are very similar to other stories around the world with comparable themes. "Water monsters" are part of Native American mythology from California to the Carolinas. Ethnologist James Mooney wrote of water monsters in Cherokee lore on the Tuckasegee River in Jackson County and in Madison County on the French Broad River, 6 miles above Warm Springs, and on the Little Tennessee River between Graham and Swain counties, all in North Carolina.[53] The Water Monster was a feared supernatural creature said to eat both horse and rider if they got too close to the Water Monster's lair.

A water monster, described as a "giant leech," is said by the Cherokee to have lived in a deep hole in Valley River, in North Carolina. Mooney records the story:

51. Budge, E.A. Wallis. *Babylonian Life and History*. New York: Barnes & Noble Books 2005, 109.
52. As quoted in *Mermaids and Mastodons* by Richard Carrington, published by Rinehart & Company New York, 1957, page 22.
53. Mooney, James, *Myths of the Cherokee*. New York: Dover Publications 1995, 404-406. A reprint of the 1900 publication "Nineteenth Annual Report of the Bureau of American Ethnology, 1897-98.

> "Just above the junction (of the river) is a deep hole...and above it is a ledge of rock running across the stream, over which people used to go on a bridge....One day some men going along the trail saw a great red object, full as large as a house, lying on the rock ledge in the middle of the stream below them. As they stood wondering what it could be they saw it unroll — and then they knew it was alive — and stretch itself out along the rock until it looked like a great leech with red and white stripes along its body.... at last (it) crawled down the rock and was out of sight in the deep water. The water began to boil and foam, and a great column of white spray was thrown high in the air and came down like a waterspout upon the very spot where the men had been standing, and would have swept them all into the water but that they say saw it in time and ran from the place."[54]

Legend says that many people lost their lives on this bridge and their bodies were later found with parts of their faces eaten off.

Among the Plains Indians a "water dragon" was said to rise up from a lake to destroy his enemy's children while the parents were away. A skilled hunter killed the dragon by throwing red-hot stones into its mouth. This mythic theme of a battle between water and fire is common from the Dakotas to British Columbia. The Lakota believed that water spirits and water monsters were of the same nature — "Bad gods".

Water monsters especially are bad as they adversely affected the lives of the people. According to Short Feather, who wrote about such things in 1898, "water monsters make the floods. They spew them out of their mouths. They make springs. They inhabit swampy places....When they take people or animals down to their places, they eat them. Or they may keep them. They took a girl down in the Missouri River and kept her for a long time. Her father threw a white dog in the river and the monster took the dog and gave up the girl."[55]

Here we see an offering being made to the water monster in exchange for the girl. The fact that the accepted offer was a dog is important in that dogs have been linked to the Otherworld throughout time and among most cultures. Dogs were a common sacrificial item in many wells throughout Great Britain, Europe and the Mediterranean up to the first few centuries of the Christian era.

Other beings today regarded as "water monsters" were a century or two ago regarded in a more respectful light. In a monumental report commissioned by President James Buchanan, written in 1857 by early ethnologist Henry Rowe Schoolcraft, the Dakotah Indians reportedly worshipped water gods named *Onkteri*. Schoolcraft wrote, "the significance of the name of this class (*Onkteri*) of Dakotah gods is unknown. In their external manifestation, they resemble the ox, but are very large. They can instantaneously extend their tail and horns so as to reach the skies, and these are the seat of their power. They are male and female, and propagate their kind like ani-

---

54. Ibid.
55. Walker, James R. *Lakota Belief and Ritual.* Lincoln: University of Nebraska Press 1991, 116.

mals, and are mortal....It is believed that the earth is animated by the spirit of the *Onkteri* goddess, while the water, and the earth beneath the water, is the dwelling-place of the male god. Hence the Dakotahs, in their addresses to the water, in religious acts, give to it the name of Grandfather, and that of the Grandmother to the earth."[56]

Contemporary Indian lore equates these beings to "water spirits" rather than high gods and they are characteristically bad. Schoolcraft's description of the *Onkteri* would appear, in fact to be that of the water monster rather than a god or goddess. Schoolcraft related an incident of a flood being caused by such a spirit, which lived under St. Anthony Falls on the Mississippi river. Evidently, when the spirit swam through the waters it caused the water to rush "down with a tremendous force which swept all before it; and a cabin which stood on the low bank of the river, near the fort, was carried away, with a soldier in it, who was never afterwards heard of....the soldier was taken by him for food, as he feeds upon human souls." The following chant, which is much used in the medicine-dance, shows the character of this class of the gods, in this respect:

> "I lie mysteriously across the lake,
> Decoying some souls.
> Let me eat him alive."[57]

Water-monsters may be, according to J.A. MacCulloch, remnants of tales of human sacrifice. "Here there is the trace of an abandoned custom of sacrifice," wrote MacCulloch, "and of the traditional idea of the anger of the divinity at being neglected." He goes on to say, "human sacrifice to water-divinities is suggested by the belief that water-monsters devour human beings, and by the tradition that a river claims its toll of victims every year."[58]

Taking this suggestion into consideration, there are very many other reports of these creatures that beg a different analysis. Certainly, hoaxes, miss-identifications, wishful thinking, and outright lies have been responsible for a great many "sightings" of sea monsters, but what about those reported by reputable people under excellent conditions?

Some of the rather outrageous claims include the story "from Lorn about a man who saw an eel so long that it took an entire day to pass his fishing-rock."[59]

Perhaps we should look at some of the actual accounts given over the years. Rappoport gives us the following sighting that transpired during the reign of Philip II of Spain:

56. Schoolcraft, Henry Rowe. *History of the Indian Tribes of the United States: Their Present Condition and Prospects, and a Sketch of the Ancient Status.* Philadelphia: J. B. Lippincott & Co. 1857, 649.
57. Ibid. 650.
58. MacCulloch, J.A. *The Religion of the Ancient Celts.* Mineola: Dover Publications, Inc. 2003, 190-191 (A reprint of the 1911 edition published by T & T Clark, Edinburgh).
59. Campbell, John Gregorson. *The Gaelic Otherworld.* Edinburgh: Birlinn Limited 2005, 375.

"...a gigantic whale or sea-monster appeared in the ocean which greatly differed from all others hitherto seen. Standing half in the water and half above it, it had two gigantic fins and sailed like a ship. A ship caught sight of the monster, fired and broke one of its fins. With a terrible noise and howling aloud the monster turned right into the Straights of Gibraltar and fell dead on the shore of Valencia. Its mouth was so large that seven men could stand in it quite comfortably and a rider on horseback could quite easily enter it. The corpses of two men were found in its stomach."[60]

In 1638, according to Rappoport, "a fisherman who tried to throw a harpoon into such a monster was killed by an electric shock emanating from the monster."[61] Perhaps the fisherman did, in fact, encounter a giant eel. Accounts of sea serpents actually attacking whales were common among sailors in the 17th, 18th and 19th centuries. Along the Isle of Skye, wrote Charles Gould in 1884, "It generally follows the tracks of whales, and in two instances observers affirm that it has been seen in combat with them."[62]

*A 19th century rendition of a sea serpent*

While accounts of these monsters surfacing from the waves to snatch lone sailors from the decks of their ships or to thrust themselves onto ships and then sinking them are many, no one has ever managed to produce any actual evidence for their existence. As far back as 1861, educated people took a cautious approach to the tantalizing subject. An unknown writer contributed the following in the March 1861 edition of *Blackwood's Edinburgh Magazine*:

"Why should we doubt the existence of the sea-serpent? The fact has been attested by many observers in various parts of the world. It is not a fact in any way contradictory of the supposed nature of things: if proved, our zoological knowledge would receive an addition, not a shake. No interests are impugned by it. No vanities can be wounded by it. Why, then, do we refuse to believe in it? Solely because we do not consider the testimony sufficient. Reports of sailors and travellers are of questionable authority. One vertebra would be more convincing than a thousand reports. But no vertebra, no vestige of the sea-serpent has ever been produced. ...as the

---

60. Rappoport, Angelo S. *The Sea: Myths and Legends*. London: Senate 1995, 211. A reprint of the 1928 edition of *Superstitions of Sailors* published by Stanley Paul & Company, London.
61. Ibid.
62. Gould, Charles. *Mythical Monsters*. London: Senate 1995, 264. A reprint of the 1886 edition.

live animal has not been captured nor the dead animal secured, we are left with the conjectures of eyewitnesses who saw the animal under delusive conditions.

"It is generally impossible to prove a negative. We cannot say that no sea-serpents exist — we can only say that there is a strong *presumption* against their existence, and no evidence strong enough to set aside that presumption."[63]

Of course, the writer's argument is a sound one. Inconsistent eye-witness accounts of everything from traffic accidents to robberies show how unreliable such testimony tends to be, especially when there is a desire to see something. However, a giant squid was recently filmed, and other "giant" specimens of certain animals may have existed that would lend a basis for these legends.[64]

---

63. Anon. *Blackwood's Edinburgh Magazine*, vol. 89 (545) Mar 1861, page 346.

64. Claims of seeing water monsters have been made in a variety of locations in the United States, including New York State, Main, New Hampshire, Arkansas, Connecticut, Kentucky, Florida, Indiana, Illinois, Wisconsin, Minnesota, Nebraska, South Dakota, Michigan, Oklahoma, Idaho, Utah, Arizona, Wyoming, Montana, Nevada, Washington, Oregon, California and Alaska.

# Chapter 3. The Forest Folk

Thoughts of Fairies and "little folk" seem to bring up scenes of the forest where they live in a cartoon world of mushroom houses, snail-carriages, flower parasols and an ambivalent co-existence with the few humans who live in the area. They are usually thought of as somewhat mischievous but harmless. However, like other nature spirits, they may also be expressions of mankind's primeval sense of the mystery and awe of nature.

Most cultures have myths of tree gods and tales of strange fairy-like creatures that live deep in dark forests or in the very trees themselves. Such stories reflect an ancient animistic belief system that gives every object in nature its own spirit and power. These vegetation spirits and gods are the foundations for classic and contemporary religious thought.

For many people the very *feel* of the forest imparts a sense of awe and wonder, inspiring thoughts of the immensity of nature and the depths of time, triggering a delighted or even fearful awareness of all that we do not know about this world. To an artistic sensibility this can suggest the presence of spirits and unseen creatures. "The edge of the forest," write Carol and Dinah Mack, "is always the boundary between the wild and domesticated, the animal and the human community. It holds its genius loci, which may appear as demonic guardian species of wilderness and wild creatures and attack trespassing hunters, mischievous fairies...and the many huge man-eating species....."[1]

This statement may be applied to any forest in the world, for they all seem to be populated with legends of these local spirits and fairies who are not often kind to human intrusion. The Cherokee, according to anthropolo-

---

1. Mack, Carol K. and Dinah Mack. *A Field Guide to Demons, Fairies, Fallen Angels, and Other Subversive Spirits.* New York: Owl Books 1998, 91.

gist James Mooney, believed that "trees and plants also were alive and could talk in the old days, and had their place in council".[2] The intelligence of trees and plants, as well as other inanimate objects, were taken for granted by the Cherokee and the other indigenous people around the world.

"Little People" are most often thought of as residents of the woods. "In Scandinavian countries," wrote Alexander Porteous, "groves and trees were appointed as the residence of the Elves after they had been worsted in a conflict with superior beings."[3] In many parts of the world, hunters will leave small offerings of food or other items for the spirits of the forest, "just in case." "Something of the same fear is felt by the peasants for the fairies, elves, pixies, and all the tribe of little people familiar to European folk-lore,"[4] noted 19th century folklorist J.H. Philpot. In his book, *The Religion of the Ancient Celts,* J.A. MacCulloch noted that in Scandinavia the dead were called elves and that they were presumed to live in barrows or hills. He also reports that the word "elf" also means any divine spirit and that the term was later changed to "fairy".[5]

The Coos Indians along Oregon's southern coast believed that the forests were filled with ghosts and spirits. Five types of spirits were identified as residing in the forest:

1. Ghosts or spirits that "reentered a corpse and escaped into the forest to do evil things to humans, especially poor people";

2. A "mirror image" of oneself, a doppelganger. If you saw one of these, your life was supposed to be shortened;

3. Giant people who lived on the fish in the streams; they were neither good nor bad "and do not scare people";

4. A visible spirit or ghost, and

5. The "noisy ones," that are little people, usually covered in long hair; they would leave tracks along creek banks. These creatures were usually seen only at night and were said to throw rocks at people's homes. [6]

Other Oregonian tribes such as the Alsea and Yaquina believed in long-haired female wood sprites called *osun* who could give certain special powers to humans that would enable them to become shamans.[7] The "sauna fairy" of Udmurt folklore were also referred to as "the one with long hair."

2. Mooney, James. *Myths of the Cherokee.* New York: Dover Publications Inc. 1995 (A reprint of the *Nineteenth Annual Report of the Bureau of American Ethnology 1897-98* published in 1900 by the Smithsonian Institution), 231.

3. Porteous, Alexander. *The Lore of the Forest.* London: Senate 1996, 52. A Reprint of the 1928 edition published by George Allen & Unwin Ltd., London.

4. Philpot, J.H. *The Sacred Tree in Religion and Myth.* Mineola: Dover Publications 2004, 65. A reprint of the 1897 edition published by Macmillan and Co. Ltd., London and New York.

5. MacCulloch, J.A. *The Religion of the Ancient Celts.* Mineola: Dover Publications, Inc. 2003, 66. A reprint of the 1911 edition published by T &T Clark, Edinburgh.

6. Beckham, Stephen Dow. "Coos, Lower Umpqua, and Siuslaw: Traditional Religious Practices" in *Native American Religious Practices and Uses, Siuslaw National Forest.* Eugene: Heritage Research Associates Report No. 7(3), September 20, 1982, 41.

7. Ibid., 27.

Tree elves have been popular in many cultures; they have been said to inhabit the elm, oak, willow, yew, fir, holly, pine, ash, cherry, laurel, nut, apple, birch and cypress trees. Each of the tree elves is created from the specific tree and thus takes on the characteristics of that tree. While all of these species of trees have a resident elf, "the elder", writes Nancy Arrowsmith, "has without doubt the highest elf population."[8] The lives of the "elder elves" are linked directly to their tree and so they are very protective of it.

The appearance of tree elves varies according to the tree from which they originated. The oak elf will appear as a gnarled old man and the birch elf appears as a thin white female. The oak has guardians in England, Italy and Germany.

In Albania and Lithuania, certain tree fairies guard the cherry tree, while the ash tree is protected in Scandinavia by the Askafroa. The Askafroa was considered an evil fairy or spirit and was left sacrificial offerings every Ash Wednesday. In West Africa a male tree spirit known as the Huntin lives in and protects the silk-cotton tree. Nature spirits and Fairies must be propitiated with offerings of fowls and palm oil prior to the removal of the silk-cotton tree.

For some reason most tree-spirits are ambivalent at best and demonic at worst. Stories abound of tree-spirits that take savage revenge on those that dare to cut trees down. Indian legend says the Banyan tree is inhabited by spirits that will "wring the necks of all persons who approached their tree during the night."[9] The guardian spirit of the Brazilian rainforest is Corupira who is not evil but will disorient those who are intent on harming the trees and the forest animals — much like Pan. However, other tree and forest-spirits do exhibit traits of kindness towards humans. Some forest spirits were said to protect hunters and fishers, and in fact to lead game to them. It was to these spirit-gods that the forests were dedicated and sacrifices made. In other cultures, tree spirits provided the rains and sun that made crops grow.

The Mesquakie, also known as the Fox Indians of Iowa, believed that the spirits of their ancestors lived within the trees. It was said, "the murmur of the trees when the wind passes through is but the voices of our grandparents."[10] The Fox felt that all wood was sacred and that objects made from wood "were thought to contain the very essence of a tree's spiritual substance."[11]

Nature spirits, normally described as miniature people but not necessarily the same as Fairy, are common throughout most "undeveloped" societies. This is not a negative judgment of those cultures, only an observation that the more "developed" and "western" societies have reinterpreted their con-

---

8. Arrowsmith, Nancy and George Moorse. *A Field Guide to the Little People.* London: Macmillan Company 1977, 180.

9. Porteous, Alexander. *The Lore of the Forest: Myths and Legends.* London: Senate 1996, 123 (A reprint of *Forest Folklore* published in 1928 by George Allen & Unwin Ltd., London).

10. Anon. *The Spirit World.* Alexandria: Time-Life Books 1992, 90.

11. Ibid.

nection with nature in light of scientific explanations. The Gururumba, a New Guinea people, believe in certain nature spirits, some who live in the forests and others who live in the reeds along the riverbanks. Other than the location of territory, there is little difference between the two forms of nature spirit. The Gururumba say that these spirits are seldom seen because even though they reside in our world, in our reality, they appear as mist or smoke. They are also always male. While generally ambivalent to the humans who live in the area, the spirits will attack anyone who stumbles into their territory. Ethnologist Philip L. Newman, who researched the Gururumba, writes "each spirit has its own dwelling place — a certain clump of reeds, a particular configuration of boulders along the river, or the exposed roots of some tree. Anyone wandering into one of these sanctuaries is attacked by the spirit which may cause him illness or even death."[12]

The Gururumba seek to placate the nature spirits by providing a small dome-shaped house (about two feet in diameter) in an enclosure in the family garden. The Gururumba provide housing, food and information to the nature spirit in exchange for the spirit's protection of the garden and care for the Gururumba's pig herds.

While we rarely think of Australia as being forested, the Aborigines tell of a race of "little men" that they call the Tuckonie. Said to live in thickly timbered country, the Tuckonie cause the gum-tree to grow. "They are tiny little men," William Ramsay Smith relates, "but they have the wonderful power of causing the trees to grow," mostly by dancing around specific trees.[13]

Tree spirits are also commonly believed in throughout Africa. The Ashanti reportedly believe that certain nature spirits are present that animate trees, stones and other "inanimate" objects as well as animals, rivers and charms. The powers of these spirits are great and respected. John Mbiti reports, in his book *African Religions and Philosophy*, an incident that took place in Ghana in the 1960s. During the construction of a new harbor at Tema, equipment was repeatedly stolen and a company investigator, an Englishman, was sent to look into it. After his investigation was over, one of the European supervisors mentioned to him that a lone tree was causing him a great deal of trouble. All the other trees in the area had been cleared but one relatively small tree remained. Every attempt to remove it had failed, as the heavy equipment always stalled when approaching the tree. One of the African foremen said that the tree was magic and could not be removed unless the tree spirit could be persuaded to move on to another tree. A shaman was called in; he sacrificed three sheep and poured three bottles of gin onto the roots of the tree as an offering. Evidently, the ritual worked as the machinery could be started,

---

12. Newman, Philip L. *Knowing the Gururumba.* New York: Holt, Rinehart and Winston Case Studies in Cultural Anthropology 1965, 63.
13. Smith, William Ramsay. *Aborigine Myths and Legends.* London: Senate 1996, 128. A reprint of the 1930 edition published by George G. Harrap, London.

and a few of the workmen simply walked to the tree and were able to pull it up out of the earth.[14]

This story illustrates the fact that myth and folklore continue to be created in contemporary times, often utilizing traditional lore as the basis for new stories and providing more fuel for the evolution of oral culture.

14. Mbiti, John S. *African Religions and Philosophy*. Garden City: Anchor Books 1970, 255.

# Chapter 4. Giants

Early natural historian Lieutenant Colonel Charles Hamilton Smith wrote in 1848, "There were, in early antiquity, nations, tribes, and families, existing in nearly every part of the earth, whose origin and affinities appear so exceedingly obscure, that they have been transferred from physical realities to poetical mythology".[1] One of these nations or tribes is that of the Giants.

In Greek mythology, the giant Titans were the offspring of Gaia, the earth goddess, and Uranus the sky god. The Titans were primordial deities that ruled over earth and heaven until overthrown by Zeus. However, many other gods and goddesses were born of the union between Zeus and Titan women or other Titan gods and goddesses. Among these were Apollo; Selene, goddess of the moon; Eos, the goddess of the dawn; Helios, god of the sun; Artemis, goddess of the wild beasts; Demeter, goddess of agriculture; Hades, god of the underworld; Poseidon, god of the sea; and Cronos, who castrated and overthrew his father Uranus. Poseidon and his Titan brothers Hades and Zeus divided the rule of the world among themselves after the death of Cronos.

The Giants in Greek myth were of human form except for snake-like legs. A distinction must be made between the Giants of old and the Titans. While both were huge in stature, the Giants were the only ones with the snake-like legs and were a younger race than the Titans. They were destroyed by Hercules with the encouragement of Zeus. The Titans were the oldest generation of the gods and were led by Cronos, the son of the sky god, Ouranos, or Ura-

---

1. Smith, Charles Hamilton. *The Natural History of the Human Species.* Edinburgh: W.H. Lizars 1848, 134

nus. Both races were ultimately subdued or destroyed by Zeus and the other gods and goddess on Olympus. The Titans were beaten in a mighty ten-year battle, following the defeat of the Giants, that shook the universe.

In Mesoamerican lore giants were considered to be the "first race." They are still believed to exist as forest cannibals in some locations and are said to be so large that they must sleep sitting up, as they have no room to stretch out.[2] The belief in a race of giant cannibals is fairly common in Native American lore although, according to ethnologist James Mooney, the giants are "comparatively few in number while the 'little people' are legion."[3]

Tales of giants are almost as numerous in Native American lore as those about the little people. Many of these tales most likely are metaphorical in nature; that is, they are the explanations for geological formations and natural oddities that they could not explain. At least that is the primary theory of contemporary anthropologists and folklorists.

In addition, in most cases, these giants are "stony-skinned" and physically are more like stone than flesh and blood. A Cherokee legend from Tennessee speaks of the Spear-Finger, a huge evil woman with a lethal index finger whose skin was like stone. She "had great powers over stone and she could easily lift and carry immense rocks and could bond them together by merely striking one stone against another. To get across the rough country more easily, she built a great rock bridge through the air from the Tree Rock, on the Hiwassee [River], over to Whiteside Mountain, on the Blue Ridge."[4] Rocky promontories supposed to be pieces of this great bridge can still be seen today.

The Miwok Indians of California's Sierra Nevadas believed that a great stone giant by the name of Chehalumche lived in nearby caves. According to the Miwok, Chehalumche "sallies forth at night in search of food. He preys, by preference, on people, but when he cannot get people, takes deer or other animals. He never eats his victims in the open but carries them into the caves and there devours them."[5]

Shamans were reportedly turned into ice-giants among the Maliseet-Passamaquoddy tribes. According to tradition, a "witch" is a shaman who employees a spirit helper to assist him or her in acquiring powers over other shamans. The spirit helper normally takes an animal form and is sent out by its shaman master in dreams to acquire the necessary information the shaman needs. The body of a shaman killed by another does not rot but stays "alive" and is capable of eating anyone who passes by. "When the corpse had

2. Bierhorst, John. *The Mythology of Mexico and Central America.* New York: William Morrow and Company, Inc. 1990, 172.

3. Mooney, James. *Myths of the Cherokee.* New York: Dover Publications, Inc. 1995, 501 A reprint of the 1900 publication "Nineteenth Annual Report of the Bureau of American Ethnology, 1897-98.

4. Atalie, Princess. *The Earth Speaks.* New York: Fleming H. Revell Company, 1940, 148.

5. Merriam, C. Hart. "Human Remains in California Caves" in *The American Antiquarian and Oriental Journal*, Vol. 31, 1909, pgs 152-153.

eaten three people it became *kíwahkw*, or cannibal ice giant....Female ice giants had more power than their male counterparts."[6]

In both Old World and New World mythology, the giants reportedly were destroyed when they dared to challenge the gods. In *Beowulf* the giants are drowned after they attacked the gods, and in Tarascan (Mexico) lore the giants are destroyed "when God decided to bless the world," or in the mythology of Honduras they are simply changed into animals "during God's conquest."[7] In Inca lore, the first human race created by the creator god Viracocha was the race of giants. These giant men and woman, who were not evil, lived in a world of darkness as the sun had not yet been made. According to legend, Viracocha was unhappy with his creation and destroyed the giants in a world-wide flood.[8]

In Scandinavian lore, giants were flesh and blood — but if the rays of the sun caught them, they would instantly turn to stone, much in the same way as the Night Trolls in Iceland. Similarly, the Callanish Standing Stones on the Western Isles of Scotland, according to legend, were originally giants that were turned to stone by St. Kieran when they refused to adopt Christianity.

Folklorist John Rhys notes that a huge giant that supposedly lived on the Isle of Man was responsible for throwing five huge stones over several miles from a mountain called Cronk yn Irree Laa. "I have seen," he remarks, "the marks of his huge hands impressed on the top of two massive monoliths."[9]

In China, it was said, there existed a "Country of the Giants." These giants were fifty feet tall with feet six feet in length, teeth like saws and fingers resembling hooked claws. Their bodies, however, did not resemble stone so much as huge bears. Their bodies were covered in long black hair. Chinese legend indicates that these giants lived as long as eighteen thousand years and that they were also cannibalistic — not eating their own kind but any human taken in battle. [10]

In the Philippines, a ruler by the name of Salingolop was in power when the first Spanish galleons arrived. Said to be "as tall as the highest tree in the forest" his skin was impervious to the bullets the Spanish fired at him. According to legend, "It was not until they dropped their rifles and struck his legs with bars of iron that he was conquered. As he fell, they say that he

6. Erickson, Vincent O. "Maliseet-Passamaquoddy" in *Handbook of North American Indians, Vol. 15: Northeast.* Edited by Bruce G. Trigger. Washington: Smithsonian Institution 1978, 133.

7. Bierhorst, op. cit., 9.

8. Hallam, Elizabeth, ed. *Gods and Goddesses.* New York: Macmillan 1996, 23.

9. Rhys, John. *Celtic Folklore: Welsh and Manx, Vol. 1.* New York: Gordon Press, 1974, 285.

10. Werner, E.T.C. *Myths and Legends of China.* New York: Dover Publications, Inc. 1994, 387. A reprint of the 1922 edition published by George G. Harrap & Co., Ltd., London.

struck on his side in the sea, causing the waves to make a great noise that it reached to the Cape of San Augustin."[11]

There are, however, stories about giant people that do not exhibit traits of evil or cannibalism. Mooney wrote of one account he obtained in the latter part of the 19th century:

> James Wafford, of the western Cherokee, who was born in Georgia in 1806, says that his grandmother, who must have been born about the middle of the last [17th] century, told him that she had heard from the old people long before her time a party of giants had come once to visit the Cherokee. They were nearly twice as tall as common men, and their eyes set slanting in their heads, so that the Cherokee called them... "the Slant-eyed people."...They said that these giants lived very far away in the direction in which the sun goes down. The Cherokee received them as friends, and they stayed some time, and then returned to their home in the west.[12]

Elkanah Walker, missionary to the Spokane Indians of the Pacific Northwest, wrote in 1840:

> They believe in the existence of a race of giants which inhabit a certain mountain, off to the west of us. This mountain is covered with perpetual snow. They inhabit its top....They hunt and do all their work in the night. They are men stealers. They come to people's lodged in the night, when the people are asleep and take them...to their place of abode without their even awakening...They say their track is about a foot and a half long...They frequently come in the night and steal their salmon from their nets and eat them raw. If the people are awake they always know when they are coming very near by their smell which is most intolerable.[13]

Interestingly enough, Irish mythology links giants to the Little People. Barbara Walker noted, "The Irish said giant people still lived in 'the chambered undergrounds of Tara...'"[14] According to Walker, the giants "shrank as popular belief in their powers waned before the encroachment of the new [Christian] religion. Eventually they became fairies or elves, not giants but 'little people'...This reduction in their size was surely related to a reduction in their awesomeness."[15]

I disagree with this theory because the myths of the two beings are very different; their powers, descriptions, characteristics and habitats are not similar at all but are essentially two different stories. What are we to make of the fact that tales of Little People and Giants are universal across the globe? This is a mystery and one of the most pleasing among many possible explana-

11. Cole, Mable Cook and Fay-Cooper Cole. *The Story of Primitive Man: His Earliest Appearance and Development.* Chicago: University of Knowledge, Inc. 1938, 295-296.

12. Mooney, op. cit., 391.

13. Drury, C.M., ed. *Nine Years with the Spokane Indians: The Diary, 1838-1848, of Elkanah Walker.* Glendale: Arthur H. Clark 1976, 122-123. It should be noted that many contemporary accounts of "Big Foot" also include observations of the creature giving off an "intolerable" small.

14. Walker, Barbara G. *The Women's Encyclopedia of Myths and Secrets.* Edison: Castle Books 1983, 341.

15. Ibid., 342.

tions is the thought that we may have had ancient contacts with other races, great and small, and ongoing cultural diffusion around the world. Walker's theory that the giants "shrank" due to the shrinking of their reputation does not explain those other stories across the world that speak of similar "unusual" people.

To the Netsilik Eskimo there were two giants to contend with. One, called *Amayersuik*, is a dangerous giant female "with a space in her back." Reportedly, she steals children. The *Inugpasugsuk* was a giant who was both fearful and fond of humans and was said to "take great pains not to harm them."[16] This giant no longer lives in the present world but the reason for his demise is unknown.

Some giants had the ability, like the Fairy, to change their sizes. According to Davidson, "One such figure, in Saxo's *History*, claims to be able to alter her appearance at will, becoming huge to terrify her opponents and shrinking to mortal size when taking a mortal lover."[17]

Among the Indian tribes of Tierra del Fuego, according to John Cooper, a gigantic, invisible creature called Taquàtu exists. It is said that he is "a giant who travels by day and night in a big canoe, over the sea and the rivers, and who glides as well through the air over the tops of the trees without bending the branches."[18] Should Taquàtu find a man or woman alone in the forest, "he takes them without much ado into his great boat and carries them far away from home."[19]

In addition, an evil spirit described as an "immense black man," called Yaccy-ma, was greatly feared for the havoc he occasionally caused among the West Patagonian Channel tribes. The Yaccy-ma was blamed for bad weather, famine, illness and most other calamities.[20]

According to Cooper, the Yaccy-ma was probably "a superior being who watches over moral conduct."[21] However, it is difficult to reconcile this statement with another that Cooper attributes to Admiral Fitz-Roy,[22] which calls the Yaccy-ma "an evil spirit."

In English folklore the giant is not only huge in size but also brutal to humans and, usually, extremely stupid. As Simpson and Roud tell it, "They hurled rocks at churches, but missed; carried stones for building, but dropped

16. Balikci, Asen. *The Netsilik Eskimo.* Garden City: The Natural History Press 1970, 205.

17. Davidson, H.R. Ellis. *Myths and Symbols in Pagan Europe: Early Scandinavian and Celtic Religions.* Syracuse: Syracuse University Press 1988, 96.

18. Cooper, John M. *Analytical and Critical Bibliography of the Tribes of Tierra Del Fuego and Adjacent Territory.* Bureau of American Ethnology Bulletin 63. Washington: Smithsonian Institution 1917,147.

19. Ibid.

20. Ibid.

21. Ibid., 148.

22. Robert Fitz-Roy was an explorer to the Patagonian region during the 1830s and was one of the most important authorities of the region for decades to come.

them; killed one another in stone throwing battles, or by accident when toss-ing tools across a valley."[23]

However stupid, brutal, powerful or noble — giants have left a fondness in our hearts and an everlasting thirst for more.

23. Simpson, Jacqueline and Steve Roud. *Oxford Dictionary of English Folklore.* Oxford: Oxford University Press 2000, 144.

# CHAPTER 5. COMPARATIVE FAIRY MYTHOLOGY AND FOLKLORE

Folklore is rife with stories about the "little people" and the powers that they wield. Both good and bad, malevolent and ambivalent, the Fairy both assist humankind and war against it. As symbologist J. E. Cirlot notes, "...they fulfill humble tasks, yet possess extraordinary powers."[1] There is a duality in these stories in regard with the Fairy that is similar to many sacred and unknown things in the world. The Fairy are said to steal children and at the same time assist in their birth. The Fairy are said to cause illness and they are also able to prevent it. As Richard Kieckhefer wrote, "fairies have both good and evil sides, and while they can represent primal paganism they can also be said to hold the Christian faith."[2]

This is an interesting statement since early Christian theologians used to say that Fairies were fallen angels, or, as Harry Percival Swan wrote, "the fairies were angels who had remained neutral during the great war in heaven."[3] Should we assume that a worldwide race of little people existed, in the dim recesses of time? If so, how did they become associated with evil? We do know that pagan traditions and icons were intentionally altered by the Church to reflect darker, more evil aspects in an effort to sway pagan populations away from their original beliefs and into the fold of Christianity. According to 19th century folklorist John Fiske: "Christianity, having no place

1. Cirlot, J.E. *A Dictionary of Symbols, 2nd Edition.* New York: Barnes & Noble Books 1995, 101

2. Kieckhefer, Richard. *Magic in the Middle Ages.* Cambridge: Cambridge University Press 1989, 54.

3. Swan, Harry Percival. *Highlights of the Donegal Highlands.* Belfast: H.R. Carter Publications LTD. 1955, 159.

for such beings, degraded them into something like imps..."[4] The various stories about elves and Fairies which have them both as beneficial as well as malicious towards humankind indicates the uncertainty that humans have about the little people, their origins and intent.

What we see, in reality, is that the nature of the Fairy is not unlike that of humans — comprising both good and evil, bestowing "favors or destruction according to their individual character, whim, or purpose."[5]

In an unsigned article appearing in the June 1844 edition of *Blackwood's Edinburgh Magazine*, an early folklorist quoted Dr. James Grimm: "Something superhuman, approximating them to the gods, is mingled up in them [the fairy]: they possess power to help and to hurt man. They are however, at the same time, afraid of him, because they are not his bodily match. They appear either far below the human stature, or misshapen. Almost all of them enjoy the faculty of rendering themselves invisible."[6] This chapter will focus on these various tales and we will examine similar stories from around the world.

## DESCRIPTIONS AND CHARACTERISTICS OF THE FAIRIES

While their breath is said to be "mortal in Wales, in Ireland, in Scotland, and in Prussa"[7] (as well as in Brittany), it is their physical attributes that are strikingly similar. One of the most interesting things to examine in regards to the Fairy is their actual description taken from various accounts the world over. Among the Cherokee, these strange beings came in different sizes and descriptions depending on their nature. The "Little People," who live in rocks and caves, are "hardly reaching up to a man's knee, but well shaped and handsome, with long hair falling almost to the ground."[8] The "Immortals," another Cherokee Fairy, are said to remain invisible "excepting when they wanted to be seen, and then they looked and spoke just like other Indians."[9] Among the Indian tribes of California, many of the Fairy were called "Water Babies". These creatures were described as small, dwarf-like men in traditional Indian dress with long hair. Also known in California are the "Rock Babies," these are said to look just like babies, with short black hair. Similar beings, part of Olmec culture since 1500 BCE, are those called *chaneques*. These creatures, similar to Water Babies, are still believed in today

---

4. Fiske, John. *Myths and Myth-Makers: Old Tales and Superstitions Interpreted by Comparative Mythology.* Boston: Houghton, Mifflin and Company 1881, 129.

5. Ibid., 108.

6. Anon. "Traditions and Tales of Upper Lusatia, No. 1: The Fairies' Sabbath" in *Blackwood's Edinburgh Magazine*, No. CCCXLIV, Vol. LV, June 1844, 668.

7. Ibid., 667.

8. Mooney, James. *Myths of the Cherokee.* New York: Dover Publications 1995, 333. A reprint of the 1900 publication "Nineteenth Annual Report of the Bureau of American Ethnology, 1897-98.

9. Mooney, op. cit., 331.

and are described as "old dwarfs with faces of children."[10] The chaneques live in waterfalls, dominate wild animals and fish, and are truly wild in nature.

The *hekura* are known and feared by the Yanomamö Indians in southern Venezuela and northern Brazil. Anthropologist Napoleon Chagnon, who studied this group he called "the fierce people," wrote that the *hekura* are "very tiny humanoid beings that dwell on rocks and mountains".[11] The Yanomamö view these small beings as "demons".

In Lakota lore, a mythical, malicious creature said to be similar to a goblin lived in the waters. It "presided over floods, drowning, and accidents in water."[12] It was also said to be the cause of foul water.

Another Fairy known to the Cherokee is "Little Tsăwa'sĭ." This Fairy is called upon by the hunter to give him skill to slip up behind game silently and unseen. He is said to be "a tiny fellow, very handsome, with long hair falling down to his feet."[13]

Spence noted that the Celtic Fairy are of human height while the Teutonic spirits are "usually dwarfish".[14] However, the Celtic Fairy were also known to take on diminutive animal, bird or fish forms. A distinction between the British and German Fairies and Elves was made during the early 20th century, which appears to be the result of British ethnocentricity. Contrary to Spence, Porteous wrote in 1928 that the British Fairy are "tiny creatures, ever dancing on the greensward..."[15] He went on to say "we hear very little of Fairies in Germany, at least as they were known in Britain, owing probably to the coarseness of the Teutonic mentality being unable to appreciate the delicacy of these ethereal beings."[16] Porteous was obviously biased in his treatment of Teutonic lore, more than likely due to the terrible conflict of World War I.

Also tiny are the *abatwa* fairy of Africa. These truly Little People live in anthills and are said to be visible only to children and pregnant women. [17]

The relative size of the various Fairy populations really cannot be definitive as there are many stories of Fairies who can change their size at will — becoming small and "dwarfish" or as tall as an adult human, or, like the *djinn* of Islam, able to shape-shift to the form of gigantic men. Such tales are common not only of British Fairies but of the Little People of Polynesia, the Eskimo, and the Native Americans. The Russians as well had their own form

10. Berrnal, Ignacio. *The Olmec World.* Berkeley: University of California Press 1969, 100.

11. Chagnon, Napoleon A. *Yanomamö: The Fierce People.* New York: Holt, Rinehart and Winston, Inc. Case Studies in Cultural Anthropology, 1968, 52

12. Walker, James R. *Lakota Belief and Ritual.* Lincoln: University of Nebraska Press 1991, 122.

13. Mooney, op. cit., 334.

14. Spence, Lewis. *Legends and Romances of Brittany.* Mineola: Dover Publications Inc. 1997, 74. A reprint of the Frederick A. Stokes Company edition, New York, n.d.

15. Porteous, Alexander. *The Lore of the Forest.* London: Senate 1996, 87. A Reprint of the 1928 edition published by George Allen & Unwin Ltd., London.

16. Ibid., 94.

17. O'Connell, Mark and Raje Airey. *The Complete Encyclopedia of Signs & Symbols.* London: Hermes House 2005, 134.

of size-altering Fairy. Called the *Leshy*[18], these mysterious creatures inhabit the forests and they disappear and reappear with the falling leaves and the sprouting vegetation. Described as "of human form, with horns, ears, and feet of a goat, his fingers are long claws, and he is covered with rough hair, often of a green colour."[19] They could also change their stature at will, remaining as tall as grass stalks or as tall as the tallest tree.

Each spring the *Leshy* would awaken from its hibernation and seek out travelers to cause them to become lost in the new and rich growth of vegetation. "He springs from tree to tree, and rocks himself in the branches, screeching and laughing, neighing, lowing, and barking."[20] The trees and animals of the forest, however, are under his protection. Philpot wrote, "the migrations of squirrels, field-mice, and such small deer are carried out under his guidance."[21] The animals protected the Leshy as well as he was prone to drinking and vulnerable to attacks from other woodland spirits.

To the Polynesians the various nature spirits and Fairies are widely separated by description and character. The Menehune were said to be the ancestors of the Hawaiians and were responsible for the ancient stone constructions evident around the islands. William D. Westervelt, an early 20th century collector of Hawaiian folklore, disagrees with this however, writing, "Menehunes...were classes of fairies or gnomes which did not belong to the ancestor-gods...The menehunes were fairy servants....The Hawaiians separated them almost entirely from the spirits of ancestors. They worked at night," he continues, "performing prodigious tasks which they were never supposed to touch again after the coming of dawn."[22] However, there were other spirits, also known as "fairies," said to be from six inches to four feet in height, fair to dark in complexion and with long straight hair growing to their knees. They were also very strong and, like other fairies around the world, very fond of dance and singing. [23]

Like the "fairies" of Polynesia, Chinese lore speaks of a race of "pygmies" which inhabited many of the mountainous regions of the country. Described as "less than nine inches high, but...well formed," [24] they were said to live in thatched houses that resembled ants' nests. Like many of their other small cousins, these "pygmies" worked in gold, silver, precious stones and wood. The men were distinguished by sporting "slight" beards, the women with

---

18. Also spelled as *Leshii* or *Ljeschi.*

19. Philpot, Mrs. J. H. *The Sacred Tree in Religion and Myth.* Mineola: Dover Publications Inc. 2004, 69 (A reprint of the 1897 edition published by Macmillan and Co. Ltd, New York & London).

20. Ibid.

21. Ibid.

22. Westervelt, William D. *Hawaiian Legends of Ghosts and Ghost Gods.* Honolulu: Mutual Publishing 1998, 255. A reprint of the 1916 edition.

23. Beckwith, Martha. *Hawaiian Mythology.* Honolulu: University of Hawaii Press 1970, 336.

24. Werner, E.T.C. *Myths and Legends of China.* New York: Dover Publications,Inc. 1994,386.A reprint of the 1922 edition published by George G. Harrap & Co., Ltd. London.

tresses four to five inches long. These Little People, however, did not wear green but clothes of a reddish color.

A Fairy-like race called the Patu-pai-a-rehe (wild men) are said to live in New Zealand and are described as having reddish skin, "hair with a golden tinge...eyes black or blue...full sized, dress in white...,"[25] and are very numerous.

The Russian Bania is a structure equivalent to the Finish sauna and has been world renowned since the 12th century. They have been made of wood, concrete and even dug into cliffs. However, what makes the Bania really interesting is the folklore surrounding them. Spirits known as the Bannik frequent them. Rarely seen, they have been described as "old men with hairy paws and long nails"[26] and live either behind the stove or under the benches. For the most part they are harmless but have been known to attack unsuspecting persons by throwing hot stones or water on them and, in some cases actually wrapping the victim around the hot stove. To appease these mean spirits it was common to allow the Bannik to bathe alone after you had finished your bath, and to leave offerings of soap, lye, and birch twigs. In extreme cases, a black chicken would be sacrificed to the Bannik.

What is perhaps even more amazing than the commonality of their appearance is the almost universal descriptions of the Little People's character. Another very common characteristic of the Fairy is their willingness to do the chores of their human neighbors, in record time. The Fairy of Hawaii, it is said, are "so small and industrious (that) any task undertaken must be finished in a single night."[27] As previously noted, the Cherokee *Yûñwĭ Tsunsdi'*, or the "Little People," were known to also help the Indians with their work at night.

Similar stories of helpful Little People were common in Britain. In a submission to the December 14th, 1850 edition of the English periodical, *Notes and Queries*, "H.G.T" offered the following concerning Piskeys:[28]

> An old woman, the wife of a respectable farmer at a place called "Colmans," in the parish of Werrington, near Launceston, has frequently told my informant...of a "piskey" (for so, and not *pixy*, the creature is called here, as well as in parts of Devon) which frequently *made its appearance* in the form of a small child in the kitchen of the farm-house, where the inmates were accustomed to set a little stool for it. It would do a good deal of household work, but if the hearth and chimney corner were not kept neatly swept, it would pinch the maid. The piskey would often come into the kitchen and sit on its little stool before the fire, so that the old lady had many opportunities of seeing it. Indeed it was a familiar guest in the house for many months. At last it left the family under these circumstances. One evening

25. Ibid., 335.
26. Aaland, Mikkel. "The Russian Bania: History of the Great Russian Bath," http://www.cyberbohemia.com/Pages/russianbaniahistory.htm 1998.
27. Andersen, Johannes C. *Myths and Legends of the Polynesians.* Rutland: Charles E. Tuttle Company: Publishers 1969, 137.
28. In Devon and Cornwall the Piskey, or Pixy were believed to be the ghosts of unbaptized babies.

it was sitting on the stool as usual, when it suddenly started, looked up, and said —

> "*Piskey fine and Piskey gay,*
> *Now, Piskey! Run away!*"[29]
> *and vanished; after which it never appeared again.*[30]

In addition, of course, we cannot forget the Leprechauns. In an ethno-graphic study of a small Irish island made in the late 1960s, John C. Messenger, professor of anthropology at Indiana University wrote, "Fairies seldom permit themselves to be seen, but most of the islanders have experienced their presence...."[31] According to information obtain by Messenger, contrary to Spence's statement, while the descriptions of the Fairies is not always consistent, the majority are said to be of the classic image, being "knee high and wear green jackets, flat red caps and buckled shoes."[32]

Another ancient group of nature spirits (for that certainly is what the Fairy are) are the genii loci ("local spirits") that exist in an area of Ethiopia peopled by the Qemant.[33] The Qemant are a "pagan-Hebraic" group of the Agaw, which are the indigenous people of Ethiopia that have lived in this region of the world for thousands of years. These genii loci are believed to control the rain and other aspects of nature and the environment. They are considered minor deities but deities that have major control over small areas. "Community tensions caused by locusts, strife, disease, or a need to regulate rain," writes anthropologist Frederick C. Gamst of Rice University "can be eased by proper veneration of the genii loci."[34]

These nature spirits are widely worshipped and even venerated by the local Christian priests although this practice is not condoned by the Church. They admit these beings are "only indirectly apparent" but say they are believed to exist in two areas of the Qemant territory. One that is venerated is believed to increase rainfall and is said to live on a hilltop with a single large tree. Another who is sought out to reduce or end rainfall lives on a rocky pinnacle a few miles to the west. According to Gamst, "the entire community participates in ceremonies honoring [the genii], which feature sacrificial offerings by animal blood."[35] The genii are said to drink the blood as it is absorbed by the earth.

---

29. Another version of this chant is "Pixy fine, pixy gay, Pixy now will run away."
30. H.G.T., "Piskies" in *Notes and Queries*, Vol. 2 (59), December 14, 1850, 475.
31. Messenger, John C. *Inis Beag: Isle of Ireland*. Case Studies in Cultural Anthropology. New York: Holt, Rinehart and Winston 1969, 98. Note, Inis Beag is a fictitious name given in the study for an actual location.
32. Ibid.
33. The Qemant were removed to Israel during the Ethiopian civil war and no longer reside in their ancestral homeland.
34. Gamst, Frederick C. *The Qemant: A Pagan-Hebraic Peasantry of Ethiopia*. Case Studies in Cultural Anthropology. New York: Holt, Rinehart and Winston 1969, 38.
35. Ibid., 38.

## WHERE THEY LIVE

The "Little People," such as the genii loci, dwarves, elves, trolls, menehu-ene and leprechauns are closely associated with the earth. In fact, they are often referred to as "land-spirits." Most reportedly live in hills, mounds, caves and the other mysterious places we all know and fear, although a few also are said to live in trees, among waterfalls and mountain passes. The Leprechaun of Inis Beag reportedly live in torn bushes where they "spend most of their time feasting, singing, dancing, fighting, playing games, and making love."[36]

Even among the Maya, Aztecs and Olmecs these little people had many of the same features of their European relations. Among the Olmecs dwarves were occasionally featured with wings in a semblance of the gargoyle. These dwarves were said to play unpleasant tricks on humankind — much as the Fairies and other nature spirits did in the rest of the world. Even today among contemporary Mayan people in the highlands, they "believe that dwarves dwell under the surface of the earth."[37]

In some parts of the world, Little People are referred to as dwarves and trolls rather than the more refined "Fairy" terminology used elsewhere. Dwarves and trolls tend to be regarded as more crude and evil than Fairy. Thirteenth-century Icelandic poet Snorri Sturluson wrote, "The dwarfs had taken shape first and acquired life in the flesh of Ymir and were then maggots, but by decision of the gods they became conscious with intelligence and had shape of men though they live in the earth and in rocks."[38]

In all aspects, however, the Little People regardless of their names had extra-ordinary powers. These powers include invisibility, shape shifting and, according to Mesoamerican lore, the ability to move heavy objects. According to John Bierhorst, "as explained by Yucatec storytellers, the first people were dwarfs, the ones who built the ancient temples. Construction work had been easy for them because all they had had to do was whistle and heavy rocks would move into place."[39] Called "the Adjusters," like their cousins they worked in darkness, for to be struck by sunlight would result in their turning to stone. This fate is also recorded in Norse tales of trolls being turned to stone by exposure to the sun.

Similar tales occur in other parts of the world as well. Megaliths in Brittany "were raised by fairy hands," wrote folklorist Lewis Spence, "the elves collecting 'all the big stones in the country' and carrying them thither in their aprons."[40]

36. Messenger, op. cit.

37. Miller, Mary and Karl Taube. *An Illustrated Dictionary of The Gods and Symbols of Ancient Mexico and the Maya.* London: Thames and Hudson 1993, 82.

38. Sturluson, Snorri. *Edda.* London: J.M. Dent 1987, 14.

39. Bierhorst, John. *The Mythology of Mexico and Central America.* New York: William Morrow and Company, Inc. 1990, 8.

40. Spence, Lewis. *Legends and Romances of Brittany.* Mineola: Dover Publications, Inc. 1997, 50. A reprint of an undated edition published by Frederick A. Stokes Company, New York.

A race of dwarves called *Inuarugligarsuit* by the Netsilik Eskimo reportedly live in the mountains where they live like the Eskimo even to the extent of hunting tiny game animals. When these tiny people are seen by the Eskimo, they are said to "have the peculiar ability to grow in size up to the height of ordinary human beings."[41]

In the mythology of other Central American tribes, the original inhabitants of the world were tiny hunter-gatherers and the Yaqui tell of an ancient people called the *surem* who are described as "a diminutive, gentle folk who could not stand noise or conflict."[42]

Like other descriptions of Little People given in Native American lore, these dwarves of Mesoamerica were said to be very old but looked like young boys.

The Little People of the Cherokee were said to live in rock caves on the sides of mountains, the Immortals were said to live in "townhouses" under mounds of earth and the Little Tsǎwa'sǐ live in "grassy patches" on hillsides — presumably mounds. The Rock Babies of the Great Basin actually lived within rock surfaces and could transport themselves easily between the two worlds.

Likewise folklore of the Finno-Ugric peoples indicate that a race of small, black creatures called *Chudes* live in dark underground areas, holes in the earth and in abandoned houses, cellars and the woods. These Little People would often throw stones and coal at humans wandering through their land. Reportedly the Chudes rebelled against the tall humans arriving near their homes, hid themselves in their holes and were regarded as demonic by the humans.[43]

Fairies in Corsica are not considered benevolent by any means. They are believed to be "wild creatures" and "water sprites" which live in caves near water and, although they are described as being beautiful, they are "dangerous to mortal man."[44]

In Britain, many of the Fairies are reported to live in the ancient megalithic monuments; dolmen, stone circles and burrows. In fact, many native peoples of the Isles believe that these ancient stone structures were built by the Fairy or used them as homes.[45] Porteous, however, wrote, "forests were their favorite resorts, and on clear moonlight nights they and the Elves were believed to dance hand in hand around the trees, and the grass being trodden down by their aerial feet, grew up with renewed vigour, and formed green circles known as Fairy rings."[46] Similar tales exist of Fairy in Estonia that,

41. Balikci, Asen. *The Netsilik Eskimo.* Garden City: The Natural History Press 1970, 205.
42. Ibid., 9.
43. Lintrop, Aado. "On the Udmurt Water Spirit and the Formation of the Concept 'Holy" Among Permian Peoples" in *Folklore*, Vol. 26, April 2004, 16. Published by the Folk Belief & Media Group of the Estonian Literary Museum, Tartu.
44. Carrington, Dorothy. *The Dream Hunters of Corsica.* London: Phoenix 1995, 48.
45. Spence, op. cit., 49.
46. Porteous, op. cit., 88.

like their British and American cousins, dance and sing at night, play tricks on humans and steal children, leaving changelings in their place.[47]

The Fairy people of New Zealand dwell in the mountains while those that reside on the Island of Mangaia are said to be from the underworld and, like the California Rock Babies, are able to travel through special apertures in the rock.

Elves in Nordic areas reportedly live in groups and families and are led by Freyr and Freyja, two of the most important deities.

## CHILDREN & CHILDBIRTH

The dangers of childbirth to both the mother and the newborn were extreme up to recent times. In fact they still are in many parts of the world where modern medicine is kept apart from the common people. It is no wonder that rituals were created to combat those dangers — either real or imagined. The loss of children through illness and accident was a tremendous hardship. Children also simply disappeared after accidentally wandering away from their homes. Many of these tragedies were explained as deeds of the Fairy.

Contemporary folklore recorded in the United States during the 1960s indicates that ancient beliefs still survive in our "advanced" state. "If you dress boys in skirts," a belief recorded in Ohio said, "the fairies won't steal them." This practice evidently had been brought to the United States by Irish immigrants. Evans noted in his book, *Irish Folk Ways*: "The old custom of dressing boys in girls' clothes, in long frocks, until they were ten or eleven years of age has been explained as a means of deceiving the fairies, who were always on the lookout for healthy young boys whom they could replace by feeble 'changelings'".[48] This practice was still in use in the 1960s in parts of Ireland and Messenger noted that boys up to the age of 18 were sometimes dressed in petticoats to confuse the Fairy.[49]

Other extreme measures included laying a pair of shears in the baby's cradle to protect the child from being stolen by Fairies. This practice evidently was known from Canada to Salt Lake City in the 1950s and '60s. It is unknown how many babies may have been injured with this protective measure! Scottish folklore recorded during the 1970s stipulated that to keep your baby safe from the Fairies, "someone must walk around your house seven times sun wise to create an invisible barrier which the fairies cannot pass."[50] Such "perambulation" is an ancient ritual still used in Britain at holy wells. It probably originated in ancient magical rituals far older.

Protective measures taken to keep newborn children safe were sometimes complicated, sometimes expensive and sometimes bizarre. Among the

---

47. Lintrop, op. cit., 11.
48. Evans, E. Estyn. *Irish Folk Ways*. Mineola: Dover Publications Inc. 2000, 289. A reprint of the 1957 edition published by Routledge & Kegan Paul Ltd., London.
49. Messenger, op. cit. 99.
50. University of California Los Angeles Folklore Archives, record # 2_6107.

Gypsies of Transylvania, it was believed that the placenta must be burned after birth, "otherwise wicked fairies could turn them into vampires who would attack the child."[51] In Germany, herbs were loaded in the newborn's cradle the first eight days after its birth to keep the child from being stolen by Fairies. These first eight days were regarded as the most dangerous time for a newborn, in fact the most dangerous time in the child's life. After christening, however, it was no longer in danger of such calamity, indicating the partial success of the Church in interrupting if not eradicating such beliefs.

According to Celtic scholar Anne Ross, a Scottish Highland custom practiced to protect newborns from the Fairies "was to make the baby swallow a large quantity of fresh butter after birth...before baptism it must be protected against this dangerous race of beings, and other supernatural creatures."[52]

Another protective practice observed in 19th century Devon was reported in the December 14, 1850 edition of *Notes and Queries*:

> The country people in their neighborhood sometimes put a prayer-book under a child's pillow as a charm to keep away the piskies. I am told that a poor woman near Launceston was fully persuaded that one of her children was taken away and a piskey substituted, the disaster being caused by the absence of the prayer-book on one particular night.

Folklore recorded in Ohio during the 1930s called for the placing of a newborn in a "light place" for the first forty days following birth, "or the fairies will give him bad luck." Good luck, on the other hand, was also available from the Fairies. In California and Ohio, it was said that gold or a golden object should be placed inside a newborn's clothing in the first three days of its life. It was believed that during these three days the baby would "be visited by the fairies who decide what kind of life he will have. If there is gold there, the fairies will be pleased and grant a good life."[53]

While many beliefs center on the bad side of the Fairy, and how individuals can protect themselves from the Fairies' evil deeds,[54] there are other stories that lend a different aspect to the relationship between humans and Fairies. During the 19th century, it was a belief in Derbyshire, England that a Fairy midwife would suddenly arrive during a difficult pregnancy. Sidney Addy noted "the fairies come, nobody knows how, bringing with them a little fairy woman, called a midwife, whose eyes are covered with a hood. In

---

51. Long, E. Croft. "The Placenta in Lore and Legend", in *Bulletin of the Medical Library Association #51* (1963), 236.
52. Ross, Anne. *Folklore of the Scottish Highlands.* Gloucestershire: Tempus Publishing Ltd. 2000, 119.
53. Puckett, Newbell Niles. *Popular Beliefs and Superstitions: A Compendium of American Folklore from the Ohio Collection of Newbell Niles Puckett.* Edited by Wayland D. Hand. Boston 1981, 136 and UCLA Folklore Archives Record # 3_6107.
54. Such as the Scottish Highland belief that nails driven in the front of the bed will ward off elves while the woman is in "child-bed".

the same mysterious manner as the fairies bring the midwife, they fetch her away, after she has assisted the woman in labor."[55]

The opposite occurred in Estonian folklore. In this Baltic country, a human midwife was summoned to care for a Fairy woman during her delivery. Not only Fairies but also Dwarves and Water Spirits would contract with a human midwife who would be paid in gold — which promptly turned into coals or leaves.[56]

Likewise, a bit of folklore from Ohio recorded in the mid-1920s appears to indicate that parents, at times, do things to increase the likelihood of contact between a child and the Fairy. According to Puckett, "green ribbons on a christening robe make a child see fairies."[57] It was said in 1960s California, "babies who smile while sleeping are dreaming of fairies."[58]

Some lore indicates that babies are created by Fairy elves "who bring them to people who want them very much." According to this tale, "the mother pays the elves for her baby by giving them carrots (sic)."[59] What a deal! Again the dichotomy between the good, beneficent Fairy and the wicked, vengeful creature is striking.

## Fairies & Illness

Other than stealing children, Fairies are also feared for their ability to bring illness and death to humans. Wide varieties of protective measures were developed over time to combat this danger — including bribery. Dr. Max Kahn noted in an article he wrote in the *Popular Science Monthly* in 1913 that in northern Europe the Fairies "were vested with the dreaded power of inflicting disease. Fairies were supposed to be evil spirits which might be propitiated by giving them a gracious appellation."[60]

Another way to combat an illness already received was to obtain soil from a churchyard while the minister is still in the pulpit preaching and to place it on the afflicted part. [61] In Norway, it was believed that sores were caused by "black elves of the underworld" and could only be treated by placing a special stone, called a *Jorelo* in milk and rubbing the milk over the sores.

In southern Slavic countries during the 19th century, incantations were performed with water and burning coals to determine the origins of sickness. Supposedly, the "doctor" was able to determine if God, the Devil, Fairies or witches caused the illness. It is assumed that only in those cases where God caused sickness were extreme remedies not employed.

55. Addy, Sidney Oldall. *Household Tales with Other Traditional Remains Collected in the Counties of York, Lincoln, Derby, and Nottingham.* London: 1895, 134.

56. Lintrop, op. cit., 9.

57. Puckett, op. cit.

58. UCLA Folklore Archives Record # 23_6106.

59. UCLA Folklore Archives, Record Number 11-5775.

60. Kahn, Max. "Vulgar Specifics and Therapeutic Superstitions" in *Popular Science Monthly*, #83 (1913), 86.

61. Storaker, Joh. Th. "Sygdom og Forgjo/relse i den Norske Folketro", in *Norske Folkeminnelag* #20, Oslo 1932, 25.

Even into the 20th century people connected illness and death with spirits of the otherworld. It is easier to believe that some supernatural force is responsible for such tragedy rather than it being a natural occurrence. In New York it was said that "those who have tuberculosis are eventually taken by the fairies."[62]

In the Philippines, it could be more deadly to say that one had actually seen a Fairy than to be stricken by disease. According to Francisco Demetrio y Radaza, such individuals were often whipped by a priest wielding a cord and could be subject to an exorcism.[63]

While the Fairy are often blamed for sickness they are also sources for healing knowledge. "Fairy doctors," usually older women, were believed to have received their knowledge from Fairies who, Lady Wilde said, "impart to them the mystical secrets of herbs and where to find them."[64] The Fairies secrets were well kept however. They were only divulged on the death-bed and only given to the eldest member of the Fairy doctor's family. These Fairy doctors were well respected in the community, as illnesses were believed to be unable to withstand their medicines. Wilde noted that these Fairy doctors were young girls who had been kidnapped by the Fairies and kept for seven years; "when the girls grow old and ugly," she wrote, "they send them back to their kindred, giving them, however, as compensation, a knowledge of herbs and philters and secret spells, by which they can kill or cure".[65]

Reportedly these Fairy Doctors mixed their strong potions on May Eve and the potions were such that "no sickness can resist."[66]

## FAIRIES & ADULT HUMANS

Obviously, children were especially believed to be vulnerable to the powers of the Fairy. However many of the same fears were contained in the minds of adults as well. Human babies were protected from the Fairies, who were believed to steal them; so too were brides. Lady Wilde noted, "a new-married couple should retire to rest at the same time, for if the bride were left alone, the fairies would come and steal her away for the sake of her fine clothes."[67]

Similar prohibitions protecting adults from the evil ways of the Fairy were also common in the United States in the mid-twentieth century. Newbell Puckett recorded in Cleveland, Ohio the warning "if you walk through the woods at night, and if you see fairies dancing, you'll surely die."[68] Another similar bit of folklore from the same area warned people not to build

62. Jones, Louis C. "The Little People" in *New York Folklore Quarterly*, #18 (1962), 258.
63. Demetrio y Radaza, Francisco. *Dictionary of Philippine Folk Beliefs and Customs, vol.2.* Philippines: 1970, 370.
64. Wild, Lady. *Irish Cures, Mystic Charms & Superstitions.* New York: Sterling Publishing Co. Inc. 1991, 100.
65. Wild, op. cit., 105.
66. Wild, Lady. *Ancient Legends, Mystic Charms and Superstitions of Ireland.* London: Chatto and Windus 1919, 104.
67. Ibid., 64.
68. Puckett, op. cit., 1172.

their houses on Fairy rings, "because this is where the fairies dance. If you do, all your children will die."[69] In Ireland, deliberate precautions were taken to avoid this danger. According to E. Estyn Evans: "...it was at all costs necessary to avoid giving offence to the fairies by building across one of their 'pads'. In Tyrone it is said that 'no man would build a house till he had stuck a new spade into the earth'. If the fairies had not removed it overnight the site was safe."[70]

These precautions are a sign of a healthy respect for the Fairy. The Irish appear to take the approach of "request and approval" prior to any possible incursion into Fairy territory. Only a few years ago a new road scheduled to be constructed in Ireland was detoured to afford protection of a hawthorn tree said to be sacred to the Fairy. An article in the *Irish Times* reported, "One of the State's best known folklorists and story tellers...had warned that the destruction of the fairy thorn bush or 'sceach' at Latoon outside Newmarket-on-Fergus to facilitate the bypass plans could result in misfortune and in some cases death for those traveling the proposed new road."[71] According to the folklorist, the fairy thorn was a marker for the Kerry fairies to rendezvous in a battle with a group of Connacht fairies and he stressed that sacred land cannot revert to being a normal place simply because men have said it is so.

"Fairies disregard human beings most of the time," relates Messenger, "but they can harm those who disregard or speak ill of them, as well as play 'fairy pranks' out of sheer capriciousness."[72]

Swan relates one Irish tale of the doings of malevolent Fairies:

> "A girl had her face twisted through their influence, and had to go to the priest to be cured. 'He was...one of the old sort, who could work miracles, of whom there are not many nowadays'."[73]

Sacrifices to elves were common in Nordic countries well after their supposed Christianization had begun. In Norway annual feasts called *álfablót*, which means "sacrifice to the elves," was held to appease their sometimes-wicked ways.[74] Similar sacrifices were annually held in Sweden during the autumn.

Fairies are very protective of their privacy and of the land they reside on. A 19th century folklorist wrote, "Whosoever has muddied the waters of their spring, or caught them combing their hair, or counting their treasures beside their dolmen...almost inevitably dies."[75] And, of all days *not* to chance

---

69. Ibid., 158.

70. Evans, op. cit., 30.

71. Deegan, Gordon. "Fairy bush survives the motorway planners" in *The Irish Times*, Saturday, May 29, 1999.

72. Messenger, op. cit. 98.

73. Swan, op. cit., 159.

74. Davidson, H.R. Ellis. *Myths and Symbols in Pagan Europe: Early Scandinavian and Celtic Religions.* Syracuse: Syracuse University Press 1988, 40.

75. Anon. *Blackwood's...op. cit.,* 667.

upon the fairy, Saturday's are especially bad, "which day, holy to the Virgin mother, is inauspicious for their kind."[76]

## FAIRIES AND CROPS

Fairies have had a long association with vegetation and crops in particular. Like other nature spirits, the Fairy may cause plants to grow in abundance or make them wither and die — should they be slighted by the human farmer in some manner. Even the Great Potato Famine of 1846-47 in Ireland was said to be caused by the Fairy. "At the time," wrote W.Y. Evans-Wentz, "the country people in these parts attributed the famine to disturbed conditions in the fairy world."[77]

Messenger noted that on Inis Beag small whirlwinds are a sign of fairies passing by. Any farmer failing to say "God bless them" when seeing a whirlwind was likely to have his entire crop blown away.

## FAIRIES AND THE COLOR GREEN

The color green has become synonymous with Fairies in almost every culture. In Estonia, the word for Fairy is *vožo*, which according to folklorist Aado Lintrop, "means green, verdure, unripe".[78] This Udmurt word is perhaps the most telling about the perceived dual nature of the Fairy. Vožo not only means "green" but it is also the basis for the words "sacred," "holy," "evil," and "anger." Green is symbolic of both life and death.

Green has been known for untold ages as the color of the Fairy. Green was so universally recognized as the color of the Fairy that many in Scotland refused to wear it as to do so would be to invite the anger of the Fairy folk. "Greenies" and "greencoaties" were common euphemisms used in Britain for the Fairy. Green was a color shunned by many as being associated with evil fairies and witches.

But why green? Green is associated with nature, with ripening life and with fertility, paganism and the supernatural — things that the Church could not control. Perhaps more importantly green symbolized not only enchantment but also divine beings. Green is also a sacred color of many religious traditions. David Catherine wrote, "much like Sufism, which associates the colour green to a realization of Wholeness/god, Tibetan culture sees the colour green as a container for all other colours."[79]

During the formation of Christianity, nature was seen to exist for the pleasure and consumption of man. Man was regarded as supreme over na-

---

76. Ibid.
77. Evans-Wentz, W.Y. *The Fairy-Faith in Celtic Countries*. Mineola: Dover Publications Inc. 2002, 43. A reprint of the 1911 edition published by Henry Frowde, London.
78. Lintrop, op. cit. 12.
79. Catherine, David. "The Green Fingerprint: Exploring a critical signature in the quest for the authentic Self". Unpublished paper copyright 2004 by Ufudu Medicinal Arts, South Africa, 8.

ture. That nature should exist as an entity unto herself, with powers beyond those of man, was a thought that put fear into many. Later, nature was viewed as evil and anything associated with nature was seen in a similar way. "By imitative magic," wrote Barbara G. Walker, "wearing green was supposed to encourage mother earth to clothe herself in the green of abundant crops."[80] That green represented the power and fertile life of nature slowly came to be associated with evil, and thus pagan, forms bent on the torment of humanity. To the Christian church green was associated with the dead, witches and sexual promiscuity. Thus Fairies, who were mischievous entities of the underworld, part of the Old Race which inhabited many parts of the world prior to man's arrival, became, if not outright evil, close relatives of evil. Green became, over time, associated with bad luck. This is well illustrated by the 19th century writer Patrick Graham. Graham wrote of the Fairy, which he called "the men of peace," that inhabited the Scottish Highlands: "The men of peace, are believed to be always dressed in green; and are supposed to take offence, when any of mortal race presume to wear their favourite colour. The celebrated Viscount of Dundee, was dressed in green, when he commanded at the Battle of Killicrankie; and to this circumstance the Highlanders ascribe the disastrous event of that day. It is still accounted peculiarly ominous to any person of *his name*, to assume this sacred colour."[81] Graham also notes that the color green "was probably the appropriate dress of the Druidical Order...in the Battle with the Fingallians, which, according to tradition, finally decided the fortunes of the Druidical Order, their Standard was Green."[82] The Radford's note "the colour green is so allied throughout Europe with luck and protection from the tree spirits, that it is...strange to find it regarded at all as an unlucky colour."[83] This bit of propaganda was so entrenched in the minds of Europeans in the early 20th century that one "cultured man" was heard to say that the pre-World War I troubles in England all stemmed from the introduction of a green halfpenny stamp.[84] Popular superstitions about the color green were abundant in the 19th century. The December 28, 1850 issue of the English periodical *Notes and Queries* reported, "In a parish adjoining Dartmoor is a green Fairy ring of considerable size, within which a black hen and chickens are occasionally seen at nightfall." Black hens were often considered as embodiments of evil. To wear green was ill advised as green clothes put oneself in the power of the Fairy folk who, in theory, owned the color as their own.

Green as a color has been associated as well with the symbolism of new growth and greenness and it is this association which the Fairy have their

80. Walker, Barbara G. *The Women's Encyclopedia of Myths and Secrets*. Edison: Castle Books 1983, 355.
81. Graham, Patrick. *Sketches Descriptive of the Picturesque Scenery of Perthshire*. Edinburgh 1810, 107-108.
82. Ibid.
83. Radford, Edwin and Mona A. *Encyclopaedia of Superstitions*. New York: The Philosophical Library 1949, 137.
84. Ibid.

link. However, it is also this link that humankind has lost over the centuries that has been reestablished through the Green Man, the Wild Huntsman and the other legends and images of the super-natural. Green is, according to the Doel's, an "extension to the natural world — and the supernatural in both its 'Otherworld' and afterlife elements."[85]

Brian Stone, a Reader in English Literature at the Open University, most succinctly defines the importance of the color green, "it surprises me that no critic has picked up one very important medieval theological reference to green as the colour of truth...evergreen...is the colour assigned to ever-living and eternal truth."[86]

## THE NATURE OF FAIRIES

We are only capable of guessing about the origins of these tales and if, in fact, the folklore of Fairy is based on some event or people that, while not really representing a mythic race of supernatural beings, did strongly alter oral traditions. Such mythic tales may have spread rapidly through trade and cultural interactions. H.R. Ellis Davidson, historian and former president of the British Folklore Society, summarized the difficulty in her book, *Myths and Symbols in Pagan Europe:* "The idea of the fairies as a former race who remained hidden from men has been explained as memories of an earlier culture displaced by more powerful invaders, but it might also be based on traditions of the land-spirits, who, as in uninhabited Iceland, possessed the land before settlers came to live there."[87]

85. Doel, Fran & Geoff. *The Green Man in Britain.* Gloucestershire: Tempus Publishing Ltd. 2001, 25.

86. Stone, Brian. "The Common Enemy of Man", in *Sir Gawain and the Green Knight,* trans. by Brian Stone. London: Penguin Books 1974, 123.

87. Davidson, H.R. Ellis. *Myths and Symbols in Pagan Europe: Early Scandinavian and Celtic Religions.* Syracuse: Syracuse University Press 1988, 112.

# Chapter 6. Fairies and Giants: A World of Reality or World of Myth?[1]

## Fairies

Fairy lore around the world is remarkable for its uniformity between countries, cultures and times. What are the reasons for this? Are these stories just that — stories? Are the tales passed down from generation to generation to explain the unknown or to persuade children to behave in certain ways? Or are they something else? "What is remarkable about fairy belief," wrote Marc Alexander, "is that it survived so vigorously for so long, especially as it had no organized structure to support it, unlike orthodox beliefs. It outlasted other aspects of folklore, and when witches ceased to be feared fairies were still respected."[1]

In 2004, a remarkable discovery was made which may shed light on this perplexing question. On the isolated Indonesian island of Flores a cave yielded the remains of half a dozen "little people" — described as Hobbit-sized (or, more accurately, only half the size of modern humans), that had existed on the island for some 95,000 years. It is possible that for 30,000 of those years they occupied the area alongside *Homo sapiens* — modern humans. Chief paleontologist Teuku Jacob, of the University of Gajah Mada, believes that these people are, in reality, a sub-species of modern man and that the small skull is suggestive of "mental defects"[2] rather than an indication of a separate human species.

---

1. Alexander, Marc. *A Companion to the Folklore, Myths & Customs of Britain.* Gloucestershire: Sutton Publishing Limited 2002, 91.
2. Santoso, Dewi and M. Taufiqurrahman. "Archaeologists divided over 'Homo floresiensis" in *The Jakarta Post*, October 30, 2004.

Other research indicates that Jacob is incorrect and that a race, or species, of human beings with a sophisticated technology and social structure and complex mental abilities survived for thousands of years.[3] Regardless of whose theory is correct the fact that these small people probably lived an autonomous existence alongside their bigger human brothers and sisters gives credence to the theory that they may be the basis for many of the fairy stories around the world — and their existence suggests that similar groups may have existed on other continents. Another scientist, Bert Roberts, said, "the new skeleton sounded remarkably similar to the Ebu Gogo, strange hairy little people that legend says lived on Flores".[4] The cave also yielded skeletal remains of pygmy elephant and komodo dragons. These little people had amazingly small brains but they made fire, stone weapons and hunted in groups. Due to the fact that the island was not connected to the mainland, they evidently also mastered water travel in rafts or small boats.

Geological records indicate that this group of humans may have been eradicated around 11-12,000 years ago when a massive volcano erupted on the island. Evidently, other archaeological discoveries show that the next group of modern humans to arrive on the island showed up around that time, after the volcanic eruption. However, island folklore tells a different story. According to Bert Roberts, an anthropologist with the University of Wollongong in New South Wales, Australia, "The stories suggest that there may be more than a grain of truth to the idea that they were still living on Flores up until the Dutch arrived in the 1500s. The stories suggest they lived in caves. The villagers would leave gourds with food out for them to eat, but legend has it these were the guests from hell — they'd eat everything, including the gourds!"[5]

Representatives of the Indonesian Archaeologists Association believe that the group of skeletal remains proves that ancient humans, in many forms, migrated around the world.[6]

Debate continues in the scientific community between those who believe the small statured people are a distinct species and those who feel that the skeletons are anomalous examples of *Homo sapiens*. According to Dr. Robert D. Martin, primatologist and Provost of the Chicago Field Museum, "a far more likely explanation is that the bones belonged to a modern human who suffered from microcephaly, a pathological condition that causes small brain size, often associated with short stature."[7] This seems unlikely, however, as multiple skeletons have been found of such small size humans. According to Martin, the cranial size is too small to have been derived from *Homo erectus*

3. Morwood, Mike & et al. "The People Time Forgot" in *National Geographic*, April 2005, 12.

4. Santoso, op. cit.

5. Onion, Amanda. "Scientists Find Ancient Hobbit-Sized People". ABC News October 27, 2004, www.abcnews.go.Technology.

6. Santoso, op. cit.

7. "'Hobbit' claims lose ring of truth" in The Geological Society of London Geology News, http://www.geolsoc.org.uk/template.cfm?name=Flores 5/20/06

through "normal dwarfing." He also states that the stone tools found were too advanced to have been made by any other than *Homo sapiens*.

Other scientists believe that these small hominids did make advanced looking tools and that the size of the brain has little to do with innate intelligence. In fact, according to Adam Brumm of the Australian National University in Canberra, tools dating back more than 800,000 years on Flores indicates that the little people inherited tool making abilities from their ancient ancestors.[8] The argument that the tools must have been made by modern humans is one commonly given when discussing any find that is out of the ordinary. The creature's origin may not have been from *Homo erectus* at all but was, in fact, a totally distinct evolutionary branch. And, as most traditional scientist would say, something that appears to be "advanced" in tool making cannot possibly have been created by anything less than modern man. The final chapter in this debate will not be written for sometime.

This discovery has all of the elements of traditional Fairy lore. These people are exceptionally small (and not related to contemporary pygmy tribes of Africa), lived in caves, hunted and fought with dragons and received propitiations from the local residents who regarded them with fear and attributed to them supernatural characteristics. They also co-existed with "modern man" perhaps as recently as 200-500 years ago. Such co-existence would certainly have inspired much folklore. The enigma of other types of humans, large or small (and other creatures, for that matter), infrequently encountered and mysterious, would surely have left a lasting impression. If indeed such remnant peoples did co-exist with modern man, and if they had preserved rituals and skills that modern man lacked, that would add fuel to the tales and be a convenient explanation for the odd fact that so much Fairy-lore describes similar creatures with the same characteristics.

It has been theorized that the human race originally had one language. That would have fostered the spread of customs and customary explanations for the world (including what we now call myths). As writer Mike Morwood with the *National Geographic* said, "It's breathtaking to think that modern humans may still have a folk memory of sharing the planet with another species of human, like us but unfathomably different."[9] Such a possibility, though the scientific evidence for it is lacking, remains highly attractive to the human imagination.

Another Indonesian mystery involves a creature called the *orang pendek*, or "little person." Described as a species of "tiny, bipedal primate" that may live in the mountains of Indonesia around the Seblat National Park in Sumatra, the *orang pendek* is reportedly the size of a small child, covered in brown, grey or black fur, with a hairless face and large teeth. Said by the locals to run upright, no one has been able to photograph it, despite numerous attempts with camera traps. Plaster casts have been presented, purporting to represent its

---

8. "Scientists link tools to ancient 'hobbits'", Reuters http://www.msnbc.msn.com/id/13065961 May 31, 2006
9. Morwood, op. cit.

foot and hand prints, however. Even as expeditions are being launched to verify the tale, it is feared that the extensive logging in the Indonesian forests will destroy its habitat and thereby the creatures chances of survival.[10]

Native American lore in itself is specific about the existence of such a population that pre-dated the arrival of the Indian. The Mohegan Indians, who lived between the Thames and the Connecticut Rivers in what is now Connecticut, spoke of a race of "little men" that had originally occupied the territory that the Mohegan came to know as home. According to legend, this race of men had pretty much become extinct by the time the Pequot tribe worked their way down from the Hudson River area to the Sound area of Connecticut.

"Little was seen of them by the Indians," according to historian Terri Hardin, "and less was known, until after the disruption of a fractious band under Uncas, prior to 1630....These are the tribal accounts. It seems then that before long the newcomers, the Mohegans, discovered that another people, a smaller and lighter people, were the rightful tenants of their adopted home. And from this period date the original memoirs relating to the mysterious originals."[11]

Those few that were seen by the Mohegans were probably the last of the race, "leaving nothing but weird reminders in the shape of a few relics and memories among the Mohegans."[12] Those "relics" include groups of dwarf sized bones that have been washed or plowed up, some exhibiting "inscriptions claimed by the Indians to have been carved not by themselves, but by some 'other people'."[13]

Like the Little People of Flores, this group of people may have also survived in the world until approximately 300 years ago.

Nineteenth-century antiquarian Caleb Atwater wrote that excavators of the various mound structures near the Coneaught River in Ohio found evidence of a smaller race of people:

"My informant says, within this work are sometimes found skeletons of a people of small stature, which, if true, sufficiently identifies it to have belonged to that race of men who erected our tumuli."[14]

Atwater goes on to say:

"The skeletons found in our mounds never belonged to a people like our Indians. The latter are a tall, rather slender, strait limbed people; the former were short and thick. They were rarely over five feet high...."[15]

10. "Expeditions" in *National Geographic*, March 2006, Vol. 209, No. 3, 26
11. Hardin, Terri, ed. *Legends & Lore of the American Indians.* New York: Barnes & Noble, Inc. 1993, 80.
12. Ibid.
13. Ibid.,81.
14. Atwater, Caleb. *Description of the Antiquities Discovered in the State of Ohio and Other Western States.* Ohio: American Antiquarian Society 1820, 125.
15. Ibid., 209.

Atwater, of course, was unaware of the large diversity of Native populations and ethnic groups that later anthropologists and archaeologists have documented.

Stories similar to other legends of Little People around the world speak of them as running along the banks of rivers or through the forests. They reportedly had the ability to become invisible so that they could take what they wanted from their larger neighbors, unseen.

Similar legends exist among the Iroquois as well that tell of Little Men who act as protectors of deer and other game animals and who have the ability to appear or disappear at will.

The indigenous occupants of Japan, the Ainu, have similar tales of an ancient race of tiny men. An interesting tale recorded in an old book on primitive man sums up the Ainu legend. The Ainu "have a tradition...of a race of dwarfs who used to live in their country, whom their ancestors finally drove out. These dwarfs, they say, belonged in the Stone Age and occupied the pits which archaeologists have investigated all over northern Japan. These people were so small, the Ainu claim, that as many as ten of them could be sheltered under one burdock leaf [approximately four feet across] during a shower."[16]

Another legend concerning "little people" in unusual circumstances also comes from Asia. According to Michael Bradley the story originated in 1938 when Professor Chi Pu Tei of Beijing University discovered the first of 716 grooved stone discs while surveying a network of caves in mountains on the border of China and Tibet. The remainder of the discs was found in a return expedition made in 1965. The discs are nine inches in diameter and each one has a continuous spiral groove "of almost microscopic hieroglyphs."[17] The caves in which the discs were found were reportedly man-made and appeared as if they had been constructed with extreme heat. Inside the caves were a series of burials. The skeletons that were unearthed were of "tiny bodies less than four feet long with oversized heads." The discs, and burials have been dated by other Chinese scholars as being over 12,000 years old. According to local lore, "small men with thin yellow faces and bright blue eyes" came down from the clouds and were met by local tribes that hunted them down. "The area around the caves," according to Bradley, "is still occupied by two tribes.... Anthropologically they are neither Chinese nor Tibetan." "Both tribes," Bradley continues, "measure between three-feet six-inches and four-feet seven-inches and are yellow skinned, with thin bodies, disproportionately large heads, and bright blue eyes..."[18] Supposedly, according to Bradley, in 1995 China claimed that yet another tribe of "little people" had been located in the same mountains of Baian-Kara-Ula. The smallest adult reportedly was only two-feet one-inch in height.

16. Cole, Mabel Cook and Fay-Cooper Cole. *The Story of Primitive Man: His Earliest Appearance and Development.* Chicago: University of Knowledge, Inc. 1938, 339.
17. Bradley, Michael. *Guide to the World's Greatest Treasures.* New York: Barnes & Noble 2005, 69.
18. Ibid., 71.

This "legend" is presented by Bradley with no ethnographic or physical evidence; most of the information is credited to the "Ancient Astronaut Society." The Dropa story is told and retold on UFO and alien conspiracy web pages without any collaborative evidence and it has taken its place in the world's urban mythology.

Of course, even today there are "pygmies" that fit many of these stories. Pygmies live today in the Congo, the Andaman Islands, the Malay Peninsula, New Guinea and the Philippines. And, while all of these groups have been living apart from each other for thousands of years, they share many physical and social customs that suggest, perhaps, that pygmies were much more common around the world in the distant past. Perhaps the people of Flores and these other groups gave rise to the vast amount of fairy lore that is still a matter of wonder around the world.

## GIANTS

As noted in Chapter 4, stories of gigantic beings are common around the world — found in most every remote corner and among most all cultures. Are giants simply an easy explanation for the creation of the magnificent natural features of the world? Nigel Pennick wrote that the primal giant "makes the fabric of the world: his bones become the rocks, his blood the rivers and seas, his hair the plants and his skull the firmament. The giant demonstrates the relationship between the parts of our body and the structure of the world. It is an image of our oneness with the world."[19]

Giants were written of in the Old Testament, which many people accepted in lieu of history before the development of archeology and other scientific methods of inquiry. The first mention of giants occurs in Genesis 6:4:

> There were giants in the earth in those days; and also after that, when the sons of God came unto the daughters of men, and they bare children to them, the same became mighty men which were of old...

This particular passage would seem to indicate that the giants were the "sons of god" which is similar to other tales of giants from the Old World that equate them to a deity-like status.

The next passage pertaining to giants is Numbers 13:33. In this one, Hebrew spies sent to Canaan reported, "And there we saw the giants, the sons of Anak, which come of the giants; and we were in our own sight as grasshoppers, and so we were in their sight."

Joshua reports that one of the ancient kings who ruled over the vast fertile plains east of the Sea of Galilee, by the name of Og, "was of the remnant of the giants, that dwelt at Ashtaroth..." Og's bed was reportedly "nine cubits" in length (one cubit is 18–22 inches, so the bed was from 13.5 to 16.5 feet long). Og's capital city was Ashtaroth which was named for the god-

19. Pennick, Nigel. *Celtic Sacred Landscapes.* London: Thames and Hudson 1996, 20.

dess of the same name. Joshua refers to the lands of Og as the "valley of the giants".[20]

Throughout the Old Testament the giants are pursued and engaged in battle by the Hebrews and usually slain, although the New Compact Bible Dictionary claims "Giants terrorized the Israelites from their entry into Canaan until the time of David."[21]

While much of the Bible is religious propaganda and reworked mythology from other peoples, much of it also reflects historical accounts of events that took place thousands of years ago. How much is fact-based and how much is added by the story tellers remains a mystery.

Ethnologist James Mooney wrote of a story related by an aged Cherokee woman: "...a party of giants had come once to visit the Cherokee. They were nearly twice as tall as common men, and their eyes set slanting in their heads, so that the Cherokee called them... 'The Slant-eyed people,'...They said that these giants lived very far away in the direction in which the sun goes down. The Cherokee received them as friends, and they stayed some time, and then returned to their home in the west."[22]

Harvey Nettleton, an early settler of Ohio, wrote the following account of burials excavated in some of the mounds located near Conneaut, Ohio in 1844. This account was featured in the weekly *Geneva Times* during the late 1860s:

> The mounds that were situated in the eastern part of what is now the village of Conneaut and the extensive burying ground near the Presbyterian Church, appear to have had no connection with the burying places of the Indians. They doubtless refer to a more remote period and are the relics of an extinct race, of whom the Indians had no knowledge.

> These mounds were of comparatively small size, and of the same general character of those that are widely scattered over the country. What is most remarkable concerning them is that among the quantity of human bones they contain, there are found specimens belonging to men of large stature, and who must have been nearly allied to a race of giants.

> Skulls were taken from these mounds, the cavities of which were of sufficient capacity to admit the head of an ordinary man, and jaw-bones that might be fitted on over the face with equal facility. The bones of the arms and lower limbs were of the same proportions, exhibiting ocular proof of the degeneracy of the human race since the period in which these men occupied the soil which we now inhabit."

While many stories of giant skeletons may be attributed to excavated dinosaur and mammoth bones, there are those few that give credence to the

---

20. Joshua 15:8, KJV.
21. Bryant, T. Alton. Ed. *The New Compact Bible Dictionary.* Grand Rapids: Zondervan Publishing House 1967, 198
22. Mooney, James. *Myths of the Cherokee.* New York: Dover Publications, Inc. 1995, 391. A reprint of the 1900 publication "Nineteenth Annual Report of the Bureau of American Ethnology, 1897-98.

possibilities of a race of giants in the ancient past through modern times. Rupert T. Gould relates one of the original reports in his book, *Enigmas*:

> "A True Report of Hugh Hodson, of Thorneway, in Cumberland, to Sr. Robert Cewell, of a gyant found at S. Bees, in Cumb'land. Gould report-edly took this quote from Jefferson's *History and Antiquities of Allerdale above Derwent*.

> "The said gyant was buried 4 yards deep in the ground, weh is now a corn feild (*sic*). He was 4 yards and a half long, and was in complete armour, his sword and battle-axe lying by him. His sword was two spans broad, and more than 2 yards long. The head of his battle-axe a yard long, and the shaft of it all of iron, as thick as a man's thigh, and more than 2 yards long.

> "His teeth were six inches long, and 2 inches broad; his forehead was more than 2 spans and a half broad. His chine bone could contain 3 pecks of oatmeal. His armour, sword, and battle-axe are at Mr. Sand's, of Redington, and at Mr. Wyber's, at St. Bees."[23]

Tales of giants living in Patagonia were generated by Magellan's expedition in 1520. According to one of Magellan's companions, a giant sized man was seen on the beach in June of 1520: "This man," reported the sailor, "was so tall that our heads scarcely came up to his waist, and his voice was like that of a bull."[24]

Other explorers such as Sir Frances Drake, Harrington, Carmen, and Commodore Byron also reported encountering gigantic men in the same area. Some of these men were said to be from 9 to 10 feet in height.

There were serious discussions and disagreements about these giants as well as a great deal of confusion. Early 20th century ethnologist John M. Cooper noted that "A 'River of the Giants' is marked on some of the maps posterior to 1641 as situated well south of Taitao Peninsula. [There seems to be enough evidence] to establish a good presumption that the 1641 expedition encountered the Indians mentioned above in the Gulf of Peñas region. These natives were reported to be of gigantic stature and to have fought with clubs and stones. They were nicknamed 'Gabiotas,' that is, 'gulls,' by the members of the expedition, on account of a fancied resemblance of their strange speech to the call of this bird."[25] In fact, their language was not understood by the expeditionary members and it was noted at the time that it was different from the speech of other Indian groups.

Cooper, however, wrote, "No concrete measurements were taken....More-over, reports of giants are too common a feature of early Magellanic literature to be taken very seriously."[26] Cooper continues to write of the contradictory

23. Gould, Rupert T. *Enigmas: Another Book of Unexplained Facts.* New Hyde Park: University Books 1965, 16. A reprint of the 1945 edition.
24. Ibid., 18.
25. Cooper, John M. *Analytical and Critical Bibliography of the Tribes of Tierra Del Fuego and Adjacent Territory.* Bureau of American Ethnology Bulletin 63. Washington: Smithsonian Institution 1917, 123.
26. Ibid., 41.

nature of these early reports: "In fact [they]...are elsewhere described as of middle stature."[27]

However, there were other characteristics that indicated that the giants were of an entirely different race. They had beards which no other tribe around did and, in fact, Cooper notes "bearded men are not reported by other expeditions to Southern Chilean waters."[28]

Early explorers also described these giants as "somewhat white-skinned" which is contrary to the skin color of the other Indian groups in the area.

Earlier, more fantastical tales were told by Sir John Mandeville who wrote of a race of giants living on an island beyond the Ganges Valley in his book published in 1356, *The Travels of Sir John Mandeville*:

> Beyond that valley is a great isle where the folk are as big in stature as giants of twenty-eight or thirty feet tall. They have no clothes to wear except the skins of beasts, which they cover their bodies with. They eat no bread; but they eat raw flesh and drink milk, for there is an abundance of animals. ...they will more readily eat human flesh than any other. ...if they see a ship in the sea with men aboard, they will wade into the sea to take the men. We were told that there is another isle beyond that where there are giants much bigger than these, for some are fifty or sixty feet tall....some men have often seen those giants catch people in the sea and go back to the land with two in one hand and two in the other, eating their flesh raw.[29]

It is obvious that Sir John was repeating some of the urban legends of his time; however, there have been massive, gigantic hominids in the past such as Gigantopithicus that may have survived as recently as 100,000 years ago, crossing paths with early man, *Homo erectus*. Could that have been enough to sow the seeds for much of the folklore surrounding giants around the world? It remains a possibility that a race of "giants," people who were larger than their neighbors or in some way physically out of the ordinary, did exist among the more "normal" human populations of the earth. However, physical evidence of communities of such a race have never been discovered. The folklore could have grown up around this theme in an attempt to create a hero persona in some cultures. Are stories such as the Biblical stories of the Valley of Giants and Cherokee legend of the visiting giants just intended as history, or a bit of "self-puffery," history with a spin to make the listeners feel that great odds were overcome? Much of the world's myths speak of extraordinary events and people overcoming tremendous odds and giants would fit nicely into this pattern.

Supposedly other archaeological evidence for giants exists, including the Glen Rose tracks. Several human-like tracks have been found in a Cretaceous limestone formation near Glen Rose, Texas. Many appear to be of giant men. The Glen Rose tracks are 15 inches long [38.1 cm], and theoretically were made by people 8.3 feet tall. Some, 21½ inches [54.6 cm] long, would have

---

27. Ibid.
28. Ibid., 42.
29. Mandeville, Sir John. *The Travels of Sir John Mandeville*. Translated by C.W.R.D. Moseley. London: Penguin Books 1983, 175.

been made by people 11.8 feet tall. Of course, there are innumerable possible explanations for such a find; they could even be a form of "cave art" left by the local (ordinary) humans. Giant ground sloth have also been mis-identified as gigantic hominids, and their tracks are also found in fossilized form.

There are a number of documented cases of gigantism over the years. Gigantism can result from the overproduction of growth hormone during childhood or adolescence. The arms and legs grow especially long, and it is not unknown for an individual's height to surpass 2.4 m (8 ft). Gigantism is caused by a pituitary tumor that, if untreated, usually kills the patient by early adulthood. Physical characteristics may include some deformity and weakened musculature. However, if these conditions can be caused by pituitary imbalances, it seems possible that isolated populations became gigantic through selective breeding. The world has witnessed gigantic animals throughout time that lived successfully without these physical faults — why not humans? Again, one would be delighted if archeological traces could be found.

Early natural historian Charles Hamilton Smith noted some true giants in history. "The emperor Maximinus exceeded eight feet; Gabarus, an Arabian, in the time of Claudius, was nine feet nine inches high; he was shown at Rome. In the reign of Augustus, Pusio and Secondilla were ten feet three inches in height...the Emperor Andronicus was ten feet high, according to Nicetas...Charlemagne, seven feet."[30] And, as Smith sums up, "Without, therefore, vouching for the exact measurements here given, we have still sufficient evidence to show, that even in recent times, men of high stature, and of immense strength, have been historically conspicuous."[31] Much of the research from Smith's era is being re-examined in a modern light, however. Heros are often depicted as oversize characters, "larger than life," in art, history and in popular story-telling. It would be naïve to pretend that symbolic exaggerations did not occur.

Still, history is full of anecdotal lore about true giants. One of these is Aymon, a member of Archduke Ferdinand's bodyguard. According to historian Dr. C. J. S. Thompson, he "was said to have been 11 feet in height, but he did not live much beyond his fortieth year. A wooden image of this giant was preserved in the Castle of Ambras in the Tyrol."[32] Giants were a favorite of the kings and queens of Europe during the 16th and 17th centuries, who employed them as door attendants, servants and guards.

## YETI, SASQUATCH AND YOWIE — WHAT DO THEY HAVE IN COMMON?

The ancient hominid Gigantopithicus was mentioned above as a possible source for many of the tales of giants around the world. Supposedly, this

30. Smith, Charles Hamilton. *The Natural History of the Human Species.* Edinburgh: W.H. Lizars 1848, 139
31. Ibid.
32. Thompson, Dr. C.J.S. *Mystery and Lore of Monsters.* New York: Barnes & Noble 1994, 142

creature, according to Richard Leakey, "was the ancestor of some apparently very large terrestrial apes of Asia that became extinct."[33]

Fossil remains of this hominid have been found throughout Asia and, while Leakey states that it was "about the size of a modern gorilla"[34], the size of its skull indicates otherwise. The skull is almost twice as large as a modern gorilla's skull.

Some researchers have speculated that this creature was more human-like than most archaeologists have allowed. Although there is little evidence, the idea has been posed that the legends of the Sasquatch of North America, Yeti of Tibet and the Yowie of Australia refer to examples of small groups of living Gigantopithicus humanoids. "Yowie" means "Great Hairy Man" and it has most of the same characteristics of the other two mysterious creatures.

However, this cannot be the source for all of the tales of Giant Men. The Cherokee tale of the visiting giants described them as being social and civilized — speaking and living with the Cherokee for some time. Likewise, the giants of Patagonia were often involved in meetings with the European explorers. We would not expect a Gigantopithicus individual to be so agreeable or conversant!

As new and remarkable discoveries are made every day, we cannot dismiss anything out of the ordinary simply because it does not fit the established mold that scientists have been able to piece together. Unusual findings, discoveries that do not fit with accepted "facts," may suggest the model is wrong and that we still have a long way to go to understand the universe and the rich past — a past that still awaits our exploration.

33. Leakey, Richard E. *Origins*. New York: E.P. Dutton 1977, 56.
34. Ibid., 71.

# Chapter 7. Wild Men

Legends concerning a group of shaggy and primitive "Wild Men" have survived over the centuries. Some tales of the Wild Man are most likely based in reality. During the Middle Ages, a sub-culture existed on the fringes of society made up of outlaws and social outcasts. At times, individuals made their way into the towns and cities and the Wild Man-Wild Folk stories began. At the same time, the term was applied to the mythical race of dwarves who were called "Moss-Folk." One folklorist wrote, "they are considered to be dwarfs, and they live in communities. They are grey and old-looking, and are hideously overgrown with moss, giving them a hairy appearance."[1] These Moss Folk weave the moss of the forests and protect it with a vengeance. They do help some people with their knowledge of the healing plants and herbs and they help crops to grow.

In folklore these Wild Men are sometimes helpful to humans in that they will locate lost cattle and have the ability to treat the illnesses of cattle, but, according to Philpot, they are "more often mischievous, having the propensity for stealing the milk and carrying off the children of the peasants."[2]

There is another aspect of the Wild Man as a creature removed from accepted society. The Wild Man subculture came to represent those things rejected by the "civilized" elements — natural elements found in animal and vegetable life as well as those more "primitive" aspects of humanity. These very basic characteristics of nature came to be those most feared by the Christian society of the day. "For much of the Middle Ages, hairy, cannibalistic, sexually omnivorous wild men and women had represented the

---

1. Porteous, Alexander. *The Lore of the Forest: Myths and Legends.* London: Senate Publishers 1996, 93 (A reprint of the 1928 publication *Forest Folklore* published by George Allen & Unwin, London).
2. Ibid.

antithesis of the civilized Christian," wrote British historian Simon Schama.[3] The many illustrations of the Wild Man of the Middle Ages show a naked individual completely covered in long, shaggy hair with only the face, hands, elbows (and the breasts of the female) exposed. Other illustrations show this very same individual covered in leaves instead of hair or fur.

Because of the association with leaves, some writers have linked the Wild Man to the Green Man archetype. Loren Coleman states directly that, "Clearly the Green Man comes from the tradition and evolution of the art form of the burly wildmen, the woodsmen, and thus the man of the woods and greenry."[4] I disagree with this and believe that the depiction of the Wild Man covered in leaves refers more to his habitat in the forest rather than as an agricultural or fertility symbol and guardian of nature that the Green Man represents. An interesting folk-festival-ritual was held in Saxony and Thüringen at Whitsuntide called "chasing the Wild Man out of the bush." Frazer wrote, "A young fellow is enveloped in leaves or moss and called the Wild Man. He hides in the wood and the other lads of the village go out to seek him. They find him, lead him captive out of the wood, and fire at him with blank muskets. He falls dead to the ground.[5] In another village Frazer identifies as Erzgebirge there was an annual custom (at Shrovetide) that originated around 1600 CE. According to Frazer "Two men disguised as Wild Men, the one in brushwood and moss, the other in straw, were led about the streets, and at last taken to the market-place, where they were chased up and down, shot and stabbed. Before falling they reeled about with strange gestures and spirted blood on the people with bladders which they carried. When they were down, the huntsmen placed them on boards and carried them to the alehouse."[6] Frazer noted that similar customs were still carried out in Bohemia during his day. While we may never know exactly what the Wild Man rituals originally were meant to express, Frazer believed that these represented a ritualized memory of actual Wild Man hunts. "It has been assumed," he wrote, "that the mock killing of the Wild Man...in North European folk-custom is a modern substitute for an ancient custom of killing them in earnest. Those who best know the tenacity of life possessed by folk-custom and its tendency, with the growth of civilization, to dwindle from solemn ritual into mere pageant and pastime, will be least likely to question the truth of this assumption."[7]

3. Schama, Simon. *Landscape and Memory*. New York: Vintage Books 1995, 97.
4. Coleman, Loren. *Bigfoot! The True Story of Apes in America*. New York: Paraview Pocket Books 2003, 58.
5. Frazer, James G. *The Golden Bough: The Roots of Religion and Folklore*. New York: Avenal Books 1981, 243. A reprint of the two volume edition published in 1890 by Macmillan, London.
6. Ibid., 244.
7. Ibid., 250-251.

*An 1801 Illustration of a 'Wild Man' as it was thought to appear during the Middle Ages*

Contrary to Frazer, Schama believes that prior to 1600 society itself transformed the wild folk into symbolic guardians of nature. "[B]eginning in the later part of the fifteenth century...wild men were made over into exemplars of the virtuous and natural life."[8] Over the next hundred years, the wild man was "turned into conspicuously gentler creatures."[9] An example of this occurred in 1515 as part of Henry VIII's Twelfth-Night pageant at Greenwich, when eight "wylde-men, all apparayled in grene mosse sodainly came oute of a place lyke a wood"[10] and battled with the royal knights. These eight "wylde-men" were representative of tree spirits and obviously acted as "symbolic guardians of nature".

Philpot also believed that the Wild People were wood spirits. Writing over one hundred years ago, she noted, "traditions concerning the wild people of the woods are current in all the more wooded countries of Europe.... They are often of gigantic proportions, dwell in woods or mountains, and originally were no doubt closely connected with the spirits of trees....From head to foot they are clothed in moss, or covered with rough shaggy hair, their long locks floating behind them in the wind."[11] Her description is certainly one commonly applied to the Sasquatch, the Big Foot and the Yeti throughout time and distance.

The wild man became the symbol of popular discontent with the burgeoning cities and court society; he was, in a sense, a response of nature towards this unnatural existence and the destruction of the Wild Wood. According to Michael Cremo, the Wild Men "were said to be members of the animal kingdom, unable to speak or comprehend the existence of God."[12]

Many centuries earlier, however, the Wild Man was depicted on a silver Etruscan bowl, "on which," writes Cremo, "may be seen, among human hunters on horses, the figure of a large, ape-like creature."[13] Cremo notes that the wild man figure was not one of the common mythological figures but "in

---

8. Schama, op. cit., 97.

9. Ibid.

10. Philpot, Mrs. J. H. *The Sacred Tree in Religion and Myth.* Mineola: Dover Publications, Inc. 2004, 21. A reprint of the 1897 edition published by Macmillan and Co., Ltd. London.

11. Ibid., 66.

12. Cremo, Michael A. and Richard L. Thompson. *The Hidden History of the Human Race: Forbidden Archaeology.* Los Angeles: Bhaktivedanta Book Publishing, Inc. 1996, 595.

13. Ibid. 594.

the midst of a hunting party of well-armed humans mounted on horses. The creature has no satyr's tail [as some have said that the figure is that of a satyr] and appears to be carrying a crude club in one hand and a large stone, raised threateningly above his head, in the other."[14] References to "hairy creatures in desert places" also occur in the Latin Bible in Isaiah 13:21 and 34:14.

Similar club-wielding "rustics" were common figures in medieval romances and it is this image that continues on with our contemporary tales of Big Foot. They are giants of huge size, of savage character and hideous features — but guardians of nature. Beatrice White tells us that, "The prototype can be found in Chrétien de Troyes's *Yvain* (c. 1173)...where Calogrenant describes the rustic he met in a clearing...in a wood. This fellow was sitting on a stump with a great club in his hand, a lout, black, big, and hideous, in fact so ugly that he defied description."[15] According to White, it was this prototype "which was repeated *ad nauseam* from story to story — the huge, repulsive churl, the primal wild herdsman, guardian of beasts and of territory whose true ancestor is the giant Humbaba of the Babylonian epic *Gilgamesh* — a deadly, terrifying forest warden, breathing fire, whose jaws were death."[16]

In the medieval romance these common wild men, according to White, all conform "to the same convention, impressive in size, repulsive in looks and manners, lurking in caves or inaccessible places, fighting as often as not with huge, iron-shod clubs, they are libidinous, predatory, cannibalistic... 'evil in their doings.'"[17]

According to Thompson, "Aldrovandus describes several of these creatures, amongst whom were a man with his son and daughters who were brought from the Canary Islands, all covered with hair, and first shown in Bologna."[18]

In North America, the Wild Man is present in the ancient legends of Big Foot and Sasquatch[19] — huge human-like figures covered in long hair and leaves. Nineteenth-century American folklore tells of a family of Big Foot who attacked a group of gold miners in their California cabin one evening, destroying the building and tearing the men apart. Was this a response to the encroachment of "civilized" man? The characteristics of the two are very similar and they react in the same way. As Matthews writes of the Wild Man, "he can only dwell in such wild spots and avoids those places tamed by humankind, retreating ever deeper into the wilderness to escape the excesses of civilization — its cruelty, greed, and hypocrisy".[20]

14. Ibid.
15. White, Beatrice. "Cain's Kin" in *The Witch in History*, ed. by Venetia Newall. New York: Barnes & Noble 1996, 190.
16. Ibid., 191.
17. Ibid., 191.
18. Thompson, Dr. C.J.S. *Mystery and Lore of Monsters*. New York: Barnes & Noble 1994, 99.
19. "Sasquatch" is derived from the Salish, meaning "wild man of the woods."
20. Matthews, John. *The Quest for the Green Man*. Wheaton; Quest Books 2001, 110.

The Pacific Northwest forest is a breeding ground for Big Foot stories. An article in the April 1965 edition of *Western Folklore* gave the following account of an event near Eureka, California in 1958:

> Two sturdy construction workers insist they have seen "Big Foot," whose 16-inch tracks have been spotted recently in the Northern California woods. "He — or it — bounded across the road in front of our car Sunday evening," said Ray Kerr, 43. "It ran upright like a man, swinging long, hairy arms. It happened so fast, it's kind of hard to give a really close description. But it was all covered with hair. It had no clothes. It looked 8 or 10 feet tall to me."[21]

Several place names in the Pacific Northwest refer to these wood spirits. "Wampus" in Klamath County, Oregon, means "forest demon," named after "a solitary beast not unlike the far-ranging Sasquatch."[22] The *skookums* are said to be evil and powerful forest gods that reside in strange and unusual places, such as Crater Lake in southern Oregon.

Ethnologist George Gibbs wrote of Oregon's Wild Men in an 1865 account:

> One other race of beings I have classed separately, as they in particular are supposed to infest the earth, and do not appear to have been properly *Elip Tilikum* ('First People' in Chinook Jargon). They are *Tsiatko*...The belief in these beings is apparently universal among the different tribes, though there is a great discrepancy in their account of them.
>
> By some, the *Tsiatko* are described as of gigantic size, their feet eighteen inches long and shaped like a bear's. They wore no clothes, but the body is covered with hair like that of a dog, only not so thick....They are said to live in the mountains, in holes under ground, and to smell badly. They come down chiefly in the fishing season, at which time the Indians are excessively afraid of them....They are visible only at night, at which time they approach the houses, steal salmon, carry off young girls and smother children.
>
> ...Dr. Tolmie states that an Indian woman, married to a Canadian, who lived at Fort Vancouver some twenty years ago, told a story of having been taken prisoner by the *Tsiatkos* and carried into the woods between the fort and the mill...."[23]

Legends of these "timber giants" (called "Snanaik" by the Kwakiutl) are part of the Native American culture from Alaska and Canada to South America. Small children were always presumed at risk in Indian villages. "Many a

---

21. "Folklore in the News: California 'Big Foot'", in *Western Folklore*, Vol. XXIV, April, 1965, Number 2, 119.

22. Nash, Tom & Twilo Scofield. *The Well-Traveled Casket: Oregon Folklore*. Eugene: Meadowlark Press 1999, 100.

23. Gibbs, George. "Account of Indian Mythology in Oregon and Washington Territories-1865, pgs 313-314, in *Oregon Historical Quarterly 57*, 1956 edited by Ella E. Clark.

child was snatched from play," says writer Joseph Wherry, "stuffed inside a basket, and carried off never again to be seen."[24]

In Alaska, the Chilkat tribe of the Tlingit Indians spoke of the Goo-teekhl, a giant that destroyed many of their villages north of present day Juneau. Children were a favorite of this creature as well. As other tales of these forest wild men relate, the Goo-teekhl often threw large tree limbs at hunters as they sat around their campfires. Even though this Wild Man was a fearsome being, the Tlingit say that anyone who dreams of the Goo-teekhl will have good luck. According to Wherry, the Tlingit may still have totems of this giant which they feed eulachon oil on a daily basis as an offering of appeasement. [25]

The legend of a mysterious tree-creature is part of the lore of the Maidu Indians living in Butte County in Northern California. Butte County, by the way, has had several reported sightings of Big Foot over the years. Anthropologist D.L. Spencer gave this account of the *Chamlakhu*:

> "Chamlakhu was an old man living in the trees, differing from human beings only in the fact that his hands and feet were armed with long bear-like claws. Although not known to commit injury, he was greatly feared. The sight of him was sure to cause a run to camp....The Chamlakhu rarely ran on the ground, and then only in a shambling way, with his arms fanning the air like wings. He could spring a long distance from tree to tree. He had a long beard, and hair that reached to the ground."[26]

Some supernatural powers were linked to him indirectly, such as illness being the result for the person seeing him during the spring when vegetation was in bloom, but the description of a "shambling way" appears to be more a straight-forward and factual observation than anything else.

The Salish tribes who lived on the east side of Puget Sound in Washington State have tales of the "Steet-athls." These creatures were said to live in caves in the mountains and communicate with each other by whistling and, again, often carried off the Indian children. The legend of the Steet-athls goes on: "as recently as 1912 a party of loggers near Chehalis, Washington, fought a pitched battle with some wild, hairy men of the forest."[27]

A 1904 newspaper article concerning several "wild man" sightings near Myrtle Point, Oregon gave this account of the "Sixes Wild Man": [28]

> At repeated intervals during the past ten years thrilling stories have come from the rugged Sixes mining district in Coos County, Oregon, near Myrtle Point, regarding a wild man or queer and terrible monster which walks erect and which has been seen by scores of miners and prospectors....

24. Wherry, Joseph H. *Indian Masks & Myths of the West*. New York: Bonanza Books 1969, 121.

25. Ibid., 123.

26. Spencer, D.L. "Notes on the Maidu Indians of Butte County" in *Journal of American Folklore*, Vol. 21, 1908, pgs 242-245.

27. Wheery, op. cit. 124.

28. "Sixes Wild Man Again: Visits the Cabins of Miners and Frightens the Prospectors" in *The Lane County Leader*, Cottage Grove, Oregon April 7, 1904, Vol. XV, No. 51.

> A report says the wild man has been seen three times since the 10th of last month. The first appearance occurred on "Thompson Flat." Wm. Ward and a young man by the name of Burlison were sitting by the fire of their cabin one night when they heard something walking around the cabin which resembled a man walking and when it came to the corner of the cabin it took hold of the corner and gave the building a vigorous shake and kept up a frightful noise all the time — the same that has so many time warned the venturesome miners of the approach of the hairy man and caused them to flee in abject fear.

Mr. Ward fired at the creature, which ran quickly away. The newspaper goes on to note, "Many of the miners avow that the 'wild man' is a reality. They have seen him and know whereof they speak. They say he is something after the fashion of a gorilla and unlike anything else either in appearance or action. He can outrun or jump anything else that has ever been known; and not only that but he can throw rocks with wonderful force and accuracy. He is about seven feet high, has broad hands and feet and his body is covered by a prolific growth of hair. In short he looks like the very devil."

Another newspaper account from May 9th, 1851, entitled "Wild Man of the Woods," was published in the *Memphis Enquirer*:

> During March last, Mr. Hamilton, of Greene county, Arkansas, while out hunting with an acquaintance, observed a drove of cattle in a state of apparent alarm, evidently pursued by some dreaded enemy. Halting for the purpose, they soon discovered as the animals fled by them, that they were followed by an animal bearing the unmistakable likeness of humanity. He was of gigantic stature, the body being covered with hair, and the head with long locks that fairly enveloped his neck and shoulders. The "wild man," for so we must call him, after looking at them deliberately for a short time, turned and ran away with great speed, leaping from twelve to fourteen feet at a time. His foot prints measured thirteen inches each.

"This singular creature," the article goes on to say, "has long been known traditionally, in St. Francis, Greene and Poinsett counties. Arkansas sportsmen and hunters having described him so long as seventeen years since....A party was to leave Memphis in pursuit of the creature."

Algonquin legend tells of "narrow faced, hirsute creatures who live shadowy lives in the sub-Arctic scrub and forest" [29] — a very similar description to other Native American accounts of these Wild Men.

Reports of wildmen captured or killed have been made in such locations as Transylvania, China, Panama and North America. A "hairy, speechless 'fellow'" reportedly was caught in 1661 in a forest in Lithuania. According to researcher John Green, 'the creature lived there for a long time as a domesticated helper in the court of Polish kings.'"[30] Some, however, like the famous "Jacko" capture of 1884 near Yale, British Columbia, are clearly examples of urban legend.

---

29. Krickeberg, Walter & et al. *Pre-Columbian American Religions.* New York: Holt, Rinehart and Winston 1968, 158.

30. Green, John. *Year of the Sasquatch: Encounters with Bigfoot from California to Canada,* Agassiz: Cheam Publishing Ltd., 1970, 36.

Philpot noted, "The idea of a wild man of the woods also exists in Brazil. The Indians call him Curupira, and attribute to his agency all such forest sounds as they cannot understand."[31] Nearby in Belize, a small form of "Big Foot" lives, called the *Dwendis*. Said to live in the jungles in the southern part of this small nation this humanoid creature is described as being between three feet six inches and four feet six and is covered in short brown hair. The name "Dwendis" comes from the Spanish word *"Duende"* which means "goblin."[32]

One Wild Man in particular did not dwell in the wild forests but rather in the sea. Known as the Wild Man of Orford, it is said that several fishermen caught this creature in their nets during the reign of Henry II. Taken to Orford Castle in Suffolk, he was reported to be "completely naked and had the appearance of a man. The hair of his head seemed torn and rubbed, but he had a bushy beard and was shaggy about the breast."[33] This Wild Man would eat most anything it was given, but preferred fresh fish that he would squeeze between his hands until all of the moisture was drained out. According to Westwood, the Wild Man of Orford could not speak even though the local authorities hung him up and tortured him. He stayed at Orford for several months until one day he was able to slip by his guards and disappeared in the waves. At the time, it could not be decided if this Wild Man was a merman, man, fish, or evil spirit that inhabited the body of a dead sailor although fins and other fish type characteristics were never mentioned in the chronicle. An 1870 edition of *Murray's East Anglian Handbook* states, "A tradition of this monster, known as 'the wild man of Orford', still exists in the village."[34]

Reports of such sightings have become rare in England since then, but in Dartmoor sightings of a creature referred to as "Hairy Hands" have been made periodically since 1921. One account related by Ruth St. Leger-Gordon tells of a woman who was sleeping along side a road in a caravan: "...she woke to see a large hairy hand clawing up and down the window, beneath which her husband lay asleep. Sensing that evil was threatening him, she slipped from the bunk on to her knees and made the sign of the cross, whereupon 'The Hand' vanished."[35] According to St. Leger-Gordon these reports became more frequent from the 1950s to the 1970s, when she wrote about these mysterious sightings, "demonstrating that a new twentieth century superstition seems to be gradually building up along this particular Dartmoor road."[36] Some psychics have suggested that the "Hairy Hand" is an "elemental" being, a creature "nebulous and semi-formless" whose appearance is more ape-like than anything else. Other, slightly different creatures were seen along a road

---

31. Philpot, op. cit. 71.
32. Cremo, op. cit. 605.
33. Westwood, Jennifer. *Albion: A Guide to Legendary Britain*. London: Paladin Grafton Books 1985, 186.
34. Ibid.
35. St. Leger-Gordon, Ruth E. *The Witchcraft and Folklore of Dartmoor*. New York: Bell Publishing Company 1972, 121.
36. Ibid , 122.

near Crediton, in the Colebrook district. As St. Leger-Gordon noted, "a creature described as 'looking something like a red monkey' would jump out upon a passer-by, following him as far as the village, when it would disappear."[37]

Sightings of these Wild Men are not restricted to any great degree, but reported worldwide. The "Winstead (Connecticut) Wild Man" has been observed off and on from 1895 through the 1970s and perhaps beyond. First reported in a local newspaper on August 21, 1895, a witness described his account thus: "...a large man, stark naked, and covered with hair all over his body, ran out of a clump of bushes, and with fearful yells and cries made for the woods at lightening speed, where he soon disappeared."[38] The witness, a Selectman by the name of Riley Smith, added that the "man" was at least six feet tall and ran upright.

The creature was seen again in 1972 and 1974. Both times witnesses described it as being six feet in height, approximately 300 pounds and covered with dark colored hair. Both times the witnesses were terrified.

As noted, however, it is not only in North America or in Britain that stories of these mysterious wood-folk abound. Among the Yupa Indians, living in Colombia and Venezuela, a similar nature spirit is spoken of. Called the Mashiramū, or "Bush Spirit," he is described as being covered with hair with its feet turned backwards. This creature, regarded as a "devastating demon," is to be greatly feared.[39] Another Yupa spirit is the Karau, the Spirit of the Night. It too is covered with hair, has very large teeth and very cold hands. The Karau is said to rape women and to kill and eat his victims.[40]

The Wild Man and Wild Woman were also known among the Nehalem Tillamook Indians in Oregon. "The Wild Woman," wrote ethnographer Elizabeth Jacobs "was one of the most important of the supernatural beings. She was a large woman and lived in the forest."[41] Described as having "long beautiful hair and wearing lots of dentalia," Wild Woman was believed to be spiritually connected with the spruce tree. She could make people sick and die, cause insanity, or simply make a tree fall on you. Should you be on her good side however, she would grant you supernatural powers to diagnose illnesses and cure them or endow you with the skill to make beautiful baskets.

Similarly, the Wild Women of old Germany were not only kindly but "they are beautiful," writes folklorist Thomas Keightley, "have fine flowing hair, live within hills, and only appear singly or in the society of each other."[42]

---

37. Ibid., 124.
38. Philips, David E. *Legendary Connecticut.* Willimantic: Curbstone Press 1992, 175.
39. Wilbert, Johannes. *Yupa Folktales.* Los Angeles: Latin American Center, University of California 1974, 139.
40. Ibid., 138.
41. Jacobs, Elizabeth D. *The Nehalem Tillamook: An Ethnography.* Corvallis: Oregon State University Press 2003, 190.
42. Keightley, Thomas. *The World Guide to Gnomes, Fairies, Elves, and Other Little People.* New York: Gramercy Books 1978, 234. A reprint of the 1878 edition titled *Fairy*

According to local lore, the Wild Women began to appear near the German village of Grödich around the year 1753. The Wild Women would give bread to the boys and girls of the village who watched over the cattle. One day their kindness was extended to kidnapping a small boy, saying to the father, "He will be better with us, and have better care taken of him than at home."[43] Reportedly, the boy was seen by woodcutters a year later in the forest, clothed in green. He was never seen again.

In Russian folklore, the Wild Women again are regarded as "handsome females, with fine square heads, abundant tresses, and hairy bodies."[44] These Russian Wild People, both men and women, lived in communities in mountain forests and could be either dangerous (they were said to like to tickle people to death who happened upon them) or helpful. If people ventured into those mountain forests and left offerings of food, the Wild Women would harvest their grain for them; tend their children and even tidy up their homes. In addition, like the Fairies, the Wild Women could become invisible by applying certain herbal remedies and would sometimes leave golden leaves to village girls they favored.

While Wild Women were considered handsome, if not beautiful (although hairy), the Wild Man, on the other hand, is an ugly giant who lives in the forest, is known to cause sickness, but also to grant certain powers and skills.[45] Clive Hicks, however, noted that the Wild Men and Wild Woman "are not necessarily malevolent and are depicted as helping humanity in some cases....The wild man represents an asset in each of us, the whole reservoir of qualities with which each of us is endowed."[46] Again, we are faced with a paradox and one that is not likely to be resolved soon.

Similar tales of these large hairy ape-men are found in such diverse locations as the Pacific Northwest, Europe, Canada, southern Mexico, Belize, Guiana, Ecuador, Brazil, Malaysia, Indonesia, parts of Africa, and of course the Himalayas and Central Asia.

The Wild Man in Chinese lore was said to have "long, thick locks, fiery red in colour, and his body is covered with hair."[47] "Many" of these wild men were said to live in the mountainous regions of China although by 1922, as the people of China began to be a bit less isolated in the world, only a few were reported to still be in existence.

These Chinese Wild Men were said to be powerful creatures, able to break large rocks with a single blow of the fist and capable of pulling up trees by their roots. Nearby villagers were fearful. "These wild men kill and

*Mythology* published by G. Bell, London.
43. Ibid., 235.
44. Campbell, Joseph. *The Hero With a Thousand Faces.* New York: MJF Books 1949, 79.
45. Jacobs, op. cit., 182.
46. Hicks, Clive. *The Green Man: A Field Guide.* Helhoughton: COMPASSbooks 2000, 7.
47. Werner, E.T.C. *Myths and Legends of China.* New York: Dover Publications, Inc. 1994, 392. A reprint of the 1922 edition published in London by George G. Harrap & Co., Ltd.

eat all human beings they meet," wrote Werner, "and other hill tribes live in terror of meeting them."[48]

Wild men are also part of Hawaiian lore. Like other wild men, the Hawaiian Patu-pai-a-rehe live in the mountains, have reddish skin, golden hair and eyes that are black or blue. The Hawaiian wild men, however, are peaceful and are regarded as guardians of sacred places.[49]

The first "Wild Man" appearing in the world's literature was Enkidu, in the ancient Sumerian Epic of Gilgamesh. Created by the goddess Aruru (also known as Anu) to answer the prayers of the subjects of Gilgamesh, who tired of his iron hand rule, Enkidu was made to match the strength of Gilgamesh and to do battle with him — although he actually became Gilgamesh's closest ally. Historian Fred Gladstone Skinner wrote that Enkidu was "a valiant god of battle, whose entire body was covered with hair, shaggy as a woman's head. His clothes were of animal skins and, like an animal, he grazed in the fields and fought with the wild beasts for a place at the water holes."[50] According to Egyptologist E.A. Wallis Budge, Aruru "washed her hands, took some clay, spat upon it, and made a man, who was covered with hair; he lived in the forests with the beasts, which he ruled by reason of his mighty stature and strength."[51] Professor of Classics at the University of Cambridge, G.S. Kirk asks an important question about Enkidu: "We find that the main unexplained element is the insistence on Enkidu as a wild man from the desert. This at first sight arbitrary theme, inconspicuous in the Sumerian versions, is emphasized, not only in the earlier part of the poem, but also by reminiscence up to Enkidu's death. What is its point, does it serve any real purpose in the epic as a whole, and how did it become so prominent a motif in the Akkadian elaboration?"[52]

What are we to make of these hairy Wild Men and Women? Some researchers believe that they are common images to the human psyche and they represent man's psychological desire to throw off the restrictions imposed by his society or culture. An ancient and universal mythic icon, if you will, of our desire to become once again "savage."

The psychic importance of the Wild Men is clearly seen in the architectural ornaments that include his image. According to anthropologist Dr. Myra Shackley, "His image permeates every form of medieval art, from architecture to heraldry, and in the latter he is often shown as a supporter of an armorial shield. Over 200 European families have wildmen as heraldic emblems.... There is little variation in the way they are portrayed, leafy deco-

48. Ibid.

49. Beckwith, Martha. *Hawaiian Mythology.* Honolulu: University of Hawaii Press 1970, 335.

50. Skinner, Fred Gladstone. *Myths and Legends of the Ancient Near East.* New York: Barnes & Noble Books 1970, 27.

51. Budge, E.A. Wallis. *Babylonian Life and History.* New York: Barnes & Noble Books 2005, 71.

52. Kirk, G.S. *Myth: Its Meaning & Functions in Ancient & Other Cultures.* London: Cambridge University Press 1970, 145.

rations and a club being the rule."[53] Similar heraldic symbols were common in Germany, and became more so with the rise of German nationalism during the 16th century.

*Coat-of-arms depicting 'Wild Men'*

Speaking of Big Foot, Sasquatch, etc. Shackley notes, "Until proven otherwise the European Wildman, whether he is called a wodewose,[54] a green man, a satyr or anything else, remains a creature of legend. It is possible that genuine relic hominids were sighted from time to time somewhere in the world during the Middle Ages," she writes, "but *verbatim* descriptions have not survived. The European Wildman is a myth."[55]

One final bit of information may shed a completely new light on the Wild Man subject. The following appears in a book titled *Strange Stories Amazing Facts*: "Transformed, the creature appears either as an extra-large wolf, moving on all fours, or as an extremely hairy biped, retaining recognizable, although repulsive, human facial features and clawed hands."[56] The description is that of a werewolf — see Chapter 10.

53. Shackley, Myra. *Still Living? Yeti, Sasquatch and the Neanderthal Enigma.* New York: Thames and Hudson 1983, 25.
54. "wodewose" is derived from an Old English word meaning "a woodland being".
55. Shackley, op. cit. 27.
56. Anon. *Strange Stories Amazing Facts.* Pleasantville: The Readers Digest Association, Inc. 1976, 434.

# Chapter 8. Horned Beings

Perhaps the oldest concept of a god is that of a horned creature — part human and part animal. Its importance in the mythic imagery of humankind is surmised by the ancient rock art that depicts these horned beings. Some of this rock art, such as found in the Algerian Sahara, date back 7,000 years.

Horned creatures were a universal subject of those shamans who used nature's material such as rock as their canvas. We must ask yet again why is the Horned Being found around the world, representing the same thing? We have all been awed by the power of horned animals. The bull, the deer and elk, and the Big Horn Sheep are majestic creatures, exuding a sense of power and pulsing with fertility. The wild cattle that lived in Mesopotamia until the Neo-Assyrian age were six feet tall at the shoulder with massive widespread horns. The wild cattle of Europe were just as awe-inspiring. We can only guess that the horned men depicted in ancient artwork were put there as a psychic link between man and animal and thereby indirectly with the force of Creation. Images of horned male figures appear in many locations around the world and are associated with an archaic, mythical figure known as the "Master of Animals." A set of deer horns attached to part of a skull were found in Star Carr, England, dating to 8000-7500 BCE and were made to be worn, probably in a ritual dance. Among Native American's the "Master of Animals" is regarded as a supernatural ruler of wild beasts who offers them protection, especially from the men who are hunting them.

Horns were an important part of war helmets in the past and for a very good reason. They were considered to impart power derived through a link with divinity: a religious power, a power derived from an ancient supernatural force. The horned-cap was the fashion of divinity in Mesopotamia from the 3rd millennium BP. Possibly derived from the huge wild cattle mentioned above, these caps had as many as seven pairs of horns and were a general symbol of divine status.[1] As J.C. Cooper noted, "Horned gods represent warriors, fecundity in both humans and animals, and are lords of animals..."[2]

Horns have shown up in some of the more unlikely places over the years. Horns have appeared on ancient carvings of the Sacred Tree as a distinguishing sign of the Tree's divinity and as a protection against evil. They also appear on the famous head of Moses carved by Michelangelo in 1513-15. While most art commentators are silent on the presence of the horns on this statue of the leader of the Hebrews, they should not be surprised. Horns signify "supernatural power; divinity; the power of the soul or life-principle arising from the head..."[3] In fact, Moses in often depicted with such horns of power. In many standard translations of the Bible Moses is said to have come down from Mt. Sinai with his head "shining" but in Hebrew the wording is that his head was "horned." It is interesting to note that Mt. Sinai is the mountain of the moon god Sin, who was often depicted as a white-bull.

Ancient depictions of animal-human composite figures are often located in cave paintings such as the 20,000 year old "sorcerer" in the Trois Frères Cave at Ariège, France. While many have interpreted this human-like figure with deer antlers as a shaman, others believe "that such figures are neither sorcerers nor shamans, but imaginary beings with their own distinct identity. They are not wearing masks or disguises; they are composite, semi-divine creatures".[4]

Horned-gods and goddesses include Pan, the nature god; Dionysus; Hathor, the Great mother; the Celtic god Cernunnos ("Cernunnos" means "the Horned One") who is accompanied by a rams-horned serpent; and the Celtic Lord of Death, Herne. Another is the 5000-year-old seated horned god from Mohenjodaro in the Indus Valley that may have been the precursor of the Hindu god Shiva, and the Egyptian gods Set and Ammon. Another ancient horned god is the Babylonian bull-man. With a human head crowned with horns, human torso and taurine lower body and legs, the bull-man appeared in Mesopotamian art in the early part of the 3rd millennium BP. He is a "magically protective demon"[5] that evolved into a beneficent creature used in temples to ward against evil. Goddesses, even the Virgin Mary, are often shown with a crescent moon or cow horns, are Isis and Nut of Egyptian origin and other mother goddesses and the Queen of Heaven. The gods Anu, Bel, Asshur and the storm god Adad, wear horned headdresses in many of their ancient depictions.

The use of horned masks for shamanic or ritual dances was an ancient practice. One such mask known as the Dorset Ooser was perhaps the last of

1. Black, Jeremy and Anthony Green. *Gods, Demons and Symbols of Ancient Mesopotamia.* Austin: University of Texas Press 2000, 102.
2. Cooper, J.C. *An Illustrated Encyclopaedia of Traditional Symbols.* London: Thames and Hudson 1978, 84.
3. Ibid.
4. Mohen, Jean Pierre. *Prehistoric Art: The Mythical Birth of Humanity.* Paris: Pierre Terrail/ Telleri 2002, 183.
5. Black and Green, op. cit. 48-49.

its kind. Constructed around 1820, the mask was made from a single piece of wood and was wonderfully expressive. It had two horns and a shaggy head of hair. It disappeared some time after 1897 and two photographs are all that remains of it. Its purpose may have been to be worn in the Mummers plays of the day although no one knows exactly who crafted it, what it was used for or where it ended up. Local legend indicates that the mask was an object of horror and was kept near the village chapel in Melbury Osmond. A contemporary description of the mask was recorded in the December 1891 issue of *Notes and Queries for Somerset and Dorset*:

> The object itself is a wooden mask, of large size, with features grotesquely human, long flowing locks of hair on either side of the head, a beard, and a pair of bullock's horns, projecting right and left of the forehead. The mask or ooser is cut from a solid block, excepting the lower jaw, which is movable, and connected with the upper by a pair of leathern hinges. A string, attached to this movable jaw, passes through a hole in the upper jaw, and is then allowed to fall into the cavity. The Ooser is so formed that a man's head may be placed in it, and thus carry or support it while he is in motion. No provision, however, is made for his seeing through the eyes of the mask, which are not pierced. By pulling the string the lower jaw is drawn up and closed against the upper, and when the string is slackened it descends

*Antlered-man on modern pub sign, Ashland, Oregon*

The Christian image of the horned Devil is a recent one. Not one image of Satan as a horned, goat-footed demon occurs before the sixth century. However, the pagan gods of fertility and reproduction often included horns.

These gods represented "the most carnal aspect of life" — sexuality. And this, of course in the Christian mind, was most "especially connected with the Devil".[6] The perfect image in the Christian mind that replicated their concept of the Devil was that of Pan — the god of animals and nature. He was perhaps one of the most popular gods of antiquity. His powers were those of prophecy and inspiration and while he was god of nature, he was also a destructive and terrifying god. The word "panic" is derived from his name. His enormous sexual desire was the force of creation and destruction at the same time. As O'Grady wrote, "Pan seemed to be the epitome of the heathen gods. He represented excess and debauchery, the vices of the world of matter, and so was the embodiment of paganism."[7] Pan became the embodiment of Satan in Christian iconography.

In some depictions and legends of the Wild Man he is also said to have horns — not unlike Pan.

Among Native American cultures, the Hopi have two important religious societies that have been depicted on rock art as wearing horns. These are the Two Horns and the One Horn societies. The Two Horns play an important role in the completion of the annual ritual patterns played out in various Hopi ceremonies.

Horn imagery was important in the religious traditions of early cultures. The altars of the Hebrews during the period of Exodus were decorated with horns. This practice may have been borrowed from Crete as horns were placed upon their altars as cult objects. The widespread use of altar horns, found in such faraway places as Sardinia, Italy, Switzerland, Spain and Syria (used on the altar of Astarte), may have spread due to the Cretan seafarers' influence.

The fact that there are historical accounts of horned humans existing over the years would indicate that perhaps some of the mythology concerned with horned beings may be based on fact. Thompson tells us, "In the Museum of Edinburgh University is preserved a crooked horn several inches long, which was cut from the head of a woman named Elizabeth Love in 1671. "Another instance of a horned woman is that of Mary Davis of Great Saughall, near Chester, who when twenty-eight years of age commenced to develop two horns. 'After four years she cast them, then grew two more, and about four years later cast these also.'"[8] Thompson noted that a portrait of this horned-woman still exist at Oxford.

6. O'Grady, Joan. *The Prince of Darkness: The Devil in History, Religion and the Human Psyche.* New York: Barnes & Noble Books 1989, 45.
7. Ibid.
8. Thompson, C.J.S. *Mystery and Lore of Monsters.* New York: Barnes & Noble Books 1994, 62

# Chapter 9. Spirits of the Otherworld — Ghosts and Vampires!

Ghosts![1] The word alone creates images of translucent and flowing spirits, spirits that have either failed to realize that they are no longer physically alive or who intend to exact revenge from those left living. Ghosts are feared the world over, and have been since humans began to recognize realities and dimensions outside of the present one. Are they creations of our own minds?

Native American lore is filled with legends about ghosts and the Otherworld that they inhabit. Native Americans are intimately linked with nature and the world of spirit — including those beings that reside in the spirit world. To the Plains Indian, however, the interaction between humans, ghosts and spirits is considered "a normal part of life on this earth."[2] Sickness is not the result of a virus or bacteria but more likely than not, the result of "ghost illnesses" caused intentionally by a malignant spirit of a departed individual. Ghosts most often appear in dreams rather than in the physical world, although physical manifestations such as footprints and sounds are also part of their calling cards.

Ideally, if such spirits want to continue their existence they should stay in the "underworld" and live a parallel existence, unaware of and inaccessible to those still living in the physical world. But folklore has may models for exceptions to this plan. The owl was considered one of the manifestations of an evil spirit, a vengeful spirit. To see an owl at night meant that a spirit had

---

1. The word "ghost" is a derivative of the Middle English "goste" and the German "geist," both meaning "breath". The breath leaving the body at the time of death was believed to be the soul.

2. St. Pierre, Mark and Tilda Long Soldier. *Walking in the Sacred Manner*. New York: Touchstone Books 1995, 108.

announced an evil intent. To the Chiricahua Apache, "the bad ones go right into the owl, at death, at once. The others who were good through life go to the underworld."[3]

The image of the ghost appearing as a white amorphous shape is common the world over — including among Native Americans. Opler related one such sighting by an Apache man:

> "One day, after I was married, I was riding my mule back from White-tail....We got lost in the woods and could not get out before dark. We got into a canyon neither of us knew. And up among the trees I saw something white. I didn't think anything of it, but in a few minutes I saw it again."[4]

This sighting affected the man so much that he was incapacitated for some time after he was able to return to his home.

Ghosts appear in dreams usually with the same intent — to draw the person into death. There was a belief even during the early part of the twentieth century that to see the ghost of an Indian was fatal but to see the ghost of a white man would only bring sickness.[5]

The Lakota Sioux believed that to see a ghost would not result in harm, but "if they hear a ghost, bad luck will follow. If they hear a ghost mourning, then someone of the family will die soon."[6] To the Lakota the ghost may signify a future event, either success of a war party, or its failure. According to Walker, "if they sing the song of victory the party will succeed, but if they mourn, then the party had better go home."[7]

Ghosts were believed to inhabit abandoned camps and tipis, and sacrifices were often made to them before a war party set out to ensure the aid of the ghosts.

Ghosts are primarily interested in securing the deaths of people they knew in life; however, they also did other types of mischief, such as causing children to spill hot soup or coffee at meals.

To the Lakota the spirit is not what constitutes life; rather it is the ghost that defines life. "His ghost is his breath",[8] they say. The good spirit goes to the spirit world which is "at the other end of the spirit way," where it is never cold and hunger no longer exists and work is no longer necessary. The bad spirit does not go on to this land but stays behind in its ghost form.

Among the Oglala Sioux, ghosts are understood to attempt to entice the living to join them — only because they grieve for them and want to be with them once again. This is especially true in the period immediately after death. According to anthropologist William Powers, the loved ones of the deceased

---

3. Opler, Morris Edward. *An Apache Life-Way: The Economic, Social, and Religious Institutions of the Chiricahua Indians.* Chicago: The University of Chicago Press 1941, 230.
4. Ibid., 232.
5. Ibid., 237.
6. Walker, James R. *Lakota Belief and Ritual.* Lincoln: University of Nebraska Press 1991, 104.
7. Ibid.
8. Ibid., 116.

will attempt to appease the ghost by "keeping" it for one year. This is done by "feeding"[9] the ghost spirit. After a year the ghost is fed for the last time and it departs along the "ghost road," which is the Milky Way. It is said, "the aura of the Milky Way is caused by their campfires."[10]

The purpose of this ghost keeping is, according to Powers, "so that by the proper rites it will be assured a return to its origin, and because the lingering ghost will help people to be mindful of death."[11]

One of the requirements of the Oglala Sioux after the Wounded Knee massacre at Pine Ridge in 1890 was for, "all Oglalas who were currently ghost keeping to release their souls on an appointed day."[12]

The contrast between the Apache, the Lakota Sioux and the Oglala Sioux is striking. The Apache fear the ghosts, which they believe to cause death, while the Sioux "keep" them for a time to stay near their loved ones, who will help the spirit find its way along the ghost road to the spirit world.

Ghosts were also greatly feared by the Navajo. "Ghosts are," wrote anthropologist Clyde Kluckhohn, "the witches of the world of the dead, a shadowy impalpable world altogether beyond the control of the living."[13]

Only those who die of old age, the stillborn, or infants who die before they are able to utter a sound do not become ghosts in Navajo belief. Ghosts are, according to the Navajo, the "malignant" parts of the human spirit. While they may shape-shift into animal forms, such as coyotes, owls, fire, mice or even whirlwinds, they normally appear as black or very dark shapes. "Whistling in the dark," wrote Clyde Kluckhohn, "is always evidence that a ghost is near."[14] (It occurs to me that whistling, a fairly penetrating sound, is quite a natural way for humans to announce their presence — which is generally a far safer practice than surprising a wild animal in the dark! It certainly seems to be a common reaction in response to the instinctive fear that sometimes attends a walk in the dark.)

To the Cheyenne, ghosts originate with the dead but they are not spirits of particular individuals. According to anthropologist E. Adamson Hoebel, they are more poltergeist than spirit. "They make their presence known by whistling and making weird noises; in very dark places, especially in the woods, they tug at one's robe; they tap and scratch on lodge coverings. In other words, they are the night noises and sensations that make even the most skeptical of us a bit jumpy..."[15]

9. "Feeding" was done by placing food in a hole in the ground near the body.

10. Powers, William K. *Oglala Religion.* Lincoln: University of Nebraska Press 1982, 53.

11. Ibid., 93.

12. Ibid., 122.

13. Kluckhohn, Clyde and Dorothea Leighton. *The Navaho.* Garden City: Anchor Books/ The American Museum of Natural History 1962, 184.

14. Ibid., 185.

15. Hoebel, E. Adamson. *The Cheyennes: Indians of the Great Plains.* New York: Holt, Rinehart and Winston, Case Studies in Cultural Anthropology 1960, 86.

However, the Cheyenne do believe in individual spirits. Or rather, they believe in individual souls. Everyone dwells in a heaven after the spirit separates from the body according to Cheyenne belief. The soul, the *tasoom*, is the very nature, the very essence of the body and death is simply the next existence.

Illnesses have long been thought to be caused by vengeful ghosts. In ancient Mesopotamia, according to Thomsen, "The reason for a ghost to appear was mostly assumed to be irregularities during funerary rites or the cessation of the offerings to the dead....The ghost of someone who had died in an accident, of a criminal who might have been sentenced to death or of someone who had not been buried at all was especially likely to persecute the living."[16]

A cause and effect relationship between dissatisfied ghosts and the illness and death of an individual was a universal concept — from Native American society to ancient Mesopotamia, Rome and Greece. This belief was also present among the tribes of Tierra Del Fuego according to early 20th century ethnologist John Cooper. Cooper noted that malevolent spirits who reside in "forest caves send sickness or death".[17] Likewise, the rituals used to rid the land of the living of these maligned ghosts were similar. It was important to sooth the ill feelings of the ghost, to rectify the wrongs. For some spirits, this was not possible given their characteristics during life. Cooper wrote "The dead are feared, especially witch-doctors, who have power even after their death."[18] One of the Tierra del Fuego tribes, the Yahgans, "believe the soul remains near the grave or wanders over the woods and mountains, especially at night, happy or unhappy, according to moral conduct in life."[19] Other tribes in the area who also feared the ghost of the "witch-doctor," or shaman shared this belief. "The dead know what is taking place on earth," wrote Cooper, "but take no active part in human affairs, except dead witch-doctors."[20] However, the spirits of some of these feared shamans were consulted during times of need because it was believed that they still maintained power over the elements.

Ghosts in other cultural settings even played an important role in a nation's leadership:

> "According to a native account," wrote Sir James Frazer, "the origin of the power of Melanesian chiefs lies entirely in the belief that they have

16. Thomsen, Marie-Louise. "Witchcraft and Magic in Ancient Mesopotamia" in *Witchcraft and Magic in Europe: Biblical and Pagan Societies.* Philadelphia: University of Pennsylvania Press 2001, 79.

17. Cooper, John M. *Analytical and Critical Bibliography of the Tribes of Tierra del Fuego and Adjacent Territory.* Washington: Smithsonian Institution Bureau of American Ethnology Bulletin 63, 1917, 148.

18. Ibid 149.

19. Ibid 151.

20. Ibid.

communication with mighty ghosts, and wield that supernatural power whereby they can bring the influence of the ghosts to bear."[21]

It was the fear of these ghosts, however, that gave the chief his authority and enforcement abilities. Once the people began to doubt the existence of such authority based in ghostly creatures the chief's ability to rule began to crumble.

In Celtic society people were often buried under trees after they died and it was believed that the tree "embodied the ghost of the person buried under it."[22] However, as MacCulloch wonders, how then did the ghost differentiate itself from a tree spirit? It was MacCulloch's belief that trees became objects of worship because they were believed to be the embodiments of ghosts — not because they were in themselves deities. Likewise fairies may be ghosts of the dead, which is why they have so many of the same characteristics such as appearing as hovering lights, haunting certain tumuli and midnight dances. MacCulloch wrote, "generally the family ghost has become a brownie, lutin, or pooka, haunting the hearth and doing the household work. Fairy corresponds in all respects to old ancestral ghost, and the one has succeeded to the place of the other, while the fairy is even said to be the ghost of a dead person."[23] MacCulloch footnotes this statement by offering a comparison: "The mischievous brownie who overturns furniture and smashes crockery is an exact reproduction of the Poltergeist."[24]

To MacCulloch and others the ghost is the true fairy and the various nature spirits that have so much influence over individuals worldwide. While this is an attractive theory and one that does explain some of the similarities of the folklore of ghosts and fairies, it does not account for all of them. Many of the stories concerning nature spirits speak of certain "themes" or core elements of how these particular spirits, be they of the water, air, stone, forests or mountains, act. They do not seem to deviate very far from these core elements regardless of where they are found around the world. Ghosts, on the other hand, behave either as the dead individuals did in life or as some representative of an evil underworld god or as souls waiting to be reborn into this world once again. While they may have common attributes of description, they do not have common behaviors.

To MacCulloch the ghosts of the dead were the origins for most of the fertility and nature spirits. "[I]n Scandinavia, they may have been held to have an influence on fertility, as an extension of the belief that certain slain persons represented spirits of fertility, or because trees and plants growing on the barrows of the dead were thought to be tenanted by their spirits."[25]

---

21. Frazer, Sir James. *The Golden Bough: A study in magic and religion.* Hertfordshire: Wordsworth Editions 1993, 84.

22. MacCulloch, J. A. *The Religion of the Ancient Celts.* Mineola: Dover Publications, Inc. 2003, 202.

23. Ibid 166.

24. Ibid.

25. Ibid 169.

To Native American people, this fairy-spirit-ghost tie may also make sense. According to David Whitley, an expert on rock art in the American West, "Throughout far-western North America, whirlwinds were believed to contain ghosts, a particular kind of supernatural spirit."[26] We must be cautious, however, in our assignment of terms. Did/do the Native Americans believe these spirits to be ghosts or ghostly spirits? We cannot always assume that we have accurate translations of abstract terms or concepts.

The ancient Greeks believed that ghosts and werewolves were closely associated. In fact, an early second century CE tale of Pausanias ("Euthymus of Loci drives a werewolf into the sea") appears to make werewolves a sub-category of ghosts.[27] Contrary to MacCulloch's views, the Greeks felt that a ghost is a supernatural being that may alter its shape but they did not believe that it is a nature spirit. The history and lore of the werewolf will be discussed in the next chapter.

Most of our fears of ghosts, regardless of where or when we live, come from the belief that they are somehow bad, evil, wont to cause the living to suffer. Do we assume then that ghosts are inherently bad souls? According to 19th century Celtic scholar James Bonwick, "The Irish, like the ancient Jews, held that bad men, especially, could walk this earth after death..."[28]

In Hindu culture, ghosts are also considered the vengeful spirits of the dead. Pregnant women, suicides, those who have been murdered or drowned, those who have been struck by lightning and those who died hating someone are likely candidates to become ghosts. These ghosts are, as one anthropologist writes, "difficult to handle...but some of them have been tamed and are thus in the service of some persons."[29]

However, not all "ghosts" are necessarily bad. To the West African people known as the Ashanti, pregnancy is caused by the mixing of a male spirit with the woman's blood. For the first eight days after delivery, the baby is considered a "ghost child." "It is believed that a ghost mother in the spirit world has lost this child and will make an effort to get it back,"[30] wrote anthropologist Elman Service. During these eight days it is unknown if the baby will live or die but upon the eighth day a ceremony is held to formally accept the child as a human child and it is named and its patrilineal lineage established.

26. Whitley, David S. *A Guide to Rock Art Sites: Southern California and Southern Nevada.* Missoula: Mountain Press Publishing Company 1996, 75.

27. Ogden, Daniel. *Magic, Witchcraft, and Ghosts in the Greek and Roman Worlds.* Oxford: Oxford University Press 2002, 175.

28. Bonwick, James. *Irish Druids and Old Irish Religions.* New York: Barnes & Noble Books 1986, 98. A reprint of the 1894 edition.

29. Service, Elman R. *Profiles in Ethnography.* New York: Harper & Row, Publishers 1963, 479

30. Ibid., 377.

## THE VAMPIRE IN LEGEND AND LORE

Vampires are surprisingly common in folklore. They are perhaps one of the oldest supernatural creatures and one of the most widespread throughout Eastern Europe and the Middle East. Vampires are described as ghosts, ghosts that take their sustenance from warm-blooded living creatures either by drinking their blood or through cannibalistic feedings. An ancient account of the vampire comes to us from Philostratus who, in 217 CE, wrote of a female vampire whose "practice [was] to feed upon beautiful young bodies, since their blood was pure."[31] The "Empusa," the vampire in Philostratus's tale, is unlike the modern image of the cloaked, dashing count. This vampire has donkey's hoofs. Similar hoofed vampires, called *Boabhan Sith*, or "Wicked Woman Fairy," reportedly inhabited the Scottish highlands.

That the origins of the vampire legend date far back into antiquity is beyond doubt. Spence notes that even in ancient Egypt the vampire was a threat. "We do not find the vampire in any concrete form," Spence wrote, "but figured as a ghost — indeed, as the wicked or spiteful dead so common in Hindu, Burmese, and Malay mythology."[32] Egyptologist E.A. Wallis Budge elaborated on the subject in his 1883 book, *Babylonian Life and History*:

> The chief objects of all...pious acts was to benefit the dead, but underneath it all was the fervent desire of the living to keep the dead in the Underworld....Wiedemann has proved that in all ages men have believed in the existence of Vampires, and he has described the various methods which were employed in ancient and modern times to keep the dead in their graves. To this desire, he believes, is due the care that the Egyptians took to bury their dead in tombs deep in the ground and in the sides of mountains. The massive stone and wooden sarcophagi, the bandages of the mummy, the double and triple coffins, the walled-up doors of the tomb, the long shaft filled with earth and stones, etc., all were devised with the idea of making it impossible for the dead to reappear upon the earth. In very early times the body was decapitated and the limbs were hacked asunder, and in later times the viscera were removed from the body and placed in hermetically sealed jars.[33]

The vampire's most sought out victim was sleeping children whom it would kill by sucking out its breath. The most effective charm to prevent these attacks was, strangely enough, "a wreath of garlic, a plant the vampire is known to detest."[34] This charm was widely used in the Balkan countries as well to ward off the same threat — as illustrated in the many movies made over the years. Vampires also figure in Chaldean and Assyrian records that

---

31. Ogden, Daniel. "Apollonius unmasks and defeats a female 'vampire'", in *Magic, Witchcraft, and Ghosts in the Greek and Roman Worlds*. Oxford: Oxford University Press 2002, 65.

32. Spence, Lewis. *Ancient Egyptian Myths and Legends*. New York: Dover Publications, Inc. 1990, 272. A reprint of the 1915 edition published as *Myths & Legends of Ancient Egypt*, published by George G. Harrap & Company, London.

33. Budge, E.A. Wallis. *Babylonian Life and History*. New York: Barnes & Noble Books 2005, 142-143. A reprint of the 1883 publication.

34. Ibid.

speak of these creatures not as mythic beings but as a matter of fact. However, they give little information as to their origin.[35]

Vampires seem to appear differently depending on where they are located. The Transylvanian variety matches our concept of the vampire from the horror films. It is gaunt and pale, with full red lips, pointed teeth, long fingernails, a hypnotic gaze and, horror of horrors, eyebrows that meet and hair on its palms. The Russian version has a purple face, the Bulgarian has but one nostril,[36] the Albanian vampire wears high-heeled shoes and the vampire from Moravia attacks its victims in the nude.[37] And, not to be outdone, the Mexican vampire is recognized by its fleshless skull.

The most effective way to kill a vampire was not a stake through the heart but through fire or decapitation. Knowlson wrote that the vampire legend is notably absent in cultures, such as India, that burn their dead, however, vampire lore is particularly more common in areas where burial is the way of disposing of the dead.[38] The infamous stake was primarily used "to hold the unquiet corpse in its grave".[39] Nineteenth-century symbologist Thomas Inman agrees, writing, "When vampires were discovered by the acumen of any observer, they were, we are told, ignominiously killed, by a stake driven through the body; but experience showed them to have such tenacity of life that they rose again, and again, notwithstanding renewed impalement, and were not ultimately laid to rest till wholly burnt."[40] Frazer noted that the very many fire festivals popularly held around Europe were sometimes intended to keep the vampire away from herds of cattle. The "need-fire," according to Frazer, was "unmistakably nothing but a means of protecting man and beast against the attacks of maleficent creatures, whom the peasant thinks to burn or scare by the heat of the fire, just as he might burn or scare wild animals."[41] Some scholars have suggested that "the revival of cremation in Europe in mediaeval and modern times [is due to the desire] to get rid of vampires."[42] "Bodies of persons whose ghosts had become vampires," wrote Donald Mackenzie, "which attacked sleepers and sucked life-blood from

35. Knowlson, T. Sharper. *The Origins of Popular Superstitions and Customs.* London: Senate 1994, 212. A reprint of the 1930 edition published by T. Werner Laurie Ltd., London.
36. This peculiar physical "defect" also appears on the Fairies in Mull, Ireland. It was through this characteristic that allowed them to be detected, according to 19th century writer John Campbell.
37. Anon. *Strange Stories, Amazing Facts.* Pleasantville: The Reader's Digest Association, Inc. 1976, 432.
38. Ibid., 218.
39. Jordan, Katy. *The Haunted Landscape: Folklore, ghosts & legends of Wiltshire.* Bradford on Avon: Ex Libris Press 2000, 118.
40. Inman, Thomas. *Ancient Pagan and Modern Christian Symbolism.* New York: Cosimo Classics 2005, xvi. A reprint of the 1869 edition.
41. Frazer, Sir James. *The Golden Bough: A study in magic and religion.* Hertfordshire: Wordsworth Editions Ltd. 1993, 649.
42. Mackenzie, Donald A. *Crete & Pre-Hellenic Myths and Legends.* London: Senate 1995, xlii. A reprint of the 1917 edition of *Crete & Pre-Hellenic Europe* published by The Gresham Publishing Company, London.

their veins, were taken from tombs and publicly burned. The vampires were thus prevented from doing further harm."[43]

Vampirism may have been used as a smoke screen to draw attention to the dead rather than to the living who were accused of witchcraft during the Burning Times. According to Robin Briggs, "There appears to be no earlier analogue for one spectacular Hungarian trend, also found in some other areas of eastern Europe after 1700, which was for magical aggression to be attributed to vampires, recently deceased persons who emerge from their graves to suck the blood of the living. This conveniently displaced blame so that it fell on the dead, with action being taken against their corpses; this new form of counter-magic may in part be seen as a response to the growing hostility of the Habsburg state to witchcraft trials."[44]

Vampires stories are rare in England although "a veritable epidemic in mediaeval times" occurred at Berwick on Tweed.[45] Evidently, suicides were thought to be prime candidates for vampirism and they were staked out in crossroads to ensure that they remained quietly dead. While rare, the vampire was recorded in England as far back as the 12th century by William of Newburgh. According to an account by Simpson and Roud:

> It appeared at Alnwick (Northumberland) in 1196, emerging nightly from its grave to roam the streets, corrupting the air with "pestiferous breath," so that plague broke out and many died. When two bold men decided to "dig up this baneful pest and burn it with fire," they found the corpse much closer to the surface than they had expected; it had swollen to a horrifying size, its face was "turgid and suffused with blood," and its shroud in tatters. They gave it a sharp blow with a spade; from the wound gushed "such a stream of blood that it might have been taken for a leech... filled with the blood of many people." So they tore the heart out, dragged the body away and burned it; this put an end to the plague.[46]

While rare in the British Isles and elsewhere there are other vampiristic creatures in existence. Franklin tells of fairies that have such tendencies. One of these is Anchanchu, a "vampire fairy" known to the Aymará Indians of Peru. "He travels in whirlwinds," writes Franklin "and seduces his victims with pleasant smiles before draining their strength and blood."[47] The Anchanchu are not regarded as vampires among the Bolivian Aymará but rather as "evil place spirits usually associated with caves."[48] However, certain Aymará people, called *Karisiris*, believed to possess supernatural powers,

---

43. Ibid.

44. Briggs, Robin. *Witches and Neighbors: The Social and Cultural Context of European Witchcraft.* New York: Viking Penguin 1996, 123-124.

45. Jordan, op. cit., 118.

46. Simpson, Jacqueline and Steve Roud. *Oxford Dictionary of English Folklore.* Oxford: Oxford University Press 2000, 374.

47. Franklin, Anna. *The Illustrated Encyclopaedia of Fairies.* London: Paper Tiger/Chrysalis Books 2002, 14.

48. Buechler, Hans S. and Judith-Maria Buechler. *The Bolivian Aymara.* Case Studies in Cultural Anthropology. New York: Holt, Rinehart and Winston, Inc. 1971, 91.

do exhibit vampire-like characteristics. According to anthropologist Hans Buechler, these people "rob children of their fat during sleep."[49]

There is, of course, a Jungian explanation for the many tales of vampires. According to the psychoanalytical theory, the human psyche is dualistic and many of the "inferior or bad" aspects of human behavior is kept hidden in an unconscious "Shadow." "Lived unconsciously," noted O'Connell and Airey, "the Shadow appears as bad or evil figures in dreams or myths....Vampires are an image of the Shadow. Having a human appearance, they live in the darkness, with hidden desires, feeding on the blood of the living, and drawing power from what we call 'normality'."[50]

While the vampire may be a ghost or a shadow of our subconscious, it is only regionally found in its traditional vampire form, for it is absent in most other non-European countries, although there is anecdotal information for vampires in Mexico, China, Brazil and in the Rocky Mountains of the United States. The vampire is also present in Hebrew mythology. One interesting bit of folklore trivia reported by Montague Summers is that "in Germany, Serbia, and modern Greece it is believed that a werewolf is doomed to be a vampire after death."[51] Summers does caution however that the two should be evaluated on their own merits as "a vampire need not once have been a werewolf....They are entirely different, separate, and apart."[52]

This leads us to the next chapter, where we discuss the werewolf in more detail.

---

49. Ibid.

50. O'Connell, Mark and Raje Airey. *The Complete Encyclopedia of Signs & Symbols.* London: Hermes House 2005, 52.

51. Summers, Montague. *The Werewolf in Lore and Legend.* Mineola: Dover Publications, Inc. 2003, 189. A reprint of the 1933 edition published by Kegan Paul, Trench, Trubner & Co., Ltd. London.

52. Ibid., 15.

# CHAPTER 10. WEREWOLVES — NOT JUST IN TRANSYLVANIA

Werewolves have been a fear of humankind since the Neolithic age and may have originated in the shamanic rituals that seemingly transformed men into wolf-like creatures. During the Middle Ages, legends of the werewolf expanded into tales of daily occurrences. There are places in the world that even today the werewolf remains a feared creature that decimates livestock and threatens the lives of local inhabitants. The interesting thing about the folklore surrounding the werewolf is that, like the Fairies and Wild Men legends, it is a common folklore motif found around the world. Well, almost around the world. Gervase of Tilbury, according to Simpson and Roud, "wrote in 1211 that werewolves were common in England, the examples he then gave are all French." Werewolves could not have been present in England as the wolf had already been extinct for centuries.[1] "The belief" in werewolves, wrote Harvard lecturer John Fiske in 1881 "is supported by a vast amount of evidence, which can neither be argued nor pooh-poohed into insignificance."[2] Fiske cautions that the stories are a "curious mixture of mythical and historical elements." Nevertheless, why, we may ask, is the werewolf legend so universally known?

Some scholars associate the original werewolves with martial brotherhoods, which were extent in the early Greek, Persian, German, Scythian, Dacian and Celt societies. The initiates "magically assumed lupine features."[3]

---

1. Simpson, Jacqueline and Steve Roud. *Oxford Dictionary of English Folklore.* Oxford: Oxford University Press 2000, 386. There is one other exception. Lewis Spence noted in his book *Ancient Egyptian Myths and Legends* (pg. 272): "So far as one can judge, the idea of the werewolf or any similar form was unknown in ancient Egypt."
2. Fiske, John. *Myths and Myth-Makers: Old Tales and Superstitions Interpreted by Comparative Mythology.* Boston: Houghton, Mifflin and Company 1881, 70.
3. White, David Gordon. *Myths of the Dog-Man.* Chicago: The University of Chicago Press 1991, 27.

This may account for many of the European tales but certainly not for those of other locations around the world.

Others believe that the werewolf legend are related to the ancient Sanskrit texts that spoke of the "howling Rakshasa" or storm-wind. According to Hindu folklore, Rakshasa is "a great misshapen giant with red beard and red hair, with pointed protruding teeth, ready to lacerate and devour human flesh; his body is covered with coarse, bristling hair, his huge mouth is open, he looks from side to side as he walks, lusting after the flesh and blood of men, to satisfy his raging hunger and quench his consuming thirst. Towards nightfall his strength increases manifold; he can change his shape at will; he haunts the woods, and roams howling through the jungle."[4]

Were-men are not confined to a wolf form, however. Depending on where the particular folklore originates these half-man half-animals may be a mix with bear, jaguar, tiger and even crocodile. Aztec shamans wore the hides, including the snout, hearts, claws, tails, and fangs, of jaguars and were said to be greatly feared because of the powers these objects transferred to the shaman.[5] This was/is a common practice in shamanism. Lapp shaman supposedly transform into demonic reindeer to fight each other. However, the cause of a person being transformed into werewolf is almost always due to an evil agent, most likely the acts of a witch or a punishment for some specific and grievous sin. William Howells, once chair of the department of anthropology at Harvard University, wrote, "Werewolves in general...are related to witchcraft in spirit if not explicitly."[6] However, there were two forms of werewolf, those who voluntarily transform into these creatures and those whose transformation is involuntary. The voluntary werewolf became one because of his or her unnatural obsession with human flesh. This person also had sufficient magical powers to affect a physical transformation. Spence wrote of this form of werewolf: "In Teutonic and Slavonic countries it was complained by men of learning that the were-wolves did more damage than real wild animals, and the existence of a regular 'college' or institution for the practice of the art of animal transformation among were-wolves was affirmed."[7] The involuntary werewolf was transformed by an evil magician or was sentenced to become such a beast for a certain number of years to atone for the commission of a sin. These individuals "were no malevolent beasts," notes Michael Kerrigan, "but tragic victims of evil magic."[8] Kerrigan goes on to say that, "The willing werewolf was a terrible man-beast, ravening de-

4. Fiske, op. cit. 77.
5. Miller, Mary and Karl Taube. *An Illustrated Dictionary of The Gods and Symbols of Ancient Mexico and the Maya.* London: Thames and Hudson Ltd., 1993, 102.
6. Howells, William. *The Heathens: Primitive Man and His Religions.* New York: Doubleday Books 1962, 124.
7. Spence, Lewis. *Legends and Romances of Brittany.* Mineola: Dover Publications, Inc. 1997, 291. A reprint of the Frederick A. Stokes Company publications, no date, New York.
8. Kerrigan, Michael. "The Faces of the Changeling" in *Forests of the Vampire: Slavic Myth.* New York: Barnes & Noble Books 1999, 120.

stroyer of anything in its path. Those changed by another's curse, however, were submissive creatures, clinging hard to their old human nature....Gentle in their ways, and protective of family and friends, they killed only when driven to desperation by hunger."[9]

However, it was only through Christianity that the belief in werewolves became synonymous with witchcraft. Fiske wrote that the belief in werewolves "did not reach its complete development, or acquire its most horrible features, until the pagan habits of thought which had originated it were modified by contact with Christian theology. To the ancient there was nothing necessarily diabolical in the transformation of a man into a beast. But Christianity, which retained such a host of pagan conceptions under such strange disguises...did not fail to impart a new and fearful character in the belief in werewolves. Lycanthropy became regarded as a species of witchcraft...and hundreds of persons were burned alive or broken on the wheel for having availed themselves of the privilege of beast-metamorphosis."[10]

It may be, in fact, the influence of Christianity that induced such a strong belief in werewolves in the first place. Such belief is particularly strong in Navajo culture. Anthropologist Harold Driver wrote "Witches are thought to roam at night as were-animals (wolves, coyotes, bears, and owls), to meet in witches' Sabbaths to plan and perform rites to kill or injure people, to have intercourse with dead women, to initiate new members, and to practice cannibalism."[11] As with the indigenous religions of Mesoamerica, Christianity has tainted the original belief systems and has made them into a mimicry of Christian theology along with the same gods, devils and traditions. Undoubtedly the belief in these were-animals and the powers that the shamans had to shape-change are drastically changed from their original nature. There is one bit of Christian folklore that even claims that St. Patrick caused this metamorphosis. According to the story, a family's lack of faith so displeased St. Patrick that he turned the entire clan into a pack of werewolves.[12]

Obviously, Christianity cannot be credited entirely with the belief in werewolves. Werewolves appear in nineteenth-century Eastern European Jewish folklore as well. According to the tale, "An evil spirit takes possession of a sinful woodcutter, making him into an evil sorcerer. He then transforms himself into a werewolf, who attacks children led by the Baal Shem Tov because their singing is so pure that Satan fears that it might hasten the coming of the Messiah."[13] After an attack by the werewolf, a young boy by the name of Israel ben Eliezer, later known as "the Baal Shem Tov" tracked the huge wolf prints into the forest. Suddenly the tracks turned into the tracks

9. Ibid.

10. Fiske, op. cit. 79.

11. Driver, Harold E. *Indians of North America*, 2nd edition. Chicago: University of Chicago Press 1969, 410.

12. Anon. *Strange Stories Amazing Facts*. Pleasantville: The Readers Digest Association, Inc. 1976, 435.

13. Schwartz, Howard. *Lilith's Cave: Jewish Tales of the Supernatural*. New York: Oxford University Press 1988, 250.

of a man. With the aid of Elijah, who appeared in a dream offering the Baal Shem Tov secrets to destroy the werewolf, it was finally defeated. Like other legends of the werewolf, the creature only appeared during a full moon and was the result of an intentional transformation by an evil sorcerer. According to Schwartz, "This theme is one of the most prominent in Hasidic literature" because it "establishes that the soul of the Baal Shem Tov, even as a young man, was so holy that it was a worthy adversary to Satan."[14]

That is not to say that shamans have not metamorphed into other animal forms since the Stone Age. Writing on shamanism, anthropologist and religious historian Mircea Eliade noted, "Naturally, the South American shaman, like his colleagues everywhere, can also fill the role of sorcerer; he can, for example, turn into an animal and drink the blood of his enemies. The belief in werewolves is widely disseminated in South America."[15] The shaman is able to change into an animal form but his true body does not change. In shamanism, the body appears to be in deep sleep while the soul journeys out in the form of an animal to either fight with other shamans, wreck havoc upon a local populace or to experience other spiritual transformations. This shamanic technique was known in later times also and anyone so unlucky to fall into a stupor or coma was often accused of witchcraft. "According to one mediaeval notion," wrote Fiske, "the soul of the werewolf quit its human body, which remained in a trance until its return."[16]

Such abilities are also part of Polynesian mythology. A dog on Oahu, known as Kaupe, also known as "dog-man," was said to be able to transform itself into either a man or a dog — and it was a cannibal. This is the only dog in Hawaiian lore that was malevolent. Another legend is that of Pa'e who was able to "change herself into a 'woman, a *mo'o* (lizard) or a brindled dog."[17] While Pa'e in the form of a dog did kill an elderly couple, it was in defense rather than from a malevolent nature. The Hawaiians closely linked dogs to humans. The lesser god Ku'ilio-loa was said to have been "formed from man" by the god Maui.

Leslie Spier recorded the Yuman Indian story of the Dog Pima: "Two men have a dog. While they hunt, she turns into a girl and cooks for them. They discover her and persuade her to remain a human. Their children become the Dog Pima, a tribe."[18] It is of interest that legends from Polynesia and Native America speak of werewolves with the ability to change shape at will and to remain in human form — usually female at that. Outside of European folklore, the werewolf is not savage or demonic.

14. Ibid.
15. Eliade, Mircea. *Shamanism: Archaic Techniques of Ecstasy.* Princeton: Princeton University Press 1964, 324.
16. Fiske, op. cit. 78.
17. Titcomb, Margaret. *Dog and Man in the Ancient Pacific.* Honolulu: Bernice P. Bishop Museum Special Publication 59, 1969, 20.
18. Spier, Leslie. *Yuman Tribes of the Gila River.* New York: Dover Publications, Inc. 1978, 422.

There are several tales based in reality of werewolves, or at least of insane humans who believed themselves to be such. Fiske and others believed these human werewolves to be obsessed with cannibalism and they acted out the part of wild animals to kill and eat their victims. Since we have already consulted Fiske let us again turn to him for one of these true stories:

> In the year 1598, in a wild an unfrequented spot near Caude [France], some countrymen came one day upon the corpse of a boy of fifteen, horribly mutilated and bespattered with blood. As the men approached, two wolves, which had been rending the body, bounded away into the thicket. The men gave chase immediately, following their bloody tracks till they lost them; when, suddenly crouching among the bushes, his teeth chattering with fear, they found a man half naked, with long hair and beard, and with his hands dyed in blood. His nails were long as claws, and were clotted with fresh gore and shreds of human flesh.

> This man, Jacques Roulet, was a poor, half-witted creature under the dominion of a cannibal appetite. He was employed in tearing to pieces the corpse of the boy when these countrymen came up. Whether there were any wolves in the case, except what the excited imaginations of the men may have conjured up, I will not presume to determine; but it is certain that Roulet supposed himself to be a wolf, and killed and ate several persons under the influence of the delusion. He was sentenced to death, but the parliament of Paris reversed the sentence, and charitably shut him up in a madhouse.[19]

Roulet was said to be suffering from a psychological condition known as Lycanthropy. This condition has been recorded since classical times although it is a rarity in the modern day. These unfortunate people would flee to the woods at night, howl at the moon and seek out local victims or, if no living soul was available, dig up corpses and devour them. While common in Europe during the 15th to 18th centuries this condition is also known to have occurred in Ethiopia, India, Malaysia and China. In Italy it was believed at one time that any child born on St. Paul's Night (June 29) or on the Annunciation (March 24) was likely to become a werewolf unless the infant's father or grandfather burned the child's foot or the nape of the neck with hot coal.

Other tales included that of Perrenette Gandillon. A French women, she "turned herself into a wolf and killed a child, the creature had no tail and human hands in place of front paws."[20] The rumor of 1573, again in France, was that a pack of donkey-sized wolves was attacking and eating people in an area near the village of Dôle. That such tales and charges were common in an area and a time so charged with the inquisition and witchcraft trials may not be coincidental.

Fiske notes that werewolves, or rather, the belief in werewolves was also present in North America and Africa but it was mostly in Europe where can-

19. Ibid 84.
20. Briggs, Robin. *Witches & Neighbors: The Social and Cultural Context of European Witchcraft.* New York: Viking 1996, 88.

nibalistic desires drove men to such extremes in behavior. In many Native American traditions, various gods and nature spirits were also were-men. These were not the evil cannibals mentioned above but spiritual beings. Among the Yuma tribes that live on the Gila River in the American Southwest it is said that "dogs are persons"[21] that may appear in dreams in human form to relate various pieces of information. One informant during the 1930s related that he never kicked his "really annoying curs" because they were, in fact, people.[22]

During the Classical Age Marcellus Sidetes, who lived in the reign of Hadrian, discussed the psychological condition of Lycanthropy:

> Men afflicted with the disease...go out by night in the month of February in imitation of wolves or dogs in all respects, and they tend to hang around tombs until daybreak. These are the symptoms that will allow you to recognize sufferers from this disease. They are pallid, their gaze is listless, their eyes are dry, and they cannot produce tears. You will observe that their eyes are sunken and their tongue is dry and they are completely unable to put on weight. They feel thirsty....One must recognize that lycanthropy is a form of melancholia.[23]

Originally, the werewolf was an aspect of the magical arts of the shaman. A transformation was sought in order to control others, seek revenge, or simply to experience the life of an animal to understand its powers as a spirit helper. Mircea Eliade wrote, "The shaman encounters the funerary dog in the course of his descent to the underworld, as it is encountered by the deceased or by heroes undergoing an initiatory ordeal. It is especially the secret societies based on a martial initiation...that developed and reinterpreted the mythology and magic of the dog and the wolf."[24] In the Navajo tradition, a wicked man after death may be transformed into a coyote, an owl or a crow. According to historian Marc Simmons, "Navajos believe in were-animals, or witches who transform themselves into beasts so that they may move about at night with speed and greater freedom....The guise of the werewolf, just as in the Old World, is most popular. Any Indian who comes upon a wolf with his tail hanging straight down will kill it, since to his way of thinking it has to be a witch. Real wolves, as he knows, always run holding the tail straight out behind."[25]

Like the vampire, the werewolf is supposed to have certain physical traits that give it away. A single eyebrow that stretches across the bridge of the nose is one, and hairs on the palms and between the shoulder blades are telltale signs, according to some.

---

21. Spier, op. cit., 254.
22. Ibid.
23. Ogden, Daniel. *Magic, Witchcraft, and Ghosts in the Greek and Roman Worlds.* Oxford: Oxford University Press 2002, 177.
24. Eliade, op. cit. 467.
25. Simmons, Marc. *Witchcraft in the Southwest: Spanish & Indian Supernaturalism on the Rio Grande.* Lincoln: University of Nebraska Press 1974, 138.

Slavic lore says that children born feet first and with teeth already show-ing are likely to become werewolves. The only way to defeat the werewolf, according to Slavic tradition, is by the intercession of the Kresnik, "a Good Spirit who battles demonic forces."[26]

The werewolf's continued existence in European thought might have been due to the Church using it as a convenient criminal charge to persecute nonbelievers and to intimidate people into submission. Montague Summers, writing in his most Christian manner, said, "Hateful to God and loathed of man, what other end, and what other reward could he look for than the stake, where they burned him quick, and scattered his ashes to the wind, to be swept away to nothingness and oblivion on the keen wings of the tramon-tane and the nightly storm."[27]

26. Mercatante, op. cit., 98.
27. Summers, Montague. *The Werewolf in Lore and Legend.* Mineola: Dover Publications, Inc. 2003, 123-124.

# Chapter 11. Harpies and Other Creatures of Storms and Wind

The ancient Greeks personified the savage winds and storms as Harpies, creatures with the faces of women and the bodies of vultures who could create whirlpools at sea and fierce windstorms on land. They were known to swoop down from the skies, taking away anything in their paths, including buildings, trees, animals and even people.

*Ancient Greek carving of a Harpy, carrying away an infant.*

The Harpies were sent by the gods to cause sudden and early death; their sole purpose was to inflict punishment upon humans. Because of their role in death, they were also known as messengers to the underworld, and as the transporters of the souls of the dead. Biedermann wrote that another duty of the Harpy was to "catch criminals and turn them over to the Fates for punishment." He further notes "although the Harpies serve the greater moral order, they are figures of dread."[1]

Are the Harpies purely a Greek creation? No, Harpies, or Harpy-like creatures

1. Biedermann, Hans. *Dictionary of Symbolism: Cultural Icons & The Meanings Behind Them.* New York: Meridian Books 1994, 39.

were known in ancient Mesopotamia as well. "Some Babylonian poems," note Jeremy Black and Anthony Green, "describe the dead as clothed with bird-like plumage. [The underworld] is peopled by a horde of unpleasant demons, described in graphic detail. In almost all cases these hellish demons are said to have been winged and to have had talons of birds."[2]

The original account of the Harpies says that they were orphan children of Poseidon (or Neptune) and Gaia or Thaumas and Electra, but they were raised by Aphrodite. When they matured, Aphrodite left them to find husbands for them but the Storm Winds, the Harpyiai, swept them from the earth and they themselves came to be Storm Winds. The Harpies had individual names meaning "squall," "fast flier," and "obscure." The name "Harpies" is derived from the Greek "harpazein," meaning "to snatch or carry away."[3] Other scholars say that the Harpies "delight in drinking the blood of men slain in battle",[4] much like the Celtic warrior-goddess, the Morrigin — who also appeared in the guise of a raven. J.E. Cirlot wrote, "At a deeper level, they have been defined as a representation of the 'evil harmonies of cosmic energies'."[5]

Other bird-like creatures that various cultures have attributed the creation of winds include the Garuda bird of India, the Native American Thunderbird, and the Hraesvelgre of Scandinavia. The wind deities that are responsible for destruction by tornadoes, volcanoes and other violent tempests are, according to Andrews, "predominantly male, robust and fearsome and full of raw energy."[6] Like most all aspects of nature and nature deities, the winds could be either good or evil — thus displaying the dual quality of life and nature's experience. Large birds, like the Thunderbird, are often representations of thunder and wind gods.

Not only large birds or Harpy-like creatures were believed to be the cause of winds and storms but other, more human-like gods were also associated with winds and storms. To the Yuman Indian tribes along the Gila River in Arizona, whirlwinds were not "creatures" or "gods" at all but "a ghost, that is, one of the several souls each person had."[7] To other Native Americans the winds were similar to the Four Directions, the Four Winds existed and resided in each of the Four Cardinal Points.

The Apache believed that the wind could be caused by boys playing with bull-roarers, noise makers made with sticks and string. These winds were

2. Black, Jeremy and Anthony Green. *Gods, Demons and Symbols of Ancient Mesopotamia.* Austin: University of Texas Press 1992,43.

3. Andrews, Tamra. *A Dictionary of Nature Myths.* Oxford: Oxford University Press 1998, 89.

4. Fiske, John. *Myths and Myth-Makers: Old Tales and Superstitions Interpreted by Comparative Mythology.* Boston: Houghton, Mifflin and Company 1881, 164.

5. Cirlot, J.E. *A Dictionary of Symbols.* 2nd ed., New York: Barnes & Noble Books 1995, 139.

6. Andrews, op. cit., 226.

7. Spier, Leslie. *Yuman Tribes of the Gila River.* New York: Dover Publications, Inc. 1978, 150. A reprint of the 1933 edition published by The University of Chicago Press.

no less dangerous and were believed to bring disease and illness.[8] To the Apache all things, including trees, stones, and wind, have a life of their own and must be respected to avoid catastrophe. Often Lakota shamans sought out the Spirits of the Wind to help in a quest, for it was believed that these spirits would bring messages from the gods. Bull-roarers were also used by the Australian Aboriginals to illicit the winds to "speak" and to give divine messages.

Cooper wrote "Winds are messengers of the gods and can indicate the presence of divinity, especially the whirlwind."[9] The Wind Spirit in Borneo is thought to carry the message of the impending death of an individual, and thus the arrival of the soul, to the underworld. The other souls of the underworld rush back to the surface in a boat to escort the soul to the underworld. "They stop the boat before the house of the deceased," wrote Mircea Eliade, "rush out and seize the soul, which struggles and cries out. But even before it reaches the shores of the underworld, it seems to be at peace."[10]

Other representations of the wind gods often include sacks, which hold the wind. In China, Fêng Po was the god of the Wind and was represented "as an old man with a white beard, yellow cloak, and blue and red cap. He holds a large sack, and directs the wind which comes from its mouth in any direction he pleases."[11] The Japanese god Fujin also was said to keep the winds in a bag.

Perhaps it is the wind which has played such an active role in mankind's religious development and the development of the many gods and goddesses that have existed on this planet. Was this invisible but felt presence, sometimes delicate, sometimes vicious, perhaps at the origin of man's belief in the supernatural, his belief in an ancient creative and destructive force outside of the control of man?

The moving air is still linked to the life-force in many traditions and religions as well as the spirit. In ancient India, Varuna ("All Encompassing") is the creator god, "the guardian of cosmic law and judge of human action."[12] In the Vedic era it was believed that the wind is Varuna's breath and when we breath it in we are linked directly to the god. Similarly, the principle deity of the Araona Indians of eastern Bolivia was Baba-Buada, who, according to Krickeberg, was "a wind god, who possessed the status of Creator. He was

8. Opler, Morris Edward. *An Apache Life-Way.* Chicago: The University of Chicago Press 1941, 46

9. Cooper, J.C. *An Illustrated Encyclopaedia of Traditional Symbols.* London: Thames and Hudson 1978, 192.

10. Eliade, Mircea. *Shamanism: Archaic Techniques of Ecstasy.* Princeton: Princeton University Press 1964, 359.

11. Werner, E.T.C. *Myths and Legends of China.* New York: Dover Publications, Inc. 1994, 204. A reprint of the 1922 edition published by George C. Harrap & Co., London.

12. Phillips, Charles. "The Bringer of Plenty" in *The Eternal Cycle: Indian Myth.* New York: Barnes & Noble 2005, 39.

the lord of the seasons, and determined the times for sowing and harvesting the crops."[13]

Is it any wonder if people have believed that when we die and the soul leaves the body, it is carried to heaven on the wind — or that when we breathe, we breathe in the breath expelled by god?

13. Krickeberg, Walter & et al. *Pre-Columbian American Religions.* New York: Holt, Rinehart and Winston 1968, 256

# PART TWO

# SPIRIT BEINGS OF THE ANIMAL & INSECT KIND

# INTRODUCTION

Animals and insects have figured in most of the world's religions in one way or another. Many times, they are the gods and goddesses that people worshipped, or they are the demons and devils that are feared. At other times, gods and goddesses appeared in certain animal or insect forms to accomplish certain tasks or to manipulate the world in some way. Throughout history, these creatures became symbolic of all the qualities, desires, faults or fears that humankind could imagine. Unfortunately, they also became hunted, persecuted, tortured or killed because of these qualities and fears. It was not uncommon in medieval France for pigs to be tried for attacking and killing children. One sow was actually executed after being tried at Falaise, Normandy, France in 1386. Charged with infanticide, "Defence council for the accused animal," wrote Nicholas Saunders "was provided at public expense."[1]

Fairies, shape-shifters, demons, witches, ghosts and gods have all contributed to the folklore, mythology and superstition surrounding animals. However, perhaps the biggest contributor to these stories is our own awe, fear and wonder of these creatures.

The ten animals and insects discussed in this section were chosen because of their characteristics and qualities. Characteristics and qualities that have reached out to most people around the world, reached out in a spiritual, mystical and fearful manner that inspires, touches and warns all of us.

Animals and insects are spirit creatures, messengers of the gods, symbols of life and resurrection and at the same time symbols of evil and diabolical powers. They are also seen as the spirit helpers of both man and deity.

---

1. Saunders, Nicholas J. *Animal Spirits.* London: Duncan Baird Publishers 1997, 22.

# Chapter 12. The Snake

"The snake is a main image of the vitality and continuity of life," wrote anthropologist Marija Gimbutas, "the guarantor of life energy in the home, and the symbol of family and animal life."[1] The snake means something different and yet the same in many cultures and locations. The serpent is a feared goddess of the river, a messenger and spirit being of Native America, a water spirit and god of Africa. These are similar characteristics for a universally important symbol. There is an opposite view, however. The snake is also portrayed as Satan himself in biblical lore. As historian Jean Markale wrote, "Western religious thought has been almost unanimous in making the serpent of Genesis into a concrete representation of the tempter, that is to say, of Satan himself, relying for support upon the Apocalypse where this 'great serpent'...is the image of absolute evil."[2] The serpent had been respected as a symbol of wisdom and life renewed for thousands of years — until the Hebrews and then the Christians waged successful campaigns to destroy it. "When the Hebrews introduced a male god into Canaan," says Mark O'Connell and Raje Airey, "the female deity and the snake were relegated and associated with evil."[3] Later, the Christian campaign was able to, as Page Bryant wrote, "distort a positive and ancient pagan symbol to suit the purposes of Christianity."[4]

1. Gimbutas, Marija. *The Civilization of the Goddess: The World of Old Europe.* San Francisco: HarperSanFrancisco 1991, 236.
2. Markale, Jean. *The Great Goddess: Reverence of the Divine Feminine from the Paleolithic to the Present.* Rochester: Inner Traditions 1999, 6.
3. O'Connell, Mark and Raje Airey. *The Complete Encyclopedia of Signs & Symbols.* London: Hermes House 2005, 186.
4. Bryant, Page. *Awakening Arthur!* London: The Aquarian Press 1991, 64

Even before Christianity established a toehold, however, the serpent was viewed by the Hebrews as either possessed by Satan or as Satan himself. In Jewish folklore, the original serpent walked on two legs, talked, and ate the same food that Adam and Eve did. One day the serpent witnessed Adam and Eve engaged in sexual relations and he became jealous — and persuaded Eve to eat the forbidden fruit. In punishment, according to Hebrew legend, "its hands and legs were cut off, so it had to crawl on its belly, all food it ate tasted of dust, and it became the eternal enemy of man."[5] However, the serpent also was able to have sexual relations with Eve before he was punished by God. Because of this the Israelites only became purified when they stood at Mt. Sinai and received the torah. "Gentiles, however," according to Alan Untermann, "have never been cleansed of this serpentine impurity."[6]

Christian hatred of the serpent was not universal, however. In Armenian folklore, according to Anthony S. Mercatante, "Christ himself is identified with Shahapet, a beneficent serpent spirit who inhabited olive trees and vinestocks in the ancient mythology."[7]

A graven image of a serpent suspended from a cross-like beam was erected by Moses to protect the Hebrews from the poisonous bite of serpents. Acting on God's instructions, "Moses made a serpent of brass, and put it upon a pole, and it came to pass, that if a serpent had bitten any man, when he beheld the serpent of brass, he lived."[8]

*Sinners transformed into snake creatures in Hell*

On the base of one of the ancient menhirs in Carnac an image of five snakes standing on their tails was carved. "When the site was excavated," writes archaeologist Johannes Maringer, "in 1922, five axes were found under the engravings. The blades faced upward; obviously the axes had been deliberately placed in that position. It is most likely that even

5. Untermann, Alan. *Dictionary of Jewish Lore & Legend*. New York: Thames and Hudson 1991, 176.
6. Ibid.
7. Mercatante, Anthony S. *Good and Evil in Myth & Legend*. New York: Barnes & Noble 1978, 65.
8. Numbers 21:9, KJV

in Neolithic times the serpent was a symbol of life."[9] Maringer believes that the serpent was closely associated with deceased ancestors and the five serpents engraved on the menhir probably indicated that five people were buried there along with the axes.

The duality of meanings most likely originated in the contrasting views of the serpent in Old European and Indo-European mythology. In Old European lore (prior to 4500 BCE) the serpent was benevolent, a symbol of life and fertility in both plants and animals (including humans), protective of the family and of domestic livestock. "Snakes are guardians of the springs of life and immortality," wrote Spanish scholar J.E. Cirlot, "and also of those superior riches of the spirit that are symbolized by hidden treasure."[10] The poisonous snake in Old European lore was, according to Gimbutas, "an epiphany of the goddess of Death."[11] Indo-European mythology (evolving between 4000 and 2500 BCE) contrasted this view, regarding the snake as a symbol of evil, an epiphany of the god of Death, and an adversary of the Thunder god. This was the point in time that the goddess religion began to give way to that of the male dominated religion of the sky god.

Gimbutas goes on to say, "it is not the body of the snake that was sacred, but the energy exuded by this spiraling or coiling creature which transcends its boundaries and influences the surrounding world."[12]

In the Classic world the serpent was the creator of the universe; it laid the Cosmic Egg and split it asunder to form the heavens and the earth. As Hans Leisegang wrote, "This serpent, which coiled round the heavens, biting its tail, was the cause of solar and lunar eclipses. In the Hellenistic cosmology, this serpent is assigned to the ninth, starless spheres of the planets and the zodiac. This sphere goes round the heavens and the earth and also under the earth, and governs the winds."[13] "In Christian theology," Leisegang continues, "this serpent became the prince of the world, the adversary of the transcendental god, the dragon of the outer darkness, who has barred off this world from above, so that it can be redeemed only by being annihilated."[14]

This creator-serpent, the Great Serpent, was symbolic of the sun, not evil but "the good spirit of light," as Leisegang so aptly describes it. It is this Great Serpent that is cause and ruler of the four seasons, the four winds and the four quarters of the cosmos.

9. Maringer, Johannes. *The Gods of Prehistoric Man: History of Religion.* London: Phoenix Press 2002, 170-171.

10. Cirlot. J. E. *A Dictionary of Symbols, 2nd Edition.* New York: Barnes & Noble Books 1995, 286.

11. Gimbutas, op. cit., 400.

12. Gimbutas, Marija. *The Language of the Goddess.* San Francisco: HarperSanFrancisco 1991, 121.

13. Leisegang, Hans. "The Mystery of the Serpent" in *Pagan and Christian Mysteries: Papers from the Eranos Yearbook,* edited by Joseph Campbell. New York: The Bollingen Foundation/Harper & Row Publishers 1955, 26-27.

14. Ibid., 27.

A white snake, like the salmon, was a source for wisdom and magical power and was associated with the goddess/Saint Brigit, also known in England and Scotland as Bride. On February 1st, Bride's Day, the serpent woke from its winter hibernation to bring in the change of seasons from winter to spring. Mackenzie relates an old Gaelic charm:

"To-day is the day of Bride,
The serpent shall come from his hole;
I will not molest the serpent
And the serpent will not molest me."[15]

The many serpent-like symbols found in ancient rock art the world over testify to the importance of this animal in the human mind. The zigzag and meandering lines symbolic of water, the mysterious spirals found the world over which mimic the coiled serpent, all speak of the underlying mystery that humans have felt towards the snake and the snakes place in the mythos of the Otherworld and death. However, not only death, for many the snake represented life and the renewal of life. The snake was the feared guardian of life and the forces of life as well as the messenger to and from the world of the dead. Snakes were believed to be symbolic of the departed soul to the ancient Greeks. They were also valued as guardians of temples, treasuries and oracles, their eyesight believed to be especially keen. Joseph Campbell noted that "in India...the 'serpent kings' guard both the waters of immortality and the treasures of the earth."[16]

While many a male anthropologist and archaeologist argue that the serpent is symbolic of fertility (as a phallic symbol), art historian Merlin Stone offers another view: "[The serpent] appears to have been primarily revered as a female in the Near and Middle East and generally linked to wisdom and prophetic counsel rather than fertility and growth, as is so often suggested."[17]

This statement is not entirely true. The god Ningišzida ("Lord of the Good Tree") was an important male deity in Mesopotamia. As an underworld god, he was guardian over demons and at least one Sumerian ruler regarded Ningišzida as his personal protector. While primarily a god of the underworld, there is one myth ("Adapa at the gate of heaven") that has Ningišzida as one of the guardians at the gates of heaven.[18] "The symbol and beast of Ningišzida," according to Black and Green, "was the horned snake..."[19]

The snake and the serpent have been depicted as goddesses and gods, as holy beings to be worshipped, as dragons, as devils and as symbols of lust, greed and sin — and of death. In mythic lore, Zeus appears in snake form to

15. Mackenzie, Donald A. *Ancient Man in Britain.* London: Senate 1996, 188-189. A reprint of the 1922 edition published by Blackie & Son Limited, London.
16. Campbell, Joseph. *Creative Mythology: The Masks of God Volume IV.* London: Secker & Warburg 1968, 120.
17. Stone, Merlin. *When God Was A Woman.* New York: Barnes & Noble Books 1993, 199.
18. Black, Jeremy and Anthony Green. *Gods, Demons and Symbols of Ancient Mesopotamia.* Austin: University of Texas Press 2000, 139.
19. Ibid 140.

mate with Persephone, who thereafter gives birth to Dionysus, "the god who in Crete, it so happens, was synonymous with Zeus."[20] The serpent is "the emblem of all self-creative divinities and represents the generative power of the earth. It is solar, chthonic, sexual, funerary and the manifestation of force at any level, a source of all potentialities both material and spiritual," writes J.C. Cooper, "and closely associated with the concepts of both life and death."[21]

The Giants of classic Greek and Roman mythology reportedly had snake-like legs as did the founder of Athens, Cecrops. Cecrops, a semi-serpent, was considered an innovator of his day, abolishing blood sacrifice, introducing basic laws of marriage, politics and property and encouraging the worship of Zeus and Athena.[22] Again, a duality exists between these two creatures with snake-like characteristics. The Giants were enemies of Zeus and were defeated by Hercules on behalf of the gods of Olympus and Cecrops was a champion for the causes of Zeus.

*Zeus conquers the Serpent-legged Titans*

Recent excavations in the Kenar Sandal area in Jiroft, Iran have uncovered additional serpent-legged figures. According to the *Persian Journal*,[23] the reliefs depicting two men with "snake tails instead of legs" were carved on soap-stone on a "flat stone cliff." At one time almost 5,000 years ago, Kenar Sandal was an important trade city for the Persian Gulf region, linking what is now Afghanistan, Pakistan, Iran and Tajikistan. The serpent-men reliefs indicate that this image has an ancient origin most likely outside the classic Greco-Roman world.

In support of the view that this mythic creature originated in the non-Classic World are the serpent-men of the Indian Underworld, the "demonic Cobras" called the Nagas. According to Mackenzie "they are of human form to the waist, the rest of their bodies being like those of serpents."[24] The Nagas were demi-gods to the Indian serpent worshippers and were, accord-

20. Baring, Anne and Jules Cashford. *The Myth of the Goddess: Evolution of an Image.* London: Arkana/Penguin Books 1991, 317.

21. Cooper, J.C. *An Illustrated Encyclopaedia of Traditional Symbols.* London : Thames and Hudson 1978, 147.

22. Cotterell, Arthur. *The Encyclopedia of Mythology: Classical, Celtic, Greek.* London: Hermes House 2005, 84.

23. "New Stone Reliefs Discovered in Jiroft, Iran" in *Persian Journal*, February 2, 2006. http://www.iranian.ws/iran_news/publish/article_12873.shtml

24. Mackenzie, Donald A. *India Myths & Legends.* London: Studio Editions 1993, 65.

ing to Mackenzie, "occasionally 'the friends of man', and to those they favoured they gave draughts of their nectar, which endowed them with great strength."[25]

An interesting image similar to the serpent-legged Titans and the Nagas is that carved upon the strange "Abrasax gems," magical amulets introduced in the second century that mingled early Christian and pagan themes. Originating in Alexandria, the images most certainly were inspired by the mystic powers of the man-serpent as represented by the Titans.

*Abrasax Gem Amulet*

It is interesting to note that Athens has even more connections to serpent-men in the form of Erichthonius — the first king of Athens. According to legend, this serpent being was created from the semen of the smith-god Hephaistos. Hephaistos had attempted to rape Athena but she miraculously disappeared just in time. His semen, as it fell to the earth, grew into the serpent Erichthonius. Ely offers an alternative view: "In the days of Pausanias, Hephaistos and Gaia were said to be the parents of Erichthonius." This version evidently arose from the more conservative elements of Greek society that could not abide with the original creation of the serpent-being from an act of rape.[26]

In Mesoamerican traditions, the Plumed Serpent, Quetzalcoatl, called "the wise instructor," brings culture and knowledge to the people and "takes charge or interferes in creative activities" of the world.[27] It is Quetzalcoatl who discovers corn and provides it for humankind's nourishment. While historical lore indicates that Quetzalcoatl was a man (in fact, a tall, white man with a beard), he is symbolically represented as a serpent on many temple complexes, the most notable being at Chichen-Itza in Yucatan. During certain times of the year the steps that lead up the pyramid temple cast an undulating shadow that connects with the carved stone serpent head — bringing to life the Plumed Serpent.

The serpent also represents chaos, corruption and darkness along with knowledge and spirit. It is this knowledge that the Bible uses to evict Adam and Eve from paradise and that brings the snake so much hatred. It is the symbolism of the snake, that is so closely associated with the earth and the earth's creative powers, that the followers of the sky god wished to destroy. According to Andrews, the snake "threatened the world order established

25. Ibid., 66.
26. Ely, Talfourd. *The Gods of Greece and Rome.* Mineola: Dover Publications Inc. 2003, 161. A reprint of the 1891 edition published by G.P. Putnam's Sons, New York.
27. Bierhorst, John. *The Mythology of Mexico and Central America.* New York: William Morrow and Company 1990, 145.

by the sky gods and continually tried to return the world to its original state of chaos."[28]

The serpent, in fact, threatened the order and control of the Judeo-Christian religion. As Markale suggests, Eve disobeyed the patriarchal priests and listens to the serpent, the serpent being representative of the mother goddess. "This is a case, pure and simple, of a return to the mother-goddess cult, a true 'apostasy' as it were, and thus a very grave sin against the patriarchal type of religion that Yahweh represents."[29] Markale and others, most notably the French Catholic priest André de Smet, believe that the original sin was the first battle in the long struggle between the patriarchal religion of Yahweh and the matriarchal religion of the mother goddess. The "curse against the serpent," Markale writes, "is against the mother goddess herself."[30]

The Gnostic writers viewed the serpent in a different manner. The Kabbalist Joseph Gikatila wrote in his book *Mystery of the Serpent*:

> Know and believe that the Serpent, at the beginning of creation, was indispensable to the order of the world, so long as he kept his place; and he was a great servent...and he was needed for the ordering of all the chariots, each in its place...It is he who moves the spheres and turns them from East to the West and from North to the South. Without him there would have been neither seed nor germination, nor will to produce any created thing.[31]

The Ophites, a successor group of the original Gnostics, venerated the snake. To the Ophites the serpent was made by God to be "the cause of Gnosis for mankind....It was the serpent...who taught man and woman the complete knowledge of the mysteries on high," which resulted in the serpent being "cast down from the heavens."[32] To this group the snake was the "living symbol of the celestial image that they worshipped."[33] According to Doresse, the Ophites kept and fed serpents in special baskets and met near the serpents' burrows. They would arrange loaves of bread on a table and then lure the snakes to the "offering." The Ophite followers would not partake of the bread, however until "each on kissing the muzzle of the reptile they had charmed. This, they claimed, was the perfect sacrifice, the true Eucharist."[34] To the Gnostic Christians, serpent worship was associated with the "restoration of Paradise, and release thereby from the bondages of time."[35]

The Greek island of Kefalonia reports a local phenomenon regarding snakes. They say that each August 15th, a day known as the feast of the Fall-

---

28. Andrews, Tamra. *A Dictionary of Nature Myths*. Oxford: Oxford University Press 1998, 176.

29. Markale, op. cit., 6.

30. Ibid., 7.

31. As quoted by Jean Doresse, *The Secret Books of the Egyptian Gnostics*. New York: MJF Books 1986, 292-293.

32. Ibid., 44.

33. Ibid., 45.

34. Ibid., 44.

35. Campbell, op. cit. 151.

ing Asleep of the Virgin, in the small village of Markopoulo, small snakes with a small cross-like mark on their heads slither through a churchyard, emerging near the bell tower and make their way toward the church. According to witnesses, the snakes enter the church building through bell rope holes in the wall; crawl over the furniture and even over the worshippers as they sit in the pews. The snakes continue onward to the bishop's throne and, as a group, to the icon of the Virgin.

After the service, the serpents disappear and are not seen again until the same evening a year later. The people of Markopoulo look forward to the appearance of these creatures as a sign of good luck and bountiful harvests. Only two years in recent memory did not see the return of the snakes. One was in 1940. The next year Greece was invaded by the Axis Forces. The year following their non-appearance in 1953 saw the area devastated by a catastrophic earthquake.

Normally the snakes avoid human contact, except on this day. When they visit the church at this time, the snakes appear quite tame and allow the residents to handle them at will. According to local lore, the annual serpent appearance dates to 1705 when Barbarossa pirates attacked the village. The nuns who resided in the village convent prayed to the Virgin to transform them into snakes to avoid being captured by the pirates, or worse. When the pirates finally gained access to the convent, they were shocked to see the floors, walls and icons writhing with snakes. The snakes have returned each year except for the two previously mentioned.

The serpent, as a representative of the mother goddess, is known from the serpent priestesses of Crete and various other mother goddess locations from the Neolithic. The shrine at Gournia, Crete yielded three figures of the mother goddess. One that shows the mother goddess with a serpent curled around her waist and over one shoulder.[36] The Greek mother goddess Ge or Gaia is often associated with the "earth snake."

Twenty-one figurines of serpent goddesses have been found at Poduri, Romania dating to 4800-4600 BCE, indicating that this goddess was not only an ancient one but was commonly worshiped throughout Europe and the Middle East. Archaeologist Marija Gimbutas wrote, "Their lack of arms, their snake-shaped heads, and the snakes coiling over their abdomens suggest that they represent the Snake goddess and her attendants; only one of them has an arm raised to her face, a gesture of power."[37]

"Undulating serpents or dragons signify cosmic rhythm, or the power of the waters."[38] The serpent has been associated with water since time began. They appear in Native American rock art throughout the continent symbolic of messengers of the otherworld that traverse through streams, rivers and

36. Mackenzie, Donald A. *Myths and Legends Crete & Pre-Hellenic.* London: Senate 1995, 261. A reprint of the 1917 edition published as *Crete & Pre-Hellenic Europe* by The Gresham Publishing Company, London.
37. Gimbutas, op. cit., 343.
38. Cooper, op. cit., 148.

time through the cracks in stone. It is by no accident that the Plumed Serpent of Mesoamerica is closely associated with the Cosmic Waters or that the Serpent Mound in the Ohio Valley is located near a flowing river. It is also not an accident that accounts of sea serpents are rampant in the world's maritime lore. In the Southwest, snakes were pecked or painted onto rock surfaces designating good or bad water sources. The snake was believed by Native Americans, as well as to the people of Old Europe and the ancient Near East, to bring rain when it is needed. Both the Hopi and Shasta Indians carried live snakes in their mouths for ritual dances in rainmaking ceremonies[39] and the Cheyenne also danced with poisonous snakes in their "crazy dances." "Crazy dances" were performed to aid in the cure of a sick child, to ensure victory in war or to obtain other blessings for the tribe.[40]

Snakes have also contributed to weather folklore around the world associated with rain. Nineteenth century folklorist Richard Inwards noted, "the chief characteristic of the serpents throughout the East in all ages seems to have been their power over the wind and rain, which they gave or withheld, according to their good or ill will towards man."[41] It was also possible to induce rain, according to Inwards, by hanging a dead snake on a tree.[42]

Mesoamerican traditions "have been recorded," writes anthropologist Robert Rands, "which directly connect the serpent with surface water, rain, and lightning....A few stray facts regarding the relationship of snakes to the anthropomorphic rain deities of the Maya and Mexicans may be noted. In the Maya codices, the serpent...and water are frequently shown together.... As giant celestial snakes or as partly anthropomorphized serpents, the Chicchans are rain and thunder deities of the present-day Chorti....In modern Zoque belief, snakes serve as the whips of the thunderbolts."[43]

The snake with its fluid motions is a natural symbol of flowing water. Native Americans and others saw this symbolism in the meandering streams and rivers that flow through their lands. They also saw the annual shedding of its skin as a renewal of life and of fertility, a renewal of the fertility that water also provides.

"The serpent is the foundation of the universe," writes Indian artist Jyoti Sahi. "Coiled around the navel of the cosmos, it appears to be the dynamic centre of time and space. The serpent seems always to be moving and yet

39. Kasner, Leone Letson. *Spirit Symbols in Native American Art.* Philomath: Ayers Mountain Press 1992, 113.

40. Mooney, James. *The Ghost-Dance Religion and the Sioux Outbreak of 1890.* Chicago: The University of Chicago Press 1965, 273.

41. Inwards, Richard. *Weather Lore.* London: Elliot Stock 1893.

42. Ibid.

43. Rands, Robert L. "Some Manifestations of Water in Mesoamerican Art," Anthropological Papers, No. 48, Bureau of American Ethnology Bulletin 157. Washington: Smithsonian Institution 1955, 361, pgs 265-393.

always still, like the oceans whose waves seem in perpetual turmoil and un-rest, but whose boundaries remain fixed, and whose depths are eternal."[44]

In ancient Indian mythology, the serpent becomes the victim of mankind, "in order to overcome the wilderness...and make it orderly and cultivated... [man] had to injure the serpent..."[45] Sahi says that this injury to the serpent is a "sin" and that the story really "represents the overthrowing of pre-Aryan serpent worship."[46]

In the ancient Mesopotamian city of Ur, the snake god Irhan was wor-shipped. To these people Irhan was representative of the Euphrates River. The mildly poisonous horned vipers of the Middle East gradually assumed the dragon form that we still recognize today.

A snake-dragon called *mušuššu*, or "furious snake" was worshipped in Babylon at least during the reign of Nebuchadnezzar II (604-562 BCE). This creature with the body and neck of a serpent, lion's forelegs and a bird's hind legs, was originally an attendant of the city god Ninazu of Ešnunna. The snake-dragon was transferred as an attendant of Ninazu to several other national gods through the years, surviving as a protective pendant through the Hellenistic Period.[47]

The serpent was present in the liturgy and symbolism of the Mithraic re-ligion as well. Mithraism almost dominated Christianity during the 2nd and 3rd centuries and many Christian symbols are derived from this ancient reli-gion. The snake appears often in paintings and carvings of Mithras hunting, the serpent is present as a companion to the god. Some depict the serpent seeking the flowing sacrificial blood of the bull that was slain in Mithraic baptisms. This, according to writer D. Jason Cooper, "seems to indicate the snake is seeking salvation."[48]

*Mithras and his salvation seeking serpent*

Snakes are also associated with healing. The caduceus, the staff with two intertwined serpents, is found not only in the healing temples of Greece, but also in Native American, Mesoamerican and Hindu symbolism. The snake with its

---

44. Sahi, Jyoti. *The Child and the Serpent: Reflections on Popular Indian Symbols.* London: Arkana/Penguin Books 1980, 161.

45. Ibid., 165.

46. Ibid., 166.

47. Jeremy and Anthony Green. *Gods, Demons and Symbols of Ancient Mesopotamia.* Austin: University of Texas Press 2000, 166.

48. Cooper, D. Jason. *Mithras: Mysteries and Initiation Rediscovered.* York Beach: Samuel Weiser, Inc. 1996, 74.

annual shedding of its skin was a logical symbol for life, renewal and protection. In Celtic lands as well the snake was, like the sacred well, associated with healing. To the Sumerians the caduceus was the symbol of life. The caduceus was also an important symbol to some Gnostic Christians who, according to Barbara Walker, "worshipped the serpent hung on a cross...or Tree of Life, calling it Christ the Savior, also a title of Hermes the Wise Serpent represented by his own holy caduceus..."[49] According to Wallis Budge, "the symbol of [the Babylonian god of healing, Ningishzida] was a staff round which a double-sexed, two-headed serpent called Sachan was coiled, and a form of this is the recognized mark of the craft of the physician at the present day."[50] The Greek god of healing, Aesculapius, was also depicted in a statue at Epidaurus "holding a staff in one hand, while his other hand rested on the head of a snake..."[51]

In Africa the spirits of the waters are, simply said, snakes. As they are symbolic of healing, they are also believed to "call" to healers to whom they give wisdom and knowledge.[52] According to anthropologist Penny Bernard, "the water spirits have been attributed a pivotal role in the calling, initiation and final induction of certain diviners in the Eastern Cape. Hence the implication that they are the key to certain forms of 'sacred' knowledge."[53]

Tornadoes and waterspouts were believed to be the physical appearance of the African serpent god Inkanyamba. Inkanyamba was believed to be an enormous serpent that twisted and writhed to and fro as it reached from the earth to the sky. Tamra Andrews noted that the Zulu "believed that he grew larger and larger as he rose out of his pool and then grew smaller and smaller when he retreated back into it."[54]

In other African cultures, the snake is considered the spirit of a departed human. Referred to as the "living-dead," the snake is prohibited from being killed, as it is representative of the soul of a relative or friend that is visiting the land of the living.[55]

According to Sumatran and Norse mythology, the vast Cosmic Snake that encircles the world in the cosmic river will eventually destroy it. However, from the destruction comes a new world, a renewal of life. The old gods die with the Cosmic Serpent but "earth will rise again from the waves, fertile, green, and fair as never before, cleansed of all its sufferings and evil."[56]

49. Walker, Barbara G. *The Women's Encyclopedia of Myths and Secrets.* Edison: Castle Books 1996, 131.

50. Budge, E.A. Wallis. *Babylonian Life and History.* New York: Barnes & Noble Books 2005, 167.

51. Ibid.

52. Bernard, Penny. "Mermaids, Snakes and the Spirits of the Water in Southern Africa: Implications for River Health", op. cit., 3.

53. Ibid., 4.

54. Andrews, op. cit., 96.

55. Mbiti, John S. *African Religions and Philosophy.* Garden City: Anchor Books 1970, 216.

56. Davidson, H. R. Ellis. *Gods and Myths of the Viking Age.* New York: Bell Publishing Company 1981, 38.

Perhaps in no other culture than Egypt was the serpent-god so prevalent. The serpent represented both male and female deities, both benign and malevolent. The snake-god Apophis was believed to have existed before time in the primeval chaos of pre-creation. Apophis was the enemy of the sun god and attacked the heavenly ship of Ra as it sojourned across the heavens. The daily battle involved other gods, including Seth, the enemy of Osiris, in a back and forth struggle of power between light and dark and balance and chaos. Each day Apophis was defeated, cut into pieces that would revive and rejoin the struggle the next day. In his own way Apophis was a symbol of renewal — renewal brought about by the eternal conflict of the powers of the universe. Apophis was associated with natural disaster, storms, earthquakes and unnatural darkness that foretold the return of chaos. As archaeologist Richard Wilkinson wrote, "Although the god was neither worshipped in a formal cult nor incorporated into popular veneration, Apophis entered both spheres of religion as a god or demon to be protected against."[57]

The Egyptians worshiped ten other snake gods. These include Mehen, who helped protect Ra from the daily attacks of Apophis; Denwen, who was very much like a dragon and had the ability to cause a fiery conflagration; Kebehwet, who was a "celestial serpent"; Meretseger, called the "goddess of the pyramidal peak" and who presided over the necropolis at Thebes. Meretseger became an important deity of the workmen who constructed the burial temples and chambers and many representations of this serpent goddess have been found in workmen's homes and shops in the area.

Other serpent gods of the Egyptians include Nehebu-Kau, "he who harnesses the spirits."[58] Nehebu-Kau was regarded as a helpful deity and was the son of the scorpion goddess Serket. He was referred to in hieroglyph as the "great serpent, multitudinous of coils" and was sometimes depicted as a man with a serpents head. Other beneficent serpent gods include Renenutet, a guardian of the king and goddess of the harvest and fertility. She was also known as a divine nurse. The cobra goddess Wadjet ("the green one") was a goddess of the Nile Delta and was associated with the world of the living rather than the world of the dead. Wadjet was another protector of the king and had the ability to spit flames as a defensive measure. The serpent on the pharaoh's crown was that of Wadjet. Like Renenutet, Wadjet was also a nurse to the god Hathor while he was yet a divine infant. Another fiery serpent is Wepset. Wepset, meaning "she who burns," guarded the king, other gods and the Eye of Ra. It was written in ancient texts that the Egyptian island of Biga was her cult center.

The last two Egyptian serpent deities are Weret-Hekau and Yam. "Great of magic" was the name for Weret-Hekau and she may be a composite of other serpent goddesses in that she was also a nursing serpent of the kings and her symbol is associated with the other uraeus goddesses. Yam was ac-

---

57. Wilkinson, Richard H. *The Complete Gods and Goddesses of Ancient Egypt.* New York: Thames & Hudson 2003, 223.
58. Ibid., 224.

tually a Semitic god, a "tyrannical, monstrous deity of the sea," according to Wilkinson.[59] Sometimes depicted as a seven-headed sea monster, Yam was a minor Egyptian god that may have been feared mostly by sailors and fishermen rather than by people of the villages and cities. Yam was defeated in various myths by the goddess Astarte, and the Canaanite god Baal and the Egyptian god Seth.

Serapis, a deity of both the Greeks and Egyptians, associated with Osiris, Hermes, and Hades, was introduced in the 3rd century BCE as a state god for both Greeks and Egyptians. Believed by the Egyptians to be a human manifestation of Apis, a sacred bull that symbolized Osiris, he was represented as a god of fertility and medicine and the ruler of the dead to the Greeks. Serapis was also depicted as a sun god and occasionally with a serpent wrapped around his body — most likely in connection with fertility.

*Serapis*

That serpents were, and still are, an extremely important aspect of religious traditions around the world cannot be doubted. Even Ireland, a land totally devoid of snakes, is obsessed with the image of the serpent. "Is it not a singular circumstance," said 19th-century scholar Marcus Keane, "that in Ireland where no living serpent exists, such numerous legends of serpents should abound, and that figures of serpents should be so profusely used to ornament Irish sculptures?"[60] Celtic scholar James Bonwick himself noted when he visited Cashel, Ireland in the 1880s, he saw "a remarkable stone, bearing a nearly defaced sculpture of a female — head and bust — but whose legs were snakes."[61] It was Bonwick's belief that this ancient stone carving depicted an "object of former worship." The "popularity" of the serpent image in Ireland caused Bonwick to write, "That one of the ancient military symbols of Ireland should be a serpent, need not occasion surprise in us. The Druidical serpent or Ireland is perceived in the Tara brooch, popularized to the present day. Irish crosses, so to speak, were alive with serpents."[62]

Serpents were valued in Slavic countries up through the 19th century as good-luck symbols. Snakes were also valued as protective charms in Sweden,

59. Ibid., 228.
60. As quoted by James Bonwick in *Irish Druids and Old Irish Religions.* New York: Barnes & Noble Books 1986, 173. A reprint of the 1894 edition.
61. Ibid 174.
62. Ibid 168.

where they were buried under the foundations of houses and other structures. Russian peasants kept them as pets and, as in Poland, snakes were
given food and drink in exchange for their protective charms.

Snakes were associated with an ancient god of thunder in Slavic countries. The thunder god was "responsible for creating mountains and for hurl-
ing down bolts of lightning also launched storms of life-giving rain into the
earth beneath him."[63] Kerrigan writes "Awesome as his strength was, pagan belief did not characterize it as being wielded destructively: only with
the coming of Christianity did his powers become identified with those of
evil."[64]

In some Native American lore, the snake was usually considered an
animal to be avoided — one of the "bad animals" that was prohibited from
journeying to the spirit world after death.[65] To the Lakota the spirit of the
snake "presided over the ability to do things slyly, to go about unknown and
unseen, and of lying."[66]

Cherokee shamans prohibited the killing of snakes and the Apache for-
bid the killing of any snake by their own people — but would not hesitate
to ask strangers to kill them.[67] The Cherokee generic name for the snake
is *inâdû'* and they are believed to be supernatural, having close associations
with rain and the thunder gods, as well as having a certain influence over
other plants and animals. "The feeling toward snakes," wrote James Mooney,
"is one of mingled fear and reverence, and every precaution is taken to avoid
killing or offending one."[68] Certain shamans were able to kill rattlesnakes for
use in rituals or for medicinal uses. The head was always cut off and buried
an arm's length deep in the earth. If this was not done, the snake would cause
the rain to fall until the streams and rivers overflowed their banks.[69]

Specific snake lore of the Cherokee indicates that some serpents were
not only associated with rain, thunder and the supernatural but also were
very unlucky. Mooney reported that a large serpent was once said to reside
on the north bank of the Little Tennessee and the main Tennessee rivers in
Loudon county, Tennessee and it was considered an evil omen simply to see
it. "On one occasion," he wrote, "a man crossing the river...saw the snake in
the water and soon afterward lost one of his children."[70]

63. Kerrigan, Michael. "A Fierce Menagerie" in *Forests of the Vampire: Slavic Myth*. New
York: Barnes & Noble 2003, 124.
64. Ibid.
65. Walker, James R. *Lakota Belief and Ritual*. Lincoln: University of Nebraska Press
1991, 71.
66. Ibid., 122.
67. Bourke, John G. *Apache Medicine-Men*. New York: Dover Publications, Inc. 1993,
20. A reprint of the 1892 edition of *The Medicine-Men of the Apache* published in the
Ninth Annual Report of the Bureau of Ethnology to the Secretary of the Smithsonian
Institution 1887-88, Washington, pgs 443-603.
68. Mooney, James. *Myths of the Cherokee*. New York: Dover Publications 1995, 294.
69. Ibid., 296.
70. Mooney, op. cit. 414.

Illnesses were often thought to be caused by snakes, and even the act of accidentally touching the discarded skin of a snake was believed to cause sickness, especially skin ailments and perhaps even death.[71]

The Apache avoided even mentioning the snake but would sometimes use it as an invective. However, by doing even this one courted disaster. According to Opler, "If a man says in anger, 'I hope a snake bites you,' he will get sick from snakes...Before this the snakes have not bothered him, but...it's bound to make him sick."[72]

When a snake is accidentally encountered on a trail, it is, according to Opler, "accorded the greatest respect and is referred to by a relationship term: 'My mother's father, don't bother me! I'm a poor man. Go where I can't see you. Keep out of my path.'"[73]

Cherokee lore tells of strange snake-like creatures, simply told as observations and accounts of frightful encounters between men and monster. One such beast is called the Ustû'tlĭ, or "foot snake" which lived on the Cohutta Mountain. Ethnologist James Mooney recorded stories at the beginning of the 20th century about this monster and gives us the following description:

> "...it did not glide like other snakes, but had feet at each end of its body, and moved by strides or jerks, like a great measuring worm. These feet were three-cornered and flat and could hold on to the ground like suckers. It had no legs, but would raise itself up on its hind feet, with its snaky head waving high in the air until it found a good place to take a fresh hold...It could cross rivers and deep ravines by throwing its head across and getting a grip with its front feet and then swinging it body over."[74]

A similar creature called the "bouncer" (Uw'tsûñ'ta) lived on the Nantahala River in North Carolina. It too moved by "jerks like a measuring worm." According to lore this snake-like animal was so immense that it would darken the valleys between rifts as it moved across them. According to Mooney the Indians that lived in this area, fearing the snake, eventually deserted the land, "even while still Indian country."[75]

Another monstrous snake, called the Uktena, was said to be as large as a tree trunk, with horns on its head. Anyone who managed to kill the Uktena could obtain a transparent scale from the snake, said to be similar to a crystal, that was located on its forehead. To have one was to be blessed with excellent hunting, success in love, rainmaking and life prophecy.

Some Native American people viewed the snake in another way entirely. It was symbolic of the war-god who also had powers over crops and vegetation. "As the emblem of the fertilizing summer showers the lightning serpent

71. Opler, Morris Edward. *An Apache Life-Way: The Economic, Social, and Religious Institutions of the Chiricahua Indians.* Chicago: The University of Chicago Press 1941, 228.
72. Ibid.
73. Ibid., 227.
74. Mooney, op. cit. 1995, 302.
75. Ibid., 304.

was the god of fruitfulness," wrote Lewis Spence, "but as the forerunner of floods and disastrous rains it was feared and dreaded."[76]

That prehistoric Indians believed that the serpent form contained supernatural powers can be surmised by the various serpent mounds constructed in the American heartland. Three such mounds are those found in Adams County, Ohio, St. Peter's River, Iowa and another serpentine mound which extends in sections over two miles in length, also in Iowa. The Great Serpent Mound located in Adams County, Ohio is believed to be the largest serpent effigy in the world at over one-quarter of a mile in length and depicts a serpent in the act of uncoiling.[77] This unusual earthwork shows the serpent with an egg, perhaps the Cosmic Egg, in its mouth. The culture that created the Great Serpent Mound is unknown since no manmade artifact has been found in connection with the site, although Adena artifacts consisting of copper breastplates, stone points and axes, and grooved sandstone have been found within 400 feet of the mound.

*South West American Indian petroglyph of the snake with the cosmic egg*

American folklore has a number of superstitions surrounding the snake. Among these is the notion that a snake cannot cross a horsehair rope but

76. Spence, Lewis. *North American Indians Myths & Legends.* London: Senate 1994, 112. A reprint of *North American Indians* published 1914 by George G. Harrap & Company Ltd.

77. Silverberg, Robert. *Mound Builders of Ancient America: The Archaeology of a Myth.* Greenwich: New York Graphic Society Ltd. 1968, 249.

that horsehair placed in a bucket of water will turn into a snake. "A spotted serpent called the milk snake," reports folklorist Vance Randolph, "is said to live by milking cows in the pasture. I know several persons who swear they have seen these snakes sucking milk cows, and they say that a cow which has been milked by a snake is always reluctant to allow a human being to touch her thereafter."[78]

While the snake was often feared, American "hill folk" also respected it. According to Randolph, rather than say the word "snake," like the Apache, "they say 'look out for *our friends* down that way,' or 'there's a lot of *them old things* between here and the river.'"[79]

British folklore says, "if you wear a snake skin round your head, you will never have a headache," and "snakes never die until the sun goes down, however much they may be cut in pieces."[80] However, "if you kill one its mate will come looking for you."[81] Another advises that to stay young — eat snake!

In 19th-century Gaelic folklore the serpent is more evil than good. Campbell wrote,

> A serpent, whenever encountered, ought to be killed. Otherwise, the encounter will prove an evil omen.

> The head should be completely smashed...and removed to a distance from the rest of the body. Unless this is done the serpent will again come alive. The tail, unless deprived of animation, will join the body, and the head becomes a *beithir*, the largest and most deadly kind of serpent.[82]

In other cultures, like many Native American ones, there is a prohibition against killing snakes. Frazer wrote, "In Madras it is considered a great sin to kill a cobra. When this has happened, the people generally burn the body of the serpent, just as they burn the bodies of human beings. The murderer deems himself polluted for three days."[83] In other areas of the world, snakes were annually sacrificed in large numbers by burning. This occurred at Luchon in the Pyrenees on Midsummer Eve at least into the early 20th century. Considered a pagan survival, the ritual was led by the local clergy. Frazer describes the event:

> At an appointed hour — about 8 PM — a grand procession, composed of the clergy, followed by young men and maidens in holiday attire, pour forth from the town chanting hymns, and take up their position [around a

78. Randolph, Vance. *Ozark Magic and Folklore.* New York: Dover Publications, Inc. 1964, 257. A reprint of the 1947 edition of *Ozark Superstitions* published by Columbia University Press.
79. Ibid., 258.
80. Radford, Edwin and Mona A. *Encyclopaedia of Superstitions.* New York: Philosophical Library 1949, 221.
81. Simpson, Jacqueline and Steve Roud. *Oxford Dictionary of English Folklore.* Oxford: Oxford University Press 2000, 2.
82. Campbell, John Gregorson. *The Gaelic Otherworld,* edited by Ronald Black. Edinburgh: Birlinn Limited 2005, 121.
83. Frazer, Sir James. *The Golden Bough: A study in magic and religion.* Hertfordshire: Wordsworth Editions 1993, 222.

wicker-work column raised 60 feet in height]. ...bonfires are lit, with beautiful effect, in the surrounding hills. As many living serpents as could be collected are now thrown into the column, which is set on fire at the base by means of torches, armed with which about fifty boys and men dance around with frantic gestures. The serpents...wriggle their way to the top... until finally obliged to drop, their struggles for life giving rise to enthusiastic delight among the surrounding spectators.[84]

Serpents have been mercilessly hunted and killed by many cultures the world over but it is possible, according to Jyoti Sahi, that "all religions which have evolved the concept of a really personal god...have emerged out of a tradition in which serpents have been extremely important symbols of the supernatural."[85]

## THE HORNED SNAKE

Snakes with horns? They are common in Celtic artistic mythology and represent protection against all forms of catastrophe — sickness, war and all of the horrors of death. According to Miranda Green, approximately fifteen examples of horned serpents can be found in Gaul while only a handful more are seen throughout the British Isles.[86]

The ram-horned serpent almost always appears as a companion to Celtic deities such as Cernunnos, who himself is stag-horned. This monstrous snake appears on the Gundestrup Cauldron on one panel with Cernunnos and on another at the head of a military march. Miranda Green noted that the ram-horned snake appears on a carving at Haute Marne accompanying a goddess who feeds the snake from a basket on her knee and at Loire on a wooden sculpture with a possible Cernunnos figure. The serpent slides down the god's arm with its head in a basket. "The repeated prosperity-symbolism," Green writes "shown in reliefs is significant: a bronze from...Seine et Loire combines several Celtic images in curious intensity; a three-headed god sits cross-legged...[with] a ram-horned snake entwined round his body."[87]

The horned snake was also an important religious image in other areas of the world. As noted previously, the Mesopotamian god Ningišzida was depicted as a horned snake, appearing on such items as ritual cups and city seals. Images of horned snakes were commonly used in the Mesopotamian world as magically protective charms.

84. Ibid 655-656.
85. Sahi, op. cit. 166.
86. Green, Miranda. *The Gods of the Celts.* Gloucester: Alan Sutton 1986, 192.
87. Ibid.

# CHAPTER 13. THE TURTLE AND THE TORTOISE

   While the turtle is symbolic of longevity, it is also symbolic of things that we mostly find distasteful, such as cowardice, the obscene, braggarts, and to the ancient Egyptians, an enemy of the sun god. However, the turtle's larger cousin, the tortoise, is symbolic of all that is good. In ancient mythology, the tortoise carries the world on its back, while the Cosmic Tree grows out of that same carapace. The tortoise represents fertility, regeneration, the beginning of time and creation, and immortality. It is also symbolic of the moon, the waters and the earth mother. In North and South Dakota, various Indian tribes viewed the turtle as a symbol of productivity and fertility. Young girls would wear turtle charms in the hope of having children. Rock art images of turtles may have been symbolic fertility figures. Some Native American tribes called the tortoise the mother of humanity, believing that humankind originated from within the tortoise.

In Chinese mythology, the tortoise is one of four sacred animals (although Frazer wrote that the tortoise was "an animal of the very worst character"),[1] the others being the phoenix, the unicorn and the dragon. The tortoise in Chinese lore is also known for its oracular powers. In India Kashyapa is known as "Old Tortoise Man," the "creator god and father of creatures."[2] Kashyapa was the first living creature and progenitor. Another "Turtle Man" exists in Oglala lore. The Turtle Man supposedly lives in the moon but may have been derived from Iroquoian myth in which the world is created upon the turtle's back. This mythic motif is also present in Hindu lore but in this story, the tortoise has a role in the world's end. According to Fiske, "when the gods get ready to destroy mankind, the tortoise will grow weary and sink under his load, and then the earth will be overwhelmed by a deluge."[3] Similar tales from Native American lore say that earthquakes result when the Great Turtle tires from carrying the world and shifts his feet.

In Indian mythology, Vishnu takes on the form of a giant tortoise as his second incarnation to lift the world out of the depths of a flood to save the earth from drowning. Charles Phillips wrote, "Scholars believe that pre-Aryan Indians worshipped the tortoise. They are thought to have seen the animal as an embodiment of the universe — with the upper shell standing for the sky above and the lower shell standing for the earth below, while the soft body of the tortoise in between represented the atmosphere."[4]

The ancient Maya believed the turtle represented the earth. The Maya created several altars carved out of rock in the form of turtles. In addition, an illustration in the Codex Madrid shows five gods in a bloodletting ritual at such an altar, which possibly represents an annual ritual meant to fertilize the earth.[5] Among contemporary Mayans residing at Chan Kom the tortoise is closely associated with the rain gods. During droughts it is said that the tortoise "weeps for men and it is said that his tears draw the rain."[6]

During the Akkadian Period of Sumeria the turtle was associated with the god Enki, or Ea, who was god of the subterranean freshwater ocean and

1. Frazer, Sir James. *The Golden Bough: A study in magic and religion.* Hertfordshire: Wordsworth Editions 1993, 36.

2. Zimmer, Heinrich. *Myths and Symbols in Indian Art and Civilization.* Princeton: Princeton University Press-Bollinger Series VI, 1946, 104.

3. Fiske, John. *Myths and Myth-Makers: Old Tales and Superstitions Interpreted by Comparative Mythology.* Boston: Houghton, Mifflin and Company 1881, 171.

4. Phillips, Charles. "The Great Preserver" in *The Eternal Cycle: Indian Myth.* New York: Barnes & Noble Books 2005, 59

5. Miller, Mary and Karl Taube. *An Illustrated Dictionary of The Gods and Symbols of Ancient Mexico and the Maya.* London: Thames and Hudson 1993, 175.

6. Rands, Robert L. "Some Manifestations of Water in Mesoamerican Art", in *Bureau of American Ethnology Bulletin 157, Anthropological Papers Numbers 43-48.* Washington: Smithsonian Institution 1955, 349.

was especially known for his wisdom, magical incantations and for giving arts and crafts to humankind. Enki was also another of the world's creator gods.

The turtle and tortoise shell were often used for musical instruments. The Mayan and other groups in Mexico and Central America used the turtle shell as a drum and Mercury was said to have invented the lyre using a tortoise-shell. Various American Indian tribes may have used similar devices. The Cherokee reportedly had a large drum carved out of stone in the shape of a turtle shell which was kept in a townhouse in the village of Keowee and used for all of the town's dances. According to Mooney, this drum was lost in 1776 when it was hidden during the invasion by Colonel Andrew Williamson and his South Carolina Army. Mooney wrote "..but as the country was never recovered by the Cherokee the drum was lost."[7]

In Lakota belief, the Spirit of the Turtle "was the guardian of life and patron of surgery and controlled accidents."[8] The heart of the turtle was dried, powdered and mixed in a liquid that was ingested by the Lakota to treat wounds.

It may have been the guardian of life aspect of the turtle that prompted prehistoric people, in the American Southwest, to bury turtle carapaces at the feet or under the skulls of the dead.[9]

In Cherokee mythology, the land tortoise was a great warrior and because of the thickness of its legs Cherokee ball players would rub their own legs with them before entering a contest. However, the turtle inspired fear among the Apache. According to ethnologist Morris Opler, an Apache informant told him, "My people were afraid of the turtle and wouldn't touch it. Only a man who got his power from it would handle it."[10]

As it did with other ancient sacred symbols around the world, early Christian symbolism depicted the tortoise as evil.

7. Mooney, James. *Myths of the Cherokee*. New York: Dover Publications, Inc. 1995, 503. A reprint of the 1900 publication "Nineteenth Annual Report of the Bureau of American Ethnology, 1897-98.

8. Walker, James R. *Lakota Belief and Ritual*. Lincoln: University of Nebraska Press 1991, 122.

9. Webb, William S. and David L. DeJarnette. *An Archaeological Survey of Pickwick Basin in the Adjacent Portions of the States of Alabama, Mississippi and Tennessee*. Bureau of American Ethnology Bulletin 129. Washington: The Smithsonian Institution 1942.

10. Opler, Morris Edward. *An Apache Life-Way: The Economic, Social, and Religious Institutions of the Chiricahua Indians*. Chicago: The University of Chicago Press 1941, 237.

# CHAPTER 14. THE TOAD AND THE FROG

Toads and frogs. One either likes them or is repulsed by them. I rather like them. Frogs have been connected with witches because they were associated with Hecate — the goddess of witches. Frogs were also sacred to the Roman goddess Venus, who is another aspect of Hecate. Heket, the Egyptian Hecate, was a frog goddess "who assisted in fashioning the child in the womb and who presided over its birth."[1] As a sacred midwife, Hecate was depicted in Egyptian art as a frog or as a woman with a frog's head. Amulets of the goddess were simply in the image of frogs but were inscribed, "I am the Resurrection."[2] Babylonian cylinder seals depicted nine frogs as a fertility charm, the frogs representing the Ninefold goddess that ruled the nine months of gestation.

As Hecate's amulets indicated that she is synonymous with resurrection, so too is the frog which represents her. The frog also came to be regarded as the protector of mothers and newborn children in Egyptian society, and represented fertility, new life, abundance and the embryonic powers of water. The frog's association with fertility was also accepted in the Graeco-Roman world.

The toad was also sacred to the Lithuanian goddess of Death and Regeneration, Ragana. As Gimbutas wrote, "If not properly treated, the toad, it was believed even in the early 20th century, could be as dangerous as the goddess herself."[3]

1. Wilkinson, Richard H. *The Complete Gods and Goddesses of Ancient Egypt.* Lonson: Thames and Hudson Ltd. 2003, 229.
2. Budge, Sir E.A. Wallis. *Egyptian Magic.* New York: Dover Publications Inc. 1971, 63.
3. Gimbutas, Marija. *The Language of the Goddess.* San Francisco: HarperSanFrancisco 1991, 256.

These dangers included spitting on the toad, which would result in death for the spitter, making the toad angry enough so that it explodes, releasing a deadly poison, and killing the toad with ones bare hands, which changes the killers face to resemble that of the toad. "As a messenger of death," Gimbutas writes, "the toad can crawl onto the chest of a sleeping person and suck the breath from his or her body, causing certain death."[4] However, the toad is also known for its healing aspects. This is not contradictory at all as both death and regeneration are qualities of Ragana and thus of the toad.

"The goddess [of Regeneration] in the form of a frog or toad," Gimbutas tells us, "predominates in the temples, and her icons or amulets...are found throughout the Neolithic, Bronze Age, and even throughout historical times. Beliefs in the body's 'traveling womb' in the form of a frog occur widely from Egypt, Greece, and Rome, to northern Europe during the historical period and, in some places, to this day."[5]

Votive pits uncovered in Danebury and in Aquitaine indicate the ritual use of frogs and toads in Celtic traditions. In Danebury, twenty bones of seven species of frogs and toads were found in one pit and in Aquitaine a 1st century BCE cremation of toads was discovered.[6] A Roman cemetery uncovered on St. Clare Street in London revealed a 1st or 2nd century deposit of eighty frogs or toads along with two broken and two complete flagons suggesting that libations were left along with the frogs and toads as an offering.[7] Frogs were sacred to the Celts for their powers of healing; the frog was the Lord of the earth to the Celts and represented the power of healing water.

While frogs and toads may be associated with witches, they are also associated with fairies that may appear as frogs. Three guardian fairies that appear as frogs protect a healing well in Shropshire, England. As frogs and toads were utilized as votive offerings, they were also used for individual spells to harm others. Archaeologist Ralph Merrifield noted, "A black pipkin covered with a slate on which the name 'Nanney Roberts' was written was found buried in a bank on Penrhos Bradwen Farm, near Holyhead, Angelsey, in the nineteenth century; it contained the skin and bones of a frog, which had been pierced by several large pins, and was clearly intended as the image-substitute of the woman named."[8] This particular frog was sacrificed as a curse in relatively recent times.

Frogs were also associated with water and rainmaking in Mesoamerica. As Rands noted "Frogs and toads are generally thought to have a 'natural' connection with rainfall."[9] During the *chac-chaac* rainmaking ceremony of

4. Ibid.
5. Gimbutas, Marija. *The Civilization of the Goddess: The World of Old Europe.* San Francisco: HarperSanFrancisco 1991, 244.
6. Green, Miranda. *The Gods of the Celts.* Gloucester: Alan Sutton 1986, 186.
7. Merrifield, Ralph. *The Archaeology of Ritual and Magic.* New York: New Amsterdam Books 1987, 36. Other offerings in the same pit included a heron, shrews and voles.
8. Ibid., 155.
9. Rands, Robert L. "Some Manifestations of Water in Mesoamerican Art," *Anthropological Papers*, No. 48, Bureau of American Ethnology Bulletin 157.

the Maya, frog "impersonators" would mimic their croaking to add power to the rainmaking efforts. "Frogs and snakes," Rands continued "were kept in a pool at the feet of an image of Tlaloc [god of rain and lightning] and during a dance in the god's honor were caught in the mouth and swallowed."[10] Zuni lore states, "When frogs warble, they herald rain. The louder the frog, the more rain would fall. When frogs croak much, it is a sign of rain."[11]

In Vedic myth, a giant frog supported the world, as Saunders noted, this was "a metaphor for the primal state of matter."[12]

Carved images of toads, like tortoises, were incorporated in some of the massive altars of Postclassic Mayan temples. These altars were usually placed in front of stelae and were an early part of the Maya stela-altar complex.[13] That the toad was regarded as an important sacred-fertility icon in Mayan society cannot be doubted. "In recently discovered Early Classic stucco reliefs from Balamkú, Campeche," Miller and Taube write, "there are full-figure toads with upwardly facing heads. Seated lords are positioned in their mouths, as if the toads were metaphorically giving birth to the kings."[14]

While frogs were thought to have a natural link to water and to rains it was also believed to be responsible for drought. In both Australia and North America, mythic tales were told of a giant frog swallowing all the waters, creating drought and famine.

Among the Cherokee Indians, it was believed in the past that the "great frog" was responsible for solar eclipses as it attempted to swallow the sun. James Mooney tells us, "in former times it was customary on such occasions to fire guns and make other loud noises to frighten away the frog."[15] In Mongolia, earthquakes were said to be the result of a giant frog jumping across the land.

The frog in Apache lore was classified as a snake. Frogs were not eaten, as it was believed that anyone who ate a frog would "walk like a cowboy" [i.e. bowlegged]. [16]

The frog was an important mythic figure to the Indian tribes living in the Great Basin and appeared in various locations depicted in rock art. The ability of frogs and other small reptiles to crawl in and out of the cracks and breaks in rocks or to jump in and out of bodies of water "is analogous to a shaman's entry into the supernatural by metaphorically entering either a

Washington: Smithsonian Institution 1955, 360.

10. Ibid., 361.

11. Inwards, Richard. *Weather Lore*. London: Elliot Stock 1893, 145.

12. Saunders, Nicholas J. *Animal Spirits*. London: Duncan Baird Publishers 1997, 106.

13. Miller, Mary and Karl Taube. *An Illustrated Dictionary of The Gods and Symbols of Ancient Mexico and the Maya*. London: Thames and Hudson 1993, 168.

14. Ibid.

15. Mooney, James. *Myths of the Cherokee*. New York: Dover Publications, Inc. 1995, 306. A reprint of the 1900 publication "Nineteenth Annual Report of the Bureau of American Ethnology, 1897-98.

16. Opler, Morris Edward. *An Apache Lifeway: The Economic, Social, and Religious Institutions of the Chiricahua Indians*. Chicago: The University of Chicago Press 1941, 332.

rock or a spring."[17] Frogs, then, were believed to be the messengers between our physical world and the world of the supernatural. The frog was often carved or painted on stone to represent the trance state of the shaman. The image of the frog was symbolic of going underwater and thereby of death.

An interesting aside is that many of the early Olmec depictions of the were-jaguar may have been of toads, instead. The jaguar eventually became an extremely important shamanic animal as well as a prominent god in Mesoamerican religions.

Frogs and toads were often associated with witches during the Burning Times as witches' familiars — or as forms that witches were able to transform into. One witch trial held in 1665 for Rose Cullender and Amy Duny of Lowestoft, England was concerned with the bewitchment of a child. According to Robin Briggs, "One of the sick child's blankets was hung up and anything found in it thrown into the fire. A toad obligingly appeared and exploded when put in the fire, after which the suspect was discovered much scorched."[18]

Medieval Christians believed that toads were "familiars of witches, symbols of avarice and lust, and tormentors of those in Hell for these and other sins."[19]

Frog superstitions, of which there are many, include the following:

> In some parts of the country a frog was supposed to possess the soul of a dead child, and it was very unlucky therefore to kill one. The origin... probably lies in the cry of the frog if injured, which is almost human in its note.[20]

Others include the belief that cancer could be cured by swallowing a young frog. Evidently, it was thought that the frog could draw the poison of cancer into its body and eliminate the disease from human victims.

To the Christians the frog represented resurrection but also sin, evil, worldly pleasure, envy and heretics. But then, most symbols originating in ancient times became symbols of evil under Christian influence.

Strangely enough, the toad has a much darker position than the frog in European folklore. In sixteenth-century England the toad was regarded as an emissary of the Evil One and often was burned to death. Likewise, the people of Norway believed that the toad was evil, or the representative of evil, and they cast unlucky frogs and toads into the bonfires which people had danced around and jump over on St. John's Eve. This act of toad killing was believed to ward off trolls and other evil spirits that were active on that night.

---

17. Whitley, David S. *A Guide to Rock Art Sites: Southern California and Southern Nevada.* Missoula: Mountain Press Publishing Company 1996, 20.

18. Briggs, Robin. *Witches & Neighbors: The Social and Cultural Context of European Witchcraft.* New York: Viking 1996, 209.

19. Saunders, op. cit.

20. Radford, Edwin and Mona A. *Encyclopaedia of Superstitions.* New York: The Philosophical Library 1949, 127.

---

While the toad, like the frog, was regarded as a symbol of resurrection, it was also believed to represent other, less desirable things. In Iranian, Celtic and Christian lore the toad represents evil and death. And we cannot forget that Judeo-Christian lore tells of the plague of frogs that was visited upon Pharaoh.

The toad, however, like many other sacred symbols, has a dual nature. A general piece of folklore from the 1940s said, "If a toad crosses the path of a bridal party on the way to church, the couple will have prosperity and happiness." The Araucanian and Orinoco Indians of Chili and Venezuela called the toad the Lord of the Water and the toad was believed to watch over the preservation of water. Its link to water, like the frog's association to water, was a common belief. In Lincolnshire, England, toads were kept in household wells to ensure the water's purity and much effort was taken to ensure that the toad never escaped from its well enclosure.

Another common bit of lore from Herefordshire was, "If you wear a toad's heart concealed on your person, you can steal to your heart's content without being found out." I wonder how many boys were amazed at being caught even though they had a toad's heart in their pocket?

In 1892, a severe outbreak of flu ravaged Togo and it was blamed on evil spirits. To expel the spirits and remove the disease "they dragged a toad through the streets, followed by an elder scattering holy water. By this means the epidemic was concentrated in the toad, which was then cast into the nearby forest."[21]

To explore even more in the remote past frogs and toads were regarded as sacred and often were associated with goddesses. Frog-woman hybrid figures were common in Anatolia dating back to the 6th millennium BCE. Symbols of regeneration, these figures had human heads and vulvas but with a decidedly frog-like body. Such figures were etched and carved in marble, alabaster, clay, ceramics, and stone since early Neolithic times. Some of the earliest carved forms have perforations that imply that they were worn as amulets.

---

21. Radford, op. cit. 241.

# CHAPTER 15. THE EAGLE AND THE RAVEN

To most indigenous people the eagle and the raven are two of the most important creatures in existence. In the Welsh triads, the "Trioedd Ynys Prydein," the eagle and the raven are two of the three oldest animals in the world. The third is the owl. The eagle is representative of divine beings, theological concepts, spirit guardians, and lofty ideals. The raven, because it is a "talking" bird, is closely linked to prophecy and wisdom. It is also, on the other hand, associated with war, destruction and death. Sailors especially saw evil in the raven. According to Anne Ross, "a raven landing on the mast was a sure indication of witchcraft." Horseshoes were nailed to the mast to ward off the potential threat from witches, fairies and the Evil Eye.[1]

The eagle is symbolic of strength, freedom, release, royalty, authority, inspiration and spiritual principle. It is also symbolic of all of the sky gods of humankind as well as the solar disc. It is, according to Walker, the "classic soul-bird...associated with the sun god, fire, and lightning."[2] The eagle appears on the Mexican flag with a snake in its talons depicting spiritual victory over evil. The eagle represents all that is good while the serpent represents all that is evil — thus the two are symbolic of the sum total of all that is. The eagle victorious over the serpent was also present in Greek symbolism. In Homer's *Iliad*, the Greek priest Kalchas observed an eagle slowly flying in the sky with a bleeding snake in its talons. "The heavenly bird ravaging the serpent," wrote Heinrich Zimmer, "symbolized to him the victory of the patriarchal, masculine, heavenly order of the Greeks over the female

---

1. Ross, Anne. *Folklore of the Scottish Highlands.* Gloucestershire: Tempus Publishing LTD. 2000, 101.
2. Walker, Barbara. *The Women's Encyclopedia of Myths and Secrets.* Edison: Castle Books 1996, 262.

principle of Asia and Troy."[3] The various mythic tales of the eagle and the serpent reflect the change in religious power from the conversion of the ancient goddess religion to the, possibly violent, usurpation of the patriarchal sky god. Zimmer sums up the two in his book *Myths and Symbols in Indian Art*: "The eagle represents this higher, spiritual principle, released from the bondage of matter and soaring into the supreme divine being above them. On the other hand, the serpent is life-force in the sphere of life-matter. The snake is supposed to be of tenacious vitality; it rejuvenates itself by sloughing off its skin."[4] In Native American symbolism, the eagle represents the Thunder Bird, the "Universal Spirit" — the "mediator between sky and earth."[5]

Thunder Birds were gigantic creatures that created storms, sometimes violent storms, by the beating of their wings and by the shooting of lightning from their eyes and wings. Thunder Birds were, at times, beneficial to man as they brought the rain. However, they were more often than not viewed as being responsible for the destruction created by these storms.

According to D'Alviella, "The Greeks, like all the Indo-European nations, seem to have figured to themselves the light of the storm under the form of a bird of prey. When they had received the image of the Thunderbolt from Asia Minor, they placed it in the talons of the eagle, and made it the scepter, and even the symbol, of Zeus...it was, said they, the eagle that brought the Thunderbolt to Zeus, when the latter was preparing to fight the Titans."[6]

The eagle has been a symbol of Pan, who gave it up to Zeus; it was a symbol to Odin and Mithras, and to St. John and to the sons of Horus. The eagle is a vehicle for the Indian god Vishnu and is the lightning bearer for Jupiter. It is also one of the four beasts of the Apocalypse and is one of the aspects of the Babylonian god Marduk and the Celtic god Lug. Zeus and Odin took the form of an eagle in their mythic pursuits but so did Jesus, at least in some Gnostic writings. "I manifest myself in the form of an eagle," Jesus says in the Secret Book of John, "upon the Tree of Knowledge."[7]

In Late Post Classic Central Mexico, the fierce harpy eagle symbolized the sun as well as human sacrifice. It was an important figure to the Olmecs, Aztecs and Mayan cultures.

Large birds, in particularly eagles and vultures, were used as religious ritual objects and as offerings. Gimbutas noted that 88% of bird bones discovered in megalithic tombs in Orkney, Scotland were from white-tailed eagles. She believed that the bones "must have been an offering to the goddess of

3. Zimmer, Heinrich. *Myths and Symbols in Indian Art and Civilization*. Princeton: Princeton University Press-Bollinger Series VI, 1946, 74.

4. Zimmer, op. cit. 75.

5. Cooper, J.C. *An Illustrated Encyclopaedia of Traditional Symbols*. London: Thames and Hudson 1978, 58.

6. D'Alviella, Count Goblet. *The Migration of Symbols*. New York: University Books 1956, 98.

7. Doresse, Jean. *The Secret Books of the Egyptian Gnostics*. New York: MJF Books 1986, 207.

Death, who in the Scottish islands manifested herself not as a vulture...but as other large birds with awe-inspiring wingspreads..."[8]

Among the Siberian Yakut the eagle is considered to be the creator of the "first shaman" and is also known as the Supreme Being. The Supreme Being is normally depicted as a two-headed eagle. An important relationship between the eagle and the sacred tree, usually a birch, also exists. It is this sacred tree which houses the souls of future shamans.[9] Among the Yakut people the eagle is itself a symbol of the vocation of shamanism.

Double-headed eagle images were important in other areas of the world as well. The Hapsburg German Empire's emblem was that of the double-headed eagle as was that of the ancient Hittite empire.

Eagles were also companions and assistants to gods. Hino, the thunder god of the Iroquois, had two eagle helpers. One of the eagles, called Oshada-gea, carried a lake of dew on its back so that it could sprinkle the world and save it from the attacks of Fire Spirits.[10]

While most cultures view the eagle as noble and sacred, if not outright divine, a few do look upon this bird of prey with disdain. Welsh folklore says, "if eagles of Snowden hovered over the plains their visit would be followed by disease and death."[11]

To the Plains Indians eagles "are seen as important messengers between man and the Sacred Mystery, partly because they can fly into the pure, rarefied air where the sacred can communicate with them away from the contaminating influences of earth."[12]

The raven has a long tradition in religious lore as well. Because the raven is more a carrion bird than a bird of prey, it is viewed as a deity of war and death rather than of life and lofty spiritual ideals. "There is also," writes Davidson, "the image of birds receiving and rejoicing over sacrificial victims, particularly the raven."[13] The raven is closely associated with Irish battle-goddesses and the Norse valkyries. However, as noted, because it is a "talking bird" it has vast powers of prophecy and wisdom.

"Both Lug and Odin," wrote Davidson "were associated with the crow and the raven, the birds of the battlefield. Odin's two ravens brought him tidings every day, presumably from the battles of the world."[14] The raven is also closely associated with the Celtic deities Macha (which means "Ra-

---

8. Gimbutas, Marija. *The Language of the Goddess.* San Francisco: HarperSanFrancisco 1991, 189.

9. Eliade, Mircea. *Shamanism: Archaic Techniques of Ecstasy.* Princeton University Press 1964, 70.

10. Andrews, Tamra. *A Dictionary of Nature Myths.* Oxford: Oxford University Press 1998, 92.

11. Radford, Edwin and Mona A. *Encyclopaedia of Superstitions.* New York: Philosophical Library 1949, 108.

12. St. Pierre, Mark and Tilda Long Soldier. *Walking in the Sacred Manner.* New York: Touchstone Books 1995, 111.

13. Davidson, H.R. Ellis. *Myths and Symbols in Pagan Europe: Early Scandinavian and Celtic Religions.* Syracuse: Syracuse University Press 1988, 98.

14. Ibid., 90-91.

ven"), Morrigan and Babd — all which take the raven form. Green notes that, "In the Mabinogion, ravens are beneficent otherworld creatures...but their magico-divine function in Irish legend is usually concerned with war and destruction."[15] Caches of raven figures have been found throughout Britain and they may represent an underworld aspect of the Celtic sky-god (Jupiter).

Over time, the raven had become almost synonymous with death and various superstitious beliefs became associated with it. "The raven, for instance" wrote Lady Wilde, "has a world-wide reputation as the harbinger of evil and ill-luck."[16] In some cultures, the raven was not necessarily the symbol of death but it was the symbol of the human soul. According to the Radford's "the Bororos of Brazil believe that the human soul has the shape of a bird, and passes out of the body in that form — and they favour ravens."[17] To the ancient Egyptians every human soul, called the *ba*, was in the form of a human-headed bird, which would fly from the body after death and travel to the afterlife. In Indian religion the raven was also the form that fleeing souls would take after the body had died. Even King Arthur was believed to have transformed into a raven after his death and it was common practice to tip one's hat to a raven out of respect to the great king. In Cornwall, it was prohibited to kill any raven because, according to the superstition, "to shoot a raven is to shoot King Arthur."

In Siberian culture the raven guides the souls of the dead to the underworld.

Even though the raven is closely linked to death and war, and thus was incorporated in battle ritual, it was also part of fertility rites and thereby with life.

Many of the goddesses that shape-shifted to the form of a raven show their dual natures through the other animal forms that they take as well. The Morrigan, the goddess of war and death, commonly changed from her raven aspect to that of a water serpent. The Celtic Raven-goddess was also seen as a maternal figure, with nurture of both humans and the animal kingdom being her purpose.

The raven, however, has more to offer. In the Pacific Northwest Native Americans regarded the raven as a trickster and as the bringer of light and fire. The Inuit said the raven originated in the primeval darkness of creation but stayed to teach humans the knowledge they would need to succeed in the world. Ravens are also associated with fairies .and are believed to act as guardians of the Fairy treasures housed in the underworld.

It is odd to think that such a creature became the symbol of the Christian Church for those who refused a Christian burial, and as "a feeder on corruption."[18]

15. Green, Miranda. *The Gods of the Celts.* Gloucester: Alan Sutton 1986, 187-188.
16. Wilde, Lady. *Irish Cures, Mystic Charms & Superstitions.* New York: Sterling Publishing Co., Inc 1991, 92.
17. Radford, op. cit. 199.
18. Saunders, Nicholas J. *Animal Spirits.* London: Duncan Baird Publishers 1997, 117.

# CHAPTER 16. THE OWL

Like the eagle and the raven, the Owl has long been held sacred by many cultures around the world. Like the eagle and the raven it has a dual meaning. It is at once a symbol of wisdom and a symbol of darkness and death. The owl represents wisdom because of its association with the goddess and the belief that the owl was the embodiment of the goddess's knowledge. It was known as the "corpse bird" among the Celts; to the Hindu it is Yama, the god of death; it also represents death to the Japanese, Chinese, Mexicans and ancient Egyptians. To the Christian the owl was Satan and represented all of the powers of darkness. The owl is more, though. It is sacred to Minerva/Athena and the Welsh goddess Blodeuwedd as well as Lilith and Anath, the "Lady of Birth and Death." The owl, Athena's bird, was the messenger of death.

The owl is also associated with the Lord of Death and the King of the Underworld Gwyn ap Nudd who resides under the Glastonbury Tor, and the far more ancient Goddess of Death. According to Lewis Spence, "The owl, too, was employed as a symbol of wisdom, and sometimes, as by the Algonquins, was represented as the attendant of the Lord of Death.[1] Undoubtedly, it is the very nature of the owl that gives it such bad press. They are, as the Radford's say, "a tenant of the night," solitary, who both screeches and gives a melancholy hoot. "The Romans held the owl in abhorrence," wrote the Radfords, "and when it was seen and caught in the city in the daylight hours, it was burnt and its ashes publicly scattered in the Tiber."[2]

---

1. Spence, Lewis. *North American Indians Myths & Legends.* London: Senate 1994, 111. A reprint of the 1914 edition of *North American Indians* published by George G. Harrap & Company Ltd.
2. Radford, Edwin and Mona A. *Encyclopaedia of Superstitions.* New York: Philosophical Library 1949, 185.

The owl has little competition as the bearer of bad news. "In the *Book of Days*," writes the Radfords, "it is recorded that two owls 'of enormous size' warn the family of Arundel of death among them. Whenever they were seen perched on the battlements of the family mansion, it was held that a member of the family was about to die."[3] Similar beliefs were held among Native American groups. According to Spier the Yuman tribes believed that "Death or an epidemic was presaged by a horned owl seen flittering about the houses: when his mouth opened a light was seen in it."[4] This same belief was still strong among California Indians in the 1960s. Anthropologist Ruth Almstedt researched the Diegueño Indians in San Diego County (California) in 1967 and noted, "Two reports show that the belief is still strong. One person told me that in the 1950s her sister was sick at Julian. She had been thinking about this sister and wanted to visit her. One night an owl flew over her home, hooted, then flew off in the direction of Julian. The next morning she went there. Her sister died during the night. Another woman said that just prior to my visit her husband heard an owl hooting and said that someone must be dying. Sure enough, someone did die that week."[5]

The owl's ability to foretell death makes it a feared creature but it is also believed to be an "auspicious spirit helper" as it can tell not only who will die but also who will get well.

The owl was identified with the night and the underworld in Mesoamerican traditions as well. The image of the Green Owl was used in Teotihuacan on mirrors. The mirrors were symbolic of supernatural caves or passageways thus linking the owl to passageways to the underworld. "Like other birds," wrote Miller and Taube, "owls were considered as omens or messengers between humans and the divine."[6] To the Maya the owl had a dual nature. It was at once both representative of death and fertility, the owl was responsible for rain and maize as well as death. To the Quiché Maya the owl was the messenger of the gods of death.

Owls have often been associated with witches. In fact, the Romans called the owl *strix*, which means "witch." One of the terms given to the owl during the Middle Ages was "night hag," referring to the belief that the owl was a witch in the form of a bird. This has carried over to contemporary times with the image of the owl prominently used in Halloween decorations. Frazer defines the relationship of the witch and her familiar, the owl. "In every case," he writes, "the...bird with which the witch or wizard has contracted this mystic alliance is an individual, never a species; and when the individual ani-

3. Ibid.

4. Spier, Leslie. *Yuman Tribes of the Gila River*. New York: Dover Publications, Inc. 1978, 294.

5. Almstedt, Ruth Farrell. *Diegueño Curing Practices*. San Diego Museum Papers Number 10. San Diego: Museum of Man 1977, 18.

6. Miller, Mary and Karl Taube. *An Illustrated Dictionary of The Gods and Symbols of Ancient Mexico and the Maya*. London: Thames and Hudson 1993, 128.

mal dies the alliance is naturally at an end, since the death of the animal is supposed to entail the death of the man."[7]

In Hawaiian lore, the owl-god Pueo had the power to restore life to a recently murdered and buried girl called the Rainbow Maiden. In fact, the owl-god was able to restore life to the Maiden several times for every time he brought her back to life the murderer reburied the girl, until at last he determined that the spirit would no longer be able to rejoin its body.[8] It was Pueo-nui-akea who restored the life to many souls wandering on the plains of Maui.

As the owl was linked to death and the underworld in Europe, Meso-america, Asia, and Native American cultures so too was it intimately associated with death in Hawaiian and Polynesian society. In Old Hawaii, the bodies of the recently deceased were offered to Ku-kaua-kahi, an owl god, so that they could also become owls and thus become protectors of the family. "Owls (pueo) are among the oldest of these family protectors," wrote folklorist Martha Beckwith.[9]

Far from being an omen of doom, however, the owl in Hawaiian legend was a special protector that would warn against danger, especially in war. The owl was worshipped both as a class of spirits and gods and as individual protectors. One owl, the owl king of Manoa, was said to have driven the Menehune from the area.[10] The Hawaiian god Kane, according to lore, would take the form of an owl to fight the enemies of his worshippers. With the thrusts of his talons and beating of his wings he was able to turn aside their weapons.

The Sumerian goddess Inanna also took the form of an owl. She was known as the "Divine Lady Owl" to her worshippers, and goddess of the Great Above and the Great Below. According to Baring and Cashford, "Throughout Neolithic civilization the owl is an image of the goddess of the world beyond death."[11] Perhaps the most infamous of owl goddesses is Lilith (thought by some to have originated in Inanna). Called the "screech owl" in the Old Testament, Lilith, after proclaiming her equality to Adam who refuses to acknowledge it, proclaims the "magic name of god" and flies into the wilderness where she raises demons and searches for children to slay to pay for their fathers sins. Here again the owl is associated with death.

However, this aspect of the owl must be understood in its entirety. While the owl represents death and the underworld, it is this aspect that emphasizes regeneration and life renewed.

7. Frazer, Sir James. *The Golden Bough: A study in magic and religion.* Hertfordshire: Wordsworth Editions Ltd. 1993, 684.

8. Westervelt, William D. *Hawaiian Legends of Ghosts and Ghost Gods.* Honolulu: Mutual Publishing 1998, 85. A reprint of an edition originally published in 1916.

9. Beckwith, Martha. *Hawaiian Mythology.* Honolulu: University of Hawaii Press 1970, 124.

10. Ibid.

11. Baring, Anne and Jules Cashford. *The Myth of the Goddess: Evolution of an Image.* London: Arkana/Penguin Books 1991, 217-218.

# CHAPTER 17. THE DOG

"Man's best friend." Three simple words to describe the most familiar of humankind's animal companions. The domesticated dog is found in every nook and cranny on the earth, from Polynesia to New Guinea to deepest Africa and Australia to the North Pole. Perhaps it is this deep-felt relationship with the dog that is responsible for another aspect of the canine-human tie. The dog is one of the oldest and most powerful of the shaman's spirit helpers as well as one of the most feared supernatural entities in the world.

Dogs apparently were the most favored of sacrificial animals; recall that the hound is associated with the Wild Huntsman and the journey to the Underworld. As J.C. Cooper notes, "having been a companion in life it continues as such after death and intercedes and interprets between the dead and the gods of the underworld."[1] In fact during the 1800s in India and the Middle East it was customary to bring a dog to the bedside of an individual in the process of dying, "in order that the soul may be sure of a prompt escort"[2] to the land of the dead. In addition, dogs were sacred to the goddess Hecate, herself a ruler of the Underworld, and were often sacrificed to her. In India, the god of the Dead, Yama, had two dogs, each with four eyes.[3] Dogs were often depicted as the guardians of the Underworld because, says White, "the dog's place lies between one world and another."[4]

---

1. Cooper, J.C. *An Illustrated Encyclopaedia on Traditional Symbols.* London: Thames and Hudson Ltd. 1978, 52.
2. Fiske, John. *Myths and Myth-Makers: Old Tales and Superstitions Interpreted by Comparative Mythology.* Boston: Houghton, Mifflin and Company 1881, 35.
3. Mackenzie, Donald A. *India Myths & Legends.* London: Studio Editions 1993, 40.
4. White, David Gordon. *Myths of the Dog-Man.* Chicago: The University of Chicago Press 1991, 14.

To the Celts, the dog was especially esteemed and was used many times in mythology and was incorporated into the names of Celtic gods. The 200-foot-deep well at Muntham Court in Sussex had numerous dog skeletons as well as a "votive" leg, made from clay, indicating that the well was valued for its healing properties. In other wells, such as Coventina's, dog figurines were given to the well instead of actual animals. Dogs in early Celtic society were symbolic of both healing and death. These two symbolic aspects are reflective moreover, of the dogs' representation of rebirth and their sacrifice to wells, pits and ritual shafts is fitting.

Dogs were a food source in Hawaii in addition to providing raw materials for fishhooks, jewelry and utensils. Dogs, like pigs, were both regarded as pets and as food. Titcomb notes that dogs were also suitable offerings for female deities. "Dogs were especially appropriate as offerings to the *mo'o* gods," she writes, "spirits that lived in the water."[5]

Hutton and Merrifield note that dogs were frequently sacrificed to wells at the time of the termination of the well's use — especially during the Roman occupation of Britain. A pair of dogs was sacrificed at Farnworth in Gloucestershire during the 4th century CE, two in Southwark dated to the 3rd century and eight pairs in a well in Surrey (along with red-deer antler, two complete dishes and a broken flagon).[6] A recent excavation at an ancient well at Shiptonthorpe in Yorkshire uncovered a number of dog skulls as well as the remains of bundles of mistletoe. Because mistletoe was so important in Druidic rites, this well may have been an important ritual site.

Other dog sacrifices have been found in Holland, Germany and among Scandinavian Viking-era ship burials as well as in smaller individual graves, and in America. Davidson notes, "the most elaborate [dog sacrifice] example being from Mannhagen in Holland, where the skulls of twelve dogs were found with the skull of a horse and that of a man."[7] Contemporary dog sacrifice continues in Africa. Mbiti tells us, "Every fortnight Yoruba blacksmiths sacrifice dogs to *Ogun* the divinity of iron and war."[8] The Iroquois sacrificed white dogs, believing that the dead dogs spirit could intercede on their behalf with the Iroquois gods.

Dogs were valued as healing agents also and it is interesting that the use of dog skulls to rub ointment on the swollen legs of horses and cattle continued into 17th-century France. This method of healing was thought to be even more effective if the local priest had blessed the skull beforehand.[9]

5. Titcomb, Margaret. *Dog and Man in the Ancient Pacific.* Honolulu: Bernice P. Bishop Museum Special Publication 59 1969, 18.
6. Hutton, Ronald. *The Pagan Religions of the Ancient British Isles: Their Nature and Legacy.* Oxford: Blackwell Publishers Ltd., 1991, 231 and Merrifield, Ralph. *The Archaeology of Ritual and Magic.* New York: New Amsterdam Books 1987, 47.
7. Davidson, H. R. Ellis. *Myths and Symbols in Pagan Europe: Early Scandinavian and Celtic Religions.* Syracuse: Syracuse University Press 1988, 57.
8. Mbiti, John S. *African Religions and Philosophy.* Garden City: Anchor Books 1969, 78.
9. Briggs, Robin. *Witches & Neighbors: The Social and Cultural Context of European Witchcraft.* New York: Viking Press 1996, 121.

Images of dogs have been painted on ancient vases found in eastern Europe guarding the Tree of Life as well as on others appearing alongside images of caterpillars signifying both death and rebirth. As previously indicated dogs also guard the land of the dead and, as the Egyptian god, Anubis acts as the guide of souls to the Underworld. This concept is also present in the folklore of the Yupa Indians who inhabit areas between Columbia and Venezuela. According to anthropologist Johannes Wilbert, "the dog plays a vital part in guiding the dead to the next world, and to mistreat a dog would condemn its owner to wander for eternity somewhere between earth and 'heaven'." [10]

*Anubis, the dog deity of Egypt*

An ancient tale from New Ireland in the New Guinea chain says that dogs were originally a race of dwarfs "who were said to be very strong and active," [11] and whom the residents greatly feared. These dwarfs walked erect, ran very fast, and killed men that they overtook. Some of the Islanders cooked breadfruit seeds and laid them across the pathways that the dwarfs usually used, causing them to burn their feet and fall to their hands. According to legend, they were forever unable to walk erect again.

### DOG SYMBOLISM

The dog has been regarded as the guardian and keeper of the passageway between our physical world and that of the Underworld. The dog, often seen as a guardian of Underworld treasures, in reality is guardian of the secret knowledge of death and resurrection. As Anubis the dog is the attendant of the dead and the soul guide to the land of spirit. The dog is associated with the messenger gods as well as those gods of destruction. The dog, however, has another aspect as well. Dogs are often placed in the company of mother goddesses and healers. Dogs, like cats, were regarded as witches' familiars and, as Cooper tells us, "represent witches as rain-makers, hence 'raining cats and dogs.'" [12]

Various age-old tales exist concerning dogs and their supernatural characteristics. A Gypsy belief said that if a dog digs a big hole in your garden, there will be a death in the family. The Radfords offer some anecdotal evidence in support of this belief in the way of some mail that they received: "About 40 years ago," he wrote," I was told by a gipsy that when a dog digs a big hole in your garden, there will be a death in the family. Last week [Feb-

10. Wilbert, Johannes. *Yupa Folktales.* Latin American Studies, Volume 24. Los Angeles: University of California Los Angeles 1974, 42.
11. Titcomb, op. cit. 59.
12. Cooper op. cit.

ruary 1945] a dog came in my garden and dug a big hole. I filled it in, but he came again and dug it out. Next day, my brother-in-law's father died. I have not seen the dog since."[13]

The indigenous people of Japan, the Ainu, felt dogs had the ability to detect ghosts. Very many people around the world believe the same thing. Dogs especially among animals are seen as having the power to "observe" spirit manifestations.

Dogs have also been linked to healing as well as death. Illnesses were "transferred" to dogs by placing a hair from the ill person between two slices of bread and butter and feeding it to a dog. The dog would catch the cough, measles or whopping cough and the person would recover soon after.

In Holland, the role of dogs in healing has been well documented. In two areas of Holland along the Rhine River, ancient altars to the mother goddess Nehalennia have been found. One site, uncovered in 1647 on the Isle of Walcheren and the other discovered in 1970 on the East Scheldt Estuary, contain 120 altars, some at depths of over 80 feet. Evidently, these altars are the remains of a temple dating back to 200 CE, which sank into the sea. Nehalennia was a domestic goddess that had an impressive following. In fact, both the Romans and Gauls adopted her into their pantheon. Nehalennia invariably appears accompanied with dogs. While mother goddesses do appear with dogs, Nehalennia is pictured with them so often that she is compared to the goddess Epona who is considered a horse-goddess because she is always shown with them. "The symbolism of the dog," according to Miranda Green, "is important here: if we use the mythology of the Graeco-Roman world, the beast could represent either healing or death, both of which are functions of the mothers."[14] Nehalennia is considered a goddess of the sea and protector of fishermen and seamen. Altars that were dedicated at her temple were put there by these sea-going men — given in thanks for her protection. Other gods and goddess often shown with dogs are Diana, Aesculapius (god of healing), Cerberus, Sucellus and Nodens. Nodens actually appears as a dog as his zoomorphic attribute.

Numerous small mother goddess figurines have been found in England, Gaul and the Rhineland, which represent fertility and prosperity. According to Davidson, the goddesses carry fruit, baskets, bunches of grapes, bread and/or eggs. They also have a babe at their breasts or a small dog as a companion. While normally found in threes near rivers, springs or temples, four were found together in London in 1977.[15]

The association with dogs and healing is an ancient one. In Mesopotamia, the sitting dog was used as a divine symbol from the Old Babylonian period through the Neo-Babylonian age (1950 BCE through 539 BCE). Various inscriptions have been found over the years that identify the sitting dog figure

---

13. Radford, Edwin and Mona A. *Encyclopaedia of Superstitions.* New York: The Philosophical Library 1949, 103.
14. Green, Miranda. *The Gods of the Celts.* Gloucester: Alan Sutton 1986, 88.
15. Davidson, op. cit., 109.

"as the symbol of Gula, goddess of healing"[16] and patron of doctors. Several dog figurines have been discovered inside a temple dedicated to Gula in Babylon and another was dedicated to the Sumerian equivalent of Gula, called Ninisina (known then as "the great doctor of the black-headed," meaning "of the human beings"). Images of the dog were also commonly utilized as protective amulets in Assyria and Babylon. "Groups of five clay figurines of dogs painted different colours were prescribed as foundation deposits for either side of a gateway," report Black and Green. "Bronze dog figurines are in the same period usually found in groups of seven....Whether they were magically protective or dedicatory or served some other purpose is unclear."[17]

Dogs are also considered one of the were-animal species. The Yuman Indians regarded dogs as "people" and would not eat dogs for that reason. In Scotland, it was believed that children were occasionally transformed into white dogs by evil magicians and could only be restored to their human form by striking them with a magic wand or dressing them in shirts made of "bog-cotton."[18]

## BLACK DOGS

Perhaps one of the most intriguing legends associated with dogs is that of the Black Dog. An almost universal tale, the Black Dog is associated with sorcery, death and the damned. This bit of lore knows no boundaries — being common in Britain and the United States both among indigenous and the dominant Euro-American cultures. Most of the tales speak of a rather nondescript, sometimes large black dog that haunts certain areas — never leaving prints even in the snow. One such story is that of the Black Dog of West Peak, or Black Pond in the hills of central Connecticut. Legend has it that the dog, appearing as a "short-haired, sad-eyed...beast of vague spaniel ancestry"[19] with friendly ways spells doom for any person who sees it three times. The legends say, "if a man shall meet the Black Dog once, it shall be for joy; and if twice, it shall be for sorrow; and the third time, he shall die."[20] Accounts of savage and ghostly Black Dogs have been recorded in England as far back as 1577, often resulting in human fatalities.

Legends of mysterious black dogs also populate the lore of Native Americans. These dogs are some of the many localized supernatural beings, which are always present but normally only seen when tragedy or disaster is imminent. One such account tells of two elderly women who went to a water hole to gather juniper berries. "One of the women saw a big, black dog

16. Black, Jeremy and Anthony Green. *Gods, Demons and Symbols of Ancient Mesopotamia.* Austin: University of Texas Press 1992, 70.

17. Ibid.

18. MacKenzie, Donald A. *Ancient Man in Britain.* London: Senate 1996, 190. A reprint of the 1922 edition published by Blackie & Son Ltd, London.

19. Philips, David E. *Legendary Connecticut: Traditional Tales from the Nutmeg State.* Willimantic: Curbstone Press 1992, 237.

20. Ibid., 238.

and thought it a sheepherder's dog. 'It went down the rock into the water below and wasn't seen again'."[21] Like the Black Dog of West Peak, an old Kawaiisu story relates how "old timers saw lots of dog there, but there were no tracks."[22]

Black Dogs have the reputation of being a number of creatures, from simply "dogs" to the ghosts of humans, demons and harbingers of doom. A fifteenth-century German manuscript says "the Devil will come in the form of a black dog and will answer all questions."[23]

In addition, while not all of the legends place these apparitions near water, a great many of them are tied to wells, ponds and lakes and the bridges and entryways to these bodies of water. Folklorist Katherine Briggs, referencing Theo Brown's article in the September 1958 issue of *Folk-Lore*, divides reports of Black Dogs into three categories:

1. A shape-shifting demon, called the Barguest,
2. A black dog about calf-size, normally described as shaggy and intensely black; and
3. Black dogs which appear at certain times of the year in a calendar-cycle. [24]

Some stories of Black Dogs regard them as guardian dogs, which reportedly have protected lonely travelers. Researcher Katy Jordan describes these dogs as "usually associated with a particular stretch of road, or a stream, or places of transition like gateways or parish boundaries. They are essentially non-aggressive, kindly and protective beasts, whose role seems to be either to patrol or guard the boundary or road that is their 'beat', or to protect and guide travellers home."[25]

A well located near an untouched tomb on Cyprus in the cemetery of the ancient Greek harbor city of Bamboula, has recently yielded a discovery of three-dozen dog skeletons.[26] A pottery shard was also found in the same well with a relief depicting two men and two bulls. The reason for the presence of the dogs is unknown, however, the similarities between this Greek well and those found in Britain is striking. If there is a common reason for the dog burials or sacrifices in these wells, it would indicate a common tradition or ritual belief dating from, at least, the 13th century BCE through the 3rd century CE.

21. Zigmond, Maurice L. "The Supernatural World of the Kawaiisu" in Thomas C. Blackburn (ed.) *Flowers of the Wind: Papers on Ritual, Myth, And Symbolism in California and the Southwest.* Socorro: Ballena Press 1977.

22. Ibid.

23. Kieckhefer, Richard. *Magic in the Middle Ages.* Cambridge: Cambridge University Press 1989, 162.

24. Briggs, Katherine. *British Folktales.* New York: Pantheon Books 1977,115.

25. Jordan, Katy. *The Haunted Landscape: Folklore, ghosts & legends of Wiltshire.* Wiltshire: Ex Libris Press 2000, 174.

26. Anon. "Intact Tomb from Bronze Age Cyprus" in *Archaeology Odyssey*, May/June 2003, Vol 6 No. 3, 21.

It is believed that one reason for sacrificing dogs was to provide eternal "guardians of place".[27] The fact that many are seen near gateways and bridges would indicate that these animals are, as spirit helpers, fulfilling that intent. These explanations do not address those mysterious Black Dogs seen in the United States; however, guardian dogs are common in shamanic lore all over the world as guardians and guides to the Otherworld.

Bob Trubshaw wrote, "few myths have such world-wide parallels. We are left with the distinct impression that dogs have been protecting the ways to the Otherworld back into the origins of human beliefs."[28]

Other animals are also associated with wells, water sources, and the connection between the world of the living and the Otherworld where the dead and other creatures of mystery reside. White cattle, stags and hounds are some of those denizens of the Underworld. Like the Black Dogs the Kawaiisu also have stories about white dogs, which frequent sacred waters. Zigmond wrote about one such occurrence: "Near Paiute Ranch there is a spring where the water used to come out of the ground like a fountain. There were lots of reeds growing there and so it was called 'by the reed-water'. A white dog lived there. Old timers saw him lying off to one side. 'Maybe he lived in the water.'" [29]

Dogs played an important role in Meso-American lore as guides for the souls of the dead to the Underworld. Alexander wrote, in his "Noble Savage" account of the journey of the soul to its final resting place, "...the perils of the Underworld Way were to be passed, and the soul to arrive before Mictlantecutli, whence after four years he should fare onward until, by the aid of his dog, sacrificed at his grave, he should pass over the Ninefold Stream, and thence, hound with master, enter into the eternal house of the dead..."[30]

W.Y. Evans-Wentz interviewed an Irish man from Galway during the early 1900s who spoke of a "fairy dog":

> Steven pointed to a rocky knoll in a field not far from his home, and said: "I saw a dog with a white ring around his neck by that hill there, and the oldest men round Galway have seen him too, for he has been here for one hundred years or more. He is a dog of the *good people*, and only appears at certain times of the night."[31]

On the Isle of Man, the Fairy Dog was called the Moddey Doo (also known as the "Mauthe Doog") — Manx for "Black Dog." However, it has also been described as "white as driven snow."[32]

---

27. Another purpose recorded in Japan was to sacrifice a black dog to obtain rain.
28. Trubshaw, Bob. "Black Dogs: Guardians of the corpse ways" in *At The Edge*, August 2001 http://www.indigogroup.co.uk/edge/bdogs.htm.
29. Zigmond, op. cit. 1977.
30. Alexander, Hartley Burr. *The World's Rim: Great Mysteries of the North American Indians.* New York: Dover Publications Inc. 1999, 201-202.
31. Evans-Wentz, W.Y. *The Fairy-Faith in Celtic Countries.* Mineola: Dover Publications Inc. 2002, 40.
32. Ibid., 120.

Tales of fairy dogs seem to contradict other stories of dogs being the enemy of fairies, mermaids and demons, "especially cave-haunting demons."[33] "In the folk-stories of Scotland," wrote MacKenzie, "dogs help human beings to attack and overcome supernatural beings."[34]

However, the Fairy did in fact have their pet dogs, too. Called *cu sith*, which means "fairy dog," they acted as guides to the fairy land and to the Underworld. They could be differentiated from "normal" dogs by their color, normally green, or white with red ears. Fairy dogs were commonly believed to be a dark green in color with the ears being a darker green and the legs running a lighter green color. Its long tail, according to Campbell, was "rolled up in a coil on its back, but others have the tail flat and plaited like the straw rug of a pack-saddle."[35] The famous fairy dog of Fin mac Coul, however, had yellow feet, black sides, white belly, green back and two pointed blood-red ears. In Wales, pure white dogs are thought to be fairy dogs.

According to Anna Franklin, "The fairy dog makes its lair in the clefts of rocks and travels in a straight line. It barks only three times and by the time the third bark is heard the victim is overtaken, unless he has reached a place of safety."[36]

## Ghost Dogs

Black dogs are, of course, ghost dogs. However, there are very many stories concerning even more mysterious and ghostly apparitions of canines. One such encounter occurred in Pemiscot County, Missouri — deep in the Ozarks. According to folklorist Vance Randolph, "Some night hunters... swore they saw an enormous black dog, fully eight feet long, without any head. They came close to the creature, and one man threw his ax at it, but the ax passed right through the body of the booger dog and stuck fast in a tree."[37] Another headless dog was frequently seen near Braggadocio, Missouri running through the town on moonlit nights. "It behaves just like any other dog, but it is clearly headless," wrote Randolph.[38]

"Black Dogs," wrote Jennifer Westwood in her book *Albion*, "were in some places thought to be the ghosts of the unquiet dead. The wicked Lady Howard in Devon was so transformed..."[39]

And of course, we cannot fail to mention the hounds of the Wild Huntsman. Various locations around England, and Europe in general, claim the

33. MacKenzie, op. cit., 65.

34. Ibid., 66.

35. Campbell, John Gregorson. *The Gaelic Otherworld*, edited by Ronald Black. Edinburgh: Birlinn Ltd., 200516.

36. Franklin, Anna. *The Illustrated Encyclopaedia of Fairies.* London: Paper Tiger 2004, 68.

37. Randolph, Vance.*Ozark Magic and Folklore.* New York: Dover Publications, Inc. 1964, 224. A reprint of *Ozark Superstitions* published by Columbia University Press 1947.

38. Ibid., 225.

39. Westwood, Jennifer. *Albion: A Guide to Legendary Britain.* London: Paladin/Grafton Books 1985, 176.

Huntsman. Referred to in some locals as the "Wish Hounds" ("Wish" being a local word for the Devil)[40] these ferocious dogs with glowing red eyes accompany the Lord of Death on his swift horse — hunting for the souls of men. "Throughout all Aryan mythology," noted John Fiske, "the souls of the dead are supposed to ride on the night-wind, with their howling dogs, gathering into their throng the souls of those just dying as they pass by their houses."[41] Dogs that would sit under the window of seriously ill persons were thought to portend the coming death and it was customary in 19th-century Europe to open the windows in homes after the death of a person "in order that the soul may not be hindered in joining the mystic cavalcade."[42]

## Dog-Men

Various legends about dog-men have been related generation after generation in various locations around the world. In pre-revolutionary China there were of four clans of people called the Jung who worshipped the dog because, to them, the dog was their ancestor. According to legend, a dog requested the hand of a Chinese princess but was refused by her father unless the dog was able to change into the form of a man. This he almost did; his body was that of a man but his head remained that of a dog. Until the early 1920s the Jung wore a large headpiece that entirely covered the head, the explanation being that they still had dog features due to their dog ancestor.[43]

Similar tales of the mating between human females and male wolves or dogs, resulting in a race of dog-men, are frequently found in Native American mythology. A race of dog-men also appears in Hawaiian mythology. "Among the peoples said to have appeared during the fifth period of the Kumulipo,"[44] wrote Martha Beckwith, "are the dog people...They lived in the sand hills [on Maui and Kauai] and they had mystical power of the demigods...in the form of big war dogs. These dog people still appear on Maui in the procession of spirits known as 'Marchers of the night.' They look like other human beings but have tails like a dog."[45] These "dog people" were a well known class of Hawaiians, said to have hairless bodies and to be well versed in wrestling and "bone breaking." Some were considered professional robbers and others as cannibals. Other dog-men are described as dogs with human bodies and having supernatural power who used to terrorize the countryside.

Various myths and legends of Dog-Men exist in Hawaiian tradition. "The Great Dog Ku" is one of these. Ku, the Dog Man, was a spirit being that one

---

40. Other names for these Black Dogs are Gabriel Hounds, Dando or Dandy Dogs, and in Wales the Cwm Annwn, the Hounds of Hell.

41. Fiske, op. cit. 76.

42. Ibid.

43. Werner, E.T.C. *Myths and Legends of China.* New York: Dover Publications, Inc. 1994, 419-423.

44. The "Kumulipo" is a chant of 2,077 lines, which tells of the creation of the world and the genealogy of a young Chief by the name of Keawe who lived in the 1700s.

45. Beckwith, Martha. *Hawaiian Mythology.* Honolulu: University of Hawaii Press 1970, 343.

day "decided to come down from the clouds and visit mankind."[46] Ku was able to change at will from his dog form to that of a man. Unfortunately, Ku desired the daughter of the High Chief, who refused Ku's advances. A savage war ensued with Ku striking as lightning and he killed and devoured many of the Hawaiian people. Eventually many men fought Ku and killed him with spears and clubs. They cut Ku's body into two pieces, which were thrown far apart and turned to stone by the priests. These stones were reportedly venerated for many years by the Hawaiian people.

In many legends, it is this race of human-like dogs and wolves that are the creators of humankind. Some dog-men, such as the Egyptian jackal-headed Anubis became gods in their own right. Or, in the Christian sense, they became saints.

There are two types of dog-men. One, cynanthropy, are the Dog-men that, according to David Gordon White, are "a hybrid creature who, while more human than the domesticated dog, is nonhuman in the sense that he belongs to an 'other' or foreign race, yet human in his social behavior."[47] The second form is the Cynocephalic — human in form except it has a dog, wolf or jackal head, such as Anubis.

Monstrous races of beings were commonly believed in during the early years of the Christian church. Irish legend, according to MacCulloch, "speaks of men with cat, dog, or goat heads."[48] As with any other pagan symbol, or place or deity they became important to the Christian theology as well. St. Augustine in his writings "saved" these creatures and, as White states, they "eventually became Christendom's favorite foils in the lives of the missionary saints who pacified, converted, domesticated, and placed them in the service of the Catholic cause."[49]

One of these dog-headed beings, Christopher, became a Catholic saint, at least in Gnostic and Coptic texts. According to White, "Christopher's Christian hagiography may be summarized as follows: He is a giant belonging to a cynocephalic race, in the land of the Channeans (the 'Canines' of the New Testament), who eat human flesh and whose only form of communication is barking (*latrare*). His original name, Réprebos, 'the Condemned,' corresponds to his nature: he is black, pagan, ferocious, and dreadful."[50]

According to the Coptic text, he is persuaded by Christ to fight against the pagan armies until St. Babylus at Antioch baptized him. At this time, his skin becomes "white as milk" and he loses his canine characteristics. Christopher was depicted with a dog's head until the beginning of the 19th century on Eastern churches, bridges, city gates, etc. Most of these images were

46. Westervelt, William D. *Myths and Legends of Hawaii.* Honolulu: Mutual Publishing 1987, 202

47. White, David Gordon. *Myths of the Dog-Man.* Chicago: University of Chicago Press 1991, 16.

48. MacCulloch, J.A. *The Religion of the Ancient Celts.* Mineola: Dover Publications, Inc. 2003, 217.

49. Ibid., 19.

50. Ibid., 34.

destroyed by the iconoclasts at that time and are rare to be found except on a few illuminated manuscript pages.

The statues and carvings of Anubis in Egypt, as well as carvings dating back to 6600 BCE in the Sahara desert of a dog-headed man, are evidence of an ancient belief in dog-headed humanoids. According to French art-historian Jean-Pierre Mohen more than 140 dog-headed figures found so far "express the imaginary and symbolic relationships between man and animal rather than any hunting techniques."[51] The carvings show creatures with "superhuman" strength and, writes Mohen, "they exist to carry out sacred tasks."[52] Do these images represent the nature of the dog as the guardian of the secrets of death and rebirth? Alternatively, do they represent creatures divine in their own right?

51. Mohen, Jean-Pierre. *Prehistoric Art: The Mythical Birth of Humanity.* Paris: Pierre Terrail/Telleri 2002, 185.
52. Ibid., 184.

# CHAPTER 18. THE CAT

The cat has long been one of humankind's favored animals. It has been worshipped as a god by the Egyptians and feared as a demon by Christians terrified of witchcraft. It is both a beloved family pet and a fierce feral predator. It is a loving companion but never tamed. Like most symbols universally important in societies around the world, the cat has a dual nature, with both good and evil aspects.

*Bast, the Egyptian Cat-Goddess*

Cats represent clairvoyance, watchfulness, mystery, female malice and sensual beauty. In India, it was believed that cats could take over the bodies of women at will.[1] On the other hand, the Indian goddess of maternity and protectress of children, Sasti, is a feline goddess who rides on a cat.[2]

Chinese and Japanese folklore view the cat as symbolic of transformation. Scandinavian mythology says that the goddess Freyja's chariot is drawn by cats. In Egyptian mythology the goddess Bast, the moon goddess, is cat-headed and the cat also symbolized the protective aspects of the mother goddess, Isis.

---

1. Tresidder, Jack. *Symbols and Their Meanings.* London: Duncan Baird Publishers 2000, 59.
2. Mackenzie, Donald A. *Myths and Legends: India.* London: Studio Editions 1985, 153.

In Cambodia, the cat is carried in cages to rain-ravaged areas where it is doused with water. It is believed that the cat's howls will awaken the rain goddess Indra so that she will stop the downpour.[3]

Big cats have dominated the ancient religious traditions of Mesoamerica. Appearing as a jaguar or puma or as a composite jaguar-human figure, the cat gods were associated with caves, the night and the underworld— much as cats were viewed during the witch-hunting days of Europe.

One of the main deities of the Olmec people was the were-jaguar, half human and half jaguar. The were-jaguar was important for its rain making abilities. The Maya had more jaguar deities than any other Mesoamerican people. They regarded the jaguar as representative of the sun. Miller and Taube noted that the Mayan jaguar was the nighttime sun, and as god of the Underworld, it was also the Underworld's sun.[4] The jaguar image is frequently associated with sacrifice.

Black cats are normally thought to bring bad luck — except in England, where they have the opposite effect. Images of black cats in England are made into good luck charms. Symbologist J. C. Cooper, however, noted, "As black it is lunar, evil and death; it is only in modern times that a black cat has been taken to signify good luck."[5] Ancient Chinese tradition speaks of the black cat as representative of misfortune and, of course, Christian symbolism links the black cat with Satan, lust, laziness and witchcraft.

While cats have caused some fear among humans for their mystical character it is the cat that has paid the price more than their human companions have. According to an entry in the January 11, 1851 *Notes and Queries*, a British periodical, "In Wilts, and also in Devon, it is believed that cats born in the Month of May will catch no mice nor rats, but will, contrary to the wont of other cats, bring in snakes and slow worms. Such cats are called 'May cats,' and are held in contempt."[6] "May cats" seem to have been universally disliked in England in the 19th century. Another *Notes and Queries* entry on February 1, 1851 stated "In Hampshire, to this day, we always kill may cats," and in June another reader wrote "...may Cats are unlucky, and will suck the breath of children."[7] This last superstition is still commonly found in the Western world.

Cats are also invariably linked to the weather — and generally not good weather. The approach of wind and rain was said to be foretold by the way a cat washes itself or in what direction it sits while grooming. Greek folklore from the 1890s said, "...if a cat licks herself with her face turned towards the north, the wind will soon blow from that dangerous quarter."[8] Witch-lore

3. Keister, Douglas. *Stories in Stone.* New York: MJF Books 2004, 71.
4. Miller, Mary and Karl Taube. *The Gods and Symbols of Ancient Mexico and the Maya.* London: Thames and Hudson 1993, 104.
5. Cooper, J.C. *An Illustrated Encyclopaedia of Traditional Symbols.* London: Thames and Hudson 1978, 30.
6. *Notes and Queries*, Vol. 3, Number 63, January 11, 1851, 20.
7. *Notes and Queries*, Vol. 3, Number 87, June 28, 1851, 516.
8. Inwards, Richard. *Weather Lore.* London: Elliot Stock 1893, 126.

says that the cat familiar is a rain-maker as well as a companion to the witch. Foretelling the weather by watching a cat may not be foolproof, however. Another bit of weather-lore says, "Cats with their tails up and hair apparently electrified indicate approaching wind — or a dog."[9]

Witches have long been associated with the cat — the cat being either the witches familiar or a form into which the witch easily transforms. This relationship is an ancient one; the Greeks and Romans told of a woman who had been changed into a cat chosen as the priestess of Hecate, goddess of the Underworld, sorcery and magic. In fact, Hecate is often depicted as a cat. It is interesting that this association is today so widely known, when in reality tradition holds more stories of rabbits being associated with witches than the cat. While there is some court testimony of the 16th century concerning witches shape-shifting into cats, many other animals were also implicated such as dogs, frogs, cocks and hares. In 1587, twenty-four Aberdeen witches were tried, and eventually, "They accused one another of unnatural practices, from eating mutton on Good Friday to concourse with devils in the shape of black cats and dogs."[10]

This belief in witches assuming the form of cats was not restricted to Europe by any means. Folklorist Vance Randolph wrote in his 1947 study, *Ozark Superstitions*, that, "A witch can assume the form of any bird or animal, but cats and wolves seem to be her favorite disguises. In many a backwoods village you may hear some gossip about a woman who visits her lover in the guise of a house cat. Once inside his cabin, she assumes her natural form and spends the night with him. Shortly before daybreak she becomes a cat again, returns to her home, and is transformed into a woman at her husband's bedside."[11]

In popular folklore, the witch was said to be able to assume the form of a black cat nine times — to match the nine magical lives that the cat is supposedly blessed with. Across Medieval Europe, black cats were hunted down and killed — usually by burning. This most often occurred on Shrove Tuesday[12] and Easter.

In fact, notes Thompson, "the connection of the cat with witches was no doubt the reason for the persecution and ill-treatment of the animal in the seventeenth century."[13]

Cats have been fearfully linked to death, in part due to their ties to ancient predator animal deities around the world and to ancient gods and goddesses of the Underworld.

---

9. Ibid.

10. Parrinder, Geoffry. "The Witch as Victim" in *The Witch in History* edited by Venetia Newall. New York: Barnes & Noble 1996, 129.

11. Randolph, Vance. *Ozark Magic and Folklore*. New York: Dover Publications, Inc. 1964, 268. A reprint of *Ozark Superstitions* published 1947 by Columbia University Press.

12. Shrove Tuesday is the last day before Lent. It was a day that became popular for divination among many other activities.

13. Thompson, C.J.S. *The Hand of Destiny*. New York: Bell Publishing Company 1989, 201.

In Estonian folklore, the returning souls of dead humans, called "home wanderers," or "revenants," could appear in human or animal form. According to Estonian folklorist Eha Viluoja, cats (black, of course) accounted for 17 out of 92 reported instances of "home wanderer" observations,. Dogs were the primary ghostly object seen, accounting for 35 cases.[14]

Any cat that jumped over a body awaiting burial was a sure sign of bad luck and was immediately killed. It was believed that should a cat do such a thing the corpse would rise up to become a vampire.[15]

The cat has also been used to effect folk-cures and to provide protection — in rather strange ways. Folklorist Luc Lacourcière noted that in French Canada it was not uncommon to attempt to transfer disease from the human patient to an animal. In the case of shingles, a skinned cat was applied to the human body so that the disease could be absorbed into the body of the dead cat.[16] Other treatments include making the sign of the cross with a cat's tail over an eye afflicted with a sty. This reportedly will make the sty disappear. This treatment was used in such diverse areas as Louisiana and England.[17] It is not clear whether the cat was living or dead when its tail was used for this purpose. A broth, made from a black cat, was also drunk to cure consumption.

The mystic power of the cat was continuously sought until well into the 19th and 20th century and, most likely, into the 21st century as well. Folk-medicine practices around the world abound in strange rituals to cure certain diseases or to warn individuals away from potentially dangerous events. Many of these today seem naïve and childish — as well as cruel for the poor animals involved. In Oregon in the 1960s folklore warned, "Never allow a child to play with cats or he will become a simpleton." A similar prohibition was reported in Ohio in the 1950s, "If a boy plays with cats, it will make him stupid, for the cat's brain will go into him."[18]

Other dangers associated with playing with cats include the possibility of women becoming pregnant (recorded in Oslo during the 1930s). While some folklore warns against being overly friendly with cats, the inverse was true during the 1950s in the American Mid-West. "If you make enemies of cats during your lifetime," it was reported, "you will be accompanied to the grave by storms of wind and rain."[19]

14. Viluoja, Eha. "Manifestations of the Revenant in Estonian Folk Tradition", in *Folklore*, Vol. 2. http://www.folklore.ee/folklore/vol. 2/viluoja.htm 8/14/06

15. Guiley, Rosemary Ellen. *The Encyclopedia of Witches & Witchcraft*. New York: Checkmark Books/Facts on File 1999, 49

16. Lacourcière, Luc. "A Survey of Folk Medicine in French Canada from Early Times to the Present", in *American Folk Medicine*, edited by Wayland D. Hand. Berkeley: University of California Press 1976, 212.

17. Simpson, Jacqueline and Steve Roud. *Oxford Dictionary of English Folklore*. Oxford: Oxford University Press 2000, 50 and Elizabeth Brandon. "Folk Medicine in French Louisiana" in *American Folk Medicine*. Edited by Wayland D. Hand. Berkeley: University of California Press 1976, 200.

18. UCLA Folkmedicine Record Numbers 10_4587, 11_4890.

19. Ibid., Record Number 5_5244

Folk-medicine traditions include one from Germany during the early 20th century that said that thieves could become invisible if they would cut off the tips of the tongue of black cats and dogs, "wrap them in wax of an Easter candle, and carry them under the left arm."[20]

A rather grisly tradition in Christian England included sacrificing a cat to ward off evil forces when buildings were being constructed. Originally cats, and other animals as well as humans in pre-historic times, were killed and buried in building foundations as sacrifices to the gods and spirits to ensure protection of the structure. Over time, the "sacrificial" aspect was rationalized. Archaeologist Ralph Merrifield wrote, "the cruel practice of killing a cat as a builder's sacrifice was revived by the notion that the body of a cat set in a lifelike attitude in a hidden place would frighten vermin from the building."[21] What the actual "vermin" were is questionable however. Were rodents the focus of these efforts or was it more the spiritual "rodent" — demons and witches — that were the objects of such fear? In some instances a dead cat was found with a single rat in its mouth or near a paw.

While this use of "charms" was widespread across England from the 15th to 19th centuries it also occurred in other locations, such as Gibraltar and Sweden.

20. Hoffman-Krayer, Eduard von and Hanns Bächtold-Stäubli, eds. *Handwörterbuch des deutschen Aberglaubens.* Berlin & Leipzig 1927-1942, vol. 2, 235.
21. Merrifield, Ralph. *The Archaeology of Ritual and Magic.* New York: New Amsterdam Books 1987, 186

# Chapter 19. The Bear

All of the animal spirit helpers that have been discussed have been re-garded as such for thousands of years. However, the most ancient of the sa-cred animals is probably the bear. Cave paintings dating to 32,000-75,000 BP in France and discovery of the intentional arrangement of bear skulls on rock altars, also in caves, indicates that the bear cult was active at least 32 millennium ago in Europe. The bear cult has continued as an important part of the indigenous Ainu culture in Japan. The Ainu, direct descendents of the ancient Jomōn culture, possibly are related to the Tlingit Indians of Alaska — who are well known for their artistic renderings of the bear in their tribal art. The bear in Ainu belief is the god of the mountain, a sacred messenger and culture hero. During one of the Ainu ceremonies, called the *iyomante*, a bear is ritually slain so that its soul is sent back to the land of the gods. There are many legends among indigenous people around the world that tell of a human woman mating with a bear and producing offspring. The Ainu have a similar story. Sir James Frazer wrote, "they have a legend of a woman who had a son by a bear; and many of them who dwell in the mountains pride themselves on being descended from a bear. Such people are called "Descen-dents of the bear"..., and in the pride of their heart they will say, "As for me, I am a child of the god of the mountains..."[1]

The bear as a sacrificial animal is important not only to the Ainu but to the Delaware Indians living in Ontario, Canada. During the Big House cer-emony, which is held at Hagersville, Ontario on the first full moon in Janu-ary, a hibernating bear is driven from its den, brought to the Big House and killed with a blow to the head. The bear is eaten in a ceremonial meal and

---

1. Frazer, Sir James. *The Golden Bough: A study in magic and religion.* Hertfordshire: Wordsworth Editions 1993, 505-506.

its spirit "rises to Patamawas ('to whom prayers are offered'), bearing with it the prayers of mankind."[2] The bear is viewed as a lunar power around the world and the astronomical signs of the Big House ceremony indicate this is true to North American Indians as well.

The bear is associated with resurrection (due to its hibernating ability), and thus with rebirth and renewal. It also is known for its supernatural powers, strength, bravery and stamina. It was sacred to Artemis and Diana — both goddesses of nature. Young Greek girls used to dance to Artemis in the guise of bears, wearing bear masks and bear costumes, and were called "Arktoi," meaning "she-bears."[3] Norse warriors also dressed in bear skins for battle and were so fierce and impervious to sword and fire that they became known as "berserkers."

In Mongolian shamanism, the bear is regarded as lord of the animals and is revered as an ancestor. The bear is called *baabgai*, which means "father." Stewart tells us that the Mongolians regard the literal name for the bear as taboo, "given that the bear is recognized as an ancestor by almost all Siberian peoples."[4] While the bear is hunted at times, it is treated with great respect, the skulls placed on poles or in trees or placed on a platform as shamans are after death. Like the dog in other cultures, the bear is believed by some Siberian people to oversee the journey of the soul to the underworld.

The bear is a messenger of forest spirits in shamanism and this concept carried over to the Slavic traditions. The *Leshii*, that fairy-like shape-changer who was master of the forest and protector of animals, used both the wolf and the bear as special servants. The bear would not only serve the Leshii but protect him.

Inuit and Lapp shamans will shape-shift into bear form for their spirit journeys.

As among the Mongolians, in Apache culture the use of the "regular" name for the bear was also prohibited. According to ethnologist Morris Edward Opler, "the Chiricahua would seldom say the regular word for bear. They would call it 'mother's sibling.' It doesn't like to be called by the regular word. It gets after you when you say that."[5] In other words, the bear will cause illness if it is addressed directly with its regular name. The Apache did not hunt, eat, or use the skins of bear and avoided it as much as possible. According to one of Opler's informants, "If you come in contact with the track of a bear, or a tree where the bear has leaned, or bear manure, or if you sleep

---

2. Krickeberg, Walter & et al. *Pre-Columbian American Religions.* New York: Holt, Rinehart and Winston 1968, 166.

3. Baring, Anne and Jules Cashford. *The Myth of the Goddess: Evolution of an Image.* London: Arkana/Penguin Books 1991, 326.

4. Sarangerel (Julie Ann Stewart). *Riding Windhorses: A Journey into the Heart of Mongolian Shamanism.* Rochester: Destiny Books 2000, 33.

5. Opler, Morris Edward. *An Apache Life-Way: The Economic, Social, and Religious Institutions of the Chiricahua Indians.* Chicago: The University of Chicago Press 1941, 224.

where a bear has sat down, or if you come in contact with a bear by smell or touch, you can get sick."[6]

The reason for the avoidance of the word "bear," no matter the language, was, as E.P. Evans noted, because bears were "looked upon, not merely as rapacious brutes, whose physical strength and voracity were to be feared, but rather as incarnations of mysterious and malignant forces capable of inflicting injuries by occult and magical influences, and therefore not to be enraged or irritated in any manner. For this reason," Evans continues, "they were not called by their real names, but were propitiated by flattering epithets."[7]

Like many other sacred icons of other more ancient religions, the bear, in Christian theology, represented the Devil, evil, cruelty and carnal appetite. Evans describes one relief on the door of a cathedral in Hildesheim, carved in 1015, "which depicts a bear stand(ing) behind Pilate, whispering into his ear and filling his mind with diabolical suggestions."[8]

While it may seem incongruous that the bear, known for its size and savagery, has been worshipped for its mother goddess aspects, it is the loving relationship that the adult bear has with its young that denotes this special association. Tamra Andrews noted, "Bears were almost always connected in some way to the female life force, either being female themselves and giving birth or being the offspring of a human female. This quality reinforced the bears' intimate connection with fertility, renewal, and, often, the moon."[9]

The goddess Artio ("bear goddess"), worshipped in the Berne (Celtic for "bear") area of Switzerland during the 4th century CE, was the protectress of bears against hunters. She also protected humans from the wrath of the bear! Artio was a goddess of plenty, which ties into the bear's associations with fertility and renewal. Bear amulets have been found in North Britain and other areas and have been found in burials. A small child was found buried near Malton in Yorkshire with a tiny black bear-amulet[10] showing perhaps the belief that the bear helped the soul on its way to the underworld.

Aside from the Apache, the bear was an important spiritual totem to many Native American people. The bear is associated with sacred and powerful water sites and was regarded as a major deity and source of power. Bear doctors could shape-shift from human to bear by swimming in a special pool. Once in the water the doctor would emerge in a bear form and could only change back into his human form by submerging once again in the same pool. The bear has many of the characteristics of water. It is symbolic of rebirth and renewal; it is connected to the feminine life force and fertility. The bear was thought to be the creator of geysers in California; the spirit of the bear

6. Ibid. 225.

7. Evans, E.P. *Animal Symbolism in Ecclesiastical Architecture*. London: W. Heineman 1896, 8

8. Ibid., 88

9. Andrews, Tamra. *A Dictionary of Nature Myths*. Oxford: Oxford University Press 1998, 25.

10. Green, Miranda. *The Gods of the Celts*. Gloucester: Alan Sutton 1986, 184.

was believed to heat the water for curative purposes, which were utilized extensively by the local tribes.

In Lakota belief, the bear "is the friend of the Great Spirit. He is very wise."[11] The bear instructed the shaman in ceremonial secrets, song and medicines. To the Lakota, if a man sees a bear in his dreams or visions he must become a medicine man. The Lakota believe that the bear is the only creature that knows all things about the Great Spirit and is totally conversant in the language of the shaman. The bear is referred to as "the god the Bear," and presides over "love and hate and bravery and wounds and many kinds of medicines." He was also "the patron of mischief and fun."[12]

"The Bears" is one of the Oglala Sioux sodalities, a "dream cult" made up of individuals who have had the same vision. Called the *Mato ihanblapi* ("they dream of bears"), the members would dress for their ceremonies as bears, parade around the camp, growling like bears while they chased people. According to Powers, these "bear dreamers" were "astute curers."[13]

*The Bear Mother and her children.*

At one California Miwok site, a large standing stone called the "Northstar stone" was used for ceremonial purposes. It stands with several mortars (areas used for the grinding of food and other materials) on one side, two on the top, and with several incised lines that run the length of one side. It is believed that this stone was a central piece used during bear ceremonies thanking the Grizzly Bear and to welcome the change of season from winter to spring. The mortars were used to grind berries and other food items with the juices running down the incised lines into a catchment at the bottom. It is assumed that the Grizzly was lured into the area and would eat from the catchment, performing its part in the ritual. A bear "footprint" was carved into one portion of the Northstar stone representative of a bear walking in a docile manner, the back print overlapping with the print of the forepaw. The footprint and incised grooves on Northstar are similar to other "rain rocks" found in Northern California. A similar bear footprint carving is located in Northwestern California and a large carving representing the claw marks of

11. Walker, James R. *Lakota Belief and Ritual.* Lincoln: University of Nebraska Press 1991, 116.
12. Ibid., 121.
13. Powers, William K. *Oglala Religion.* Lincoln: University of Nebraska Press 1982, 58.

a bear can be seen at Chaw'se, Indian Grinding Rock State Park near Fiddle-town, California.

The importance of the bear in Native American culture and religion cannot be minimized. During an archaeological excavation in 1966 in the Sacramento delta area east of Oakley, California, a Plains Miwok burial of a small five-year old Indian girl was uncovered. The unusual aspect of this burial was that the child was buried with a grizzly bear cub of approximately the same size. It appeared to the excavators that the bear cub was slain deliberately to accompany the child to the afterlife. According to the excavation report, the bear was positioned directly behind and to the side of the child with one paw draped over the child's body.[14] The Plains Indians believed the bear to be the ruler of underworld creatures.

The Athapaskan Indians of British Columbia believe the bear to be the guardian of fire; however, it is the "Bear mother" that remains the most endearing characterization of this animal. Christopher Manes wrote, in *Other Creations: Rediscovering the Spirituality of Animals*, that the Bear mother is representative of the mother goddess. According to Manes:

> Invariably, the feminine animal spirit represents a force for good, even cultural heroism. In the Bear mother stories....a woman is kidnapped by a bear in the form of a man, who takes her to his village to be his bride. In her new life among the bears, the woman learns their "songs," at the same time teaching the bear spirits about human society. The woman usually gives birth to several children by her bear husband who grow up to become leaders or warriors.[15]

14. Cowan, R.A., Clewlow, C.W. Jr & et al. "An Unusual Burial of a Bear and Child From the Sacramento Delta", in Institute of Archaeology, University of California Los Angeles *Journal of New World Archaeology, Vol 1, Number 2, December 1975*, 25-30.
15. Manes, Christopher. *Other Creations: Rediscovering the Spirituality of Animals.* New York: Doubleday 1997, 162-163.

# CHAPTER 20. THE HARE AND THE RABBIT

Perhaps fittingly we come to the hare and the rabbit following on the heels of the tortoise. Both the hare and the rabbit are considered moon animals and are associated with both the moon and earth goddesses in different traditions. In Aztec lore, the moon is a rabbit and, on the other side of the world, rabbit figures were made for the Moon Festival in China. The rabbit has been depicted as a lunar symbol in Pre-Hispanic Central America, the Mayan lands and in Mimbres art of the American Southwest, as well as in Egyptian, Hindu, Burmese and Sanskrit mythology. To the Chinese the hare was associated with augury and was said to live on the moon. The hare is symbolic of fertility, rebirth, resurrection and intuition. Because of the hare's association with the moon, it has been considered an intermediary between the lunar gods and humankind. The hare also has a dual nature. The hare's foot (remember that lucky rabbit's foot you had as a child?) and head have been used as protections against witchcraft but the rabbit has also been depicted as one of the witches familiars. According to Celtic scholar Anne Ross, "the hare being a frequent shape for metamorphosis,"[1] in other words, was a favorite form for witches to shape-change into. It may be that this belief is rooted in the Church's attempt to tie the rabbit's pagan symbolism to evil and satanic traditions.

In some circles the rabbit is, and has been, considered unlucky. This is especially true among fishermen. An old superstition among English fishermen is to never say the word "rabbit" when at sea. (Why one would have occasion to do so is beyond me!) As the Native American's substituted terms for the snake, English fishermen will only refer to "long ears," or "furry things," or

---

1. Ross, Anne. *Folklore of the Scottish Highlands.* Gloucestershire: Tempus Publishing LTD., 2000, 73.

"bob-tailed bastards" while at sea.[2] This fear is undoubtedly tied to the belief that rabbits may be foreseers of death or witches who have transformed into an animal form.

In Native American lore, especially of the eastern woodlands tribes, the rabbit is one of the guises of the Trickster/cultural-hero. Anthropologist Paul Radin wrote the hare, at least in Winnebago cultural traditions, is "depicted as being born of a virgin who dies in giving birth to him, and not creating the world originally, but recreating it after it has been destroyed by a flood..."[3] Like other culture-heros the rabbit gives culture to the Indians, perhaps not intentionally but rather incidentally. "The Great Hare, Manabozho, father and guardian, is a creator and transformer," wrote philosopher J.C. Cooper, "changing man's animal nature."[4] He is, says Cooper, "Hero of the Dawn, the personification of Light...who lives in the moon with his grandmother and is 'provider of all waters, master of winds and brother of the snow.'"[5] Mooney elaborates, saying, "The Great White Rabbit is really the incarnation of the eastern dawn that brings light and life and drives away the dark shadows which have held the world in chains."[6] This then gives us some basis for the importance of the Easter Rabbit — the rabbit, like Jesus, brings light and life and "drives away the dark shadows. This was a concept that the Church could not ignore. "In European folklore," says Mooney, "...the rabbit is regarded as something uncanny and half-supernatural."[7]

The hare was an important ritual animal to the Celts, being sacrificed to the war goddess Andraste in both animal and bronze forms. Bronze hares have been found in England in an 85-foot deep shaft and at a Thistleton Dyer shrine.[8] Caesar noted that the ancient Celts forbade eating the hare, probably due to its religious usage in divination. In Sanskrit lore, the rabbit was the ambassador to and symbol of the moon goddess Chandra and, according to the Radfords, rabbits "were appointed to guard the fountain consecrated to that deity."[9]

In Chinese lore, the hare is the guardian of wild animals, the mixer of the elixir of immortality, and represents divinity, peace and prosperity, good fortune and virtuous rulers. And, once again, it is seen in the opposite way in

2. Simpson, Jacqueline and Steve Roud. *Oxford Dictionary of English Folklore.* Oxford: Oxford University Press 2000, 289.
3. Radin, Paul. *The Trickster: A Study in American Indian Mythology.* New York: Schocken Books 1972, 125.
4. Cooper, J.C. *An Illustrated Encyclopaedia of Traditional Symbols.* London: Thames and Hudson Ltd. 1978, 79.
5. Ibid.
6. Mooney, James. *Myths of the Cherokee.* New York: Dover Publications, Inc. 1995, 233. A reprint of the 1900 publication "Nineteenth Annual Report of the Bureau of American Ethnology, 1897-98.
7. Ibid., 232. Ibid
8. Green, Miranda. *The Gods of the Celts.* Gloucester: Alan Sutton 1986, 185.
9. Radford, Edwin and Mona A. *Encyclopaedia of Superstitions.* New York: Philosophical Library 1949, 195.

the Judeo-Christian tradition. To the Christian church, the hare is symbolic of lust, and to the Hebrews it is considered unclean.[10]

We mentioned the rabbit's foot, above. The origin of the lucky rabbit's foot may lie in the "belief that young rabbits are born with their eyes open, and thus have the power of the Evil Eye, and can shoo away the Evil One."[11] Writing in the 1940s, folklorists Edwin and Mona Radford stated that "a rabbit's foot is the most potent charm of the American Negroes, who, it is said, turn white with fright at the loss of one."[12] However, they then go on to relate that the use was, at least in that time, common in Britain by "hundreds of mothers" who placed one in their children's "perambulator" when going out for a stroll to protect against any possible accident. Thousands of rabbit feet were prepared in the United States and exported to England, carrying an advertisement stating that the foot was "the left hind foot of a rabbit killed in a country churchyard at midnight, during the dark of the moon, on Friday the 13th of the month, by a cross-eyed, left-handed, red-headed bow-legged Negro riding a white horse." This last statement had a convenient disclaimer — "this we do not guarantee."[13] Thompson notes, "Pepys mentions in his *Diary*, that he wore a hare's foot to avert the plague, and seems to have placed more faith in the amulet than in all the vaunted remedies that were recommended for that terrible scourge."[14]

Another rabbit ritual still in place in 1940s Britain was the "calling of rabbits." On the first day of each month people would go outside and "call rabbits" three times in rapid succession to ensure that "fortune is kind to the caller throughout the month."[15]

We mentioned the Easter Bunny or Rabbit above. This hare represents new life, dawn and resurrection. The Easter Bunny originally represented the moon goddess Oestra (or Eostre), who was depicted with a hare's head. The typical Easter celebration with the Easter Bunny and Easter Eggs certainly is not a Christian one but a pagan celebration of Spring that was taken over by the Church.

It was the goddess Hathor-Astarte who produced the first Easter Egg; actually it was the Golden Egg of the sun, Eostre. The egg was symbolic of resurrection for many Eastern European people; the Russians laid red Easter Eggs on graves as resurrection charms.[16] Eostre, for which Easter is named, is the same goddess as India's Great mother Kali. Kali is the goddess of creation

10. Cooper, op. cit., 79.
11. Radford, op. cit., 195.
12. Ibid.
13. *Folk-Lore* 19 (1908), 296.
14. Thompson, C.J. S. *The Hand of Destiny: Folklore and Superstitions for Everyday Life.* New York: Bell Publishing Company 1989, 182. A reprint of the 1932 edition published by Rider & Company, London.
15. Ibid.
16. Walker, Barbara G. *The Women's Encyclopedia of Myths and Secrets.* Edison: Castle Books 1996, 268.

and destruction as well as preservation. She both gives life and takes it, and, like the Russian Easter Eggs, her color is red.

In American folklore hunters are advised to "hunt rabbits in the light of the moon," which may hearken back to the rabbit's association with the moon.[17] Rabbits, like black cats crossing your path, are to be avoided. According to Randolph, "It is bad luck for a rabbit to cross your path from left to right," although the curse can be removed, he says, "by tearing some article of clothing just a little. If the same rabbit crosses your path *twice*, it means that you are needed at home immediately."[18] Similar warnings concerning hares crossing one's path were recorded in 17th-century England: "If an hare do but cross their way, they suspect they shall be rob'd or come to some mischance forthwith."[19] Nineteenth-century writer John Campbell wrote that this fear "no doubt arose from their [the hare] being unclean under the Levitical Law."[20] This would seem, however, an unlikely bit of folklore in a predominately-Christian country. Another bit of folklore from the Ozarks says, "when a man feels a sudden chill without any obvious reason, it means that someone or something — usually a rabbit...is walking over the spot which will ultimately be his grave."[21]

17. Koch, William E. "Hunting Beliefs and Customs from Kansas" in *Western Folklore*, Vol. XXIV, July 1965, Number 3, 168 (pgs 165-175).
18. Randolph, Vance. *Ozark Magic and Folklore*. New York: Dover Publications, Inc. 1964, 244. A reprint of *Ozark Superstitions* published in 1947 by Columbia University Press.
19. Attributed to Ramsey in 1668.
20. Campbell, John Gregorson. *The Gaelic Otherworld*, edited by Ronald Black. Edinburgh: Birlinn Limited 2005, 140.
21. Ibid., 326.

# CHAPTER 21. THE BAT

One of the few animals today that universally inspires fear is the bat. This denizen of the dark and hidden places of the earth has a dual nature though, as do many sacred symbols. In Mesoamerican tradition the bat is identified with death, darkness and sacrifice. Flint blades used in Mesoamerica often were personified with bat snouts or wings.[1]

In Chinese lore, the bat is symbolic of happiness, good luck, wealth, peace and longevity. To the Japanese the bat was associated with "unhappy restlessness" and a chaotic state of existence. And, of course, in Europe the bat was closely connected to witchcraft. Witches were said to either fly on the backs of bats or to transform into bats. "An old Scottish superstition," wrote the Radfords, "stated that if the bat is observed, while flying, to rise and then descend again earthwards, you may know that the witches' hour is come, the hour in which they have power over every human being under the sun who is not specially shielded from their influence."[2]

In English folklore a bat that flies against a window or into a room is considered very unlucky or, worse yet, an omen of death.

Bats, or rather their blood, was used during the Middle Ages as a magical ingredient in folk remedies. "To ensure keen eyesight by night as well as by day," wrote historian Richard Kieckhefer, "one should anoint one's eyes with bat's blood, which presumably imparts that animal's remarkable ability to 'see' even in the dark."[3] Bat's blood was also useful as an aphrodisiac.

---

1. Miller, Mary and Karl Taube. *An Illustrated Dictionary of The Gods and Symbols of Ancient Mexico and the Maya.* London: Thames and Hudson 1993, 45.
2. Radford, Edwin and Mona A. *Encyclopaedia of Superstitions.* New York: The Philosophical Library 1949, 28.
3. Kieckhefer. Richard. *Magic in the Middle Ages.* Cambridge: Cambridge University Press 1989, 5.

"To arose a woman's lust," Kieckhefer tells us, "soaking wool in the blood of a bat and putting it under her head while she is sleeping" will certainly do the trick![4]

From the 19th to the 21st century, the folklore of bats is almost non-existent. Its association with vampires and the Devil is mostly derived from modern day horror films. There are a few exceptions, however. At least into the 1940s the people on the Gold Coast of Africa were reported as believing that the swarms of bats that flew from the island of Tendo "are the souls of the dead who retire to the holy isle" but who must present themselves in the form of the deity Tano — which happens to be a bat.[5] Another rather peculiar piece of folklore from the Ozarks states that bedbugs are somehow derived from bats. According to Vance Randolph, "Some old-timers say that the daddy long-legs or harvestmen deposit their eggs on bats, and that these eggs hatch into bedbugs."[6]

In Apache lore, an individual who, through a supernatural experience, comes to "know" Bat becomes an excellent horseman.[7] The acquiring of animal powers through visionary experiences was common in Native American cultures. However, to be bitten by a bat means certain death for a horseman if he continues to ride. According to ethnologist Morris Opler, the Apache warn: "If a bat bites you, you had better never ride a horse anymore....If you do ride a horse after being bitten, you are just as good as dead."[8]

The bat's inherent "goodness" or "badness" depends on the religious traditions of those who pass judgment on them. The Kono of Sierra Leon, Africa have the following tale:

> "[T]here was no darkness and no cold at the beginning. The sun lit the day, and the moon lit the night. But God gave the bat darkness to carry to the moon. The bat got tired on the way and set the basket down while he went off to get food. Some animals opened the basket searching for food, and the darkness escaped. Now the bat flies at night trying to catch the dark and take it to the moon.[9]

In Christian lore, the bat is "the bird of the Devil." It is an incarnation of Satan, the Prince of Darkness. The bat represents duplicity and hypocrisy and is associated with melancholy places.

---

4. Ibid., 83.
5. Radford, Edwin and Mona A. *Encyclopaedia of Superstitions.* New York: Philosophical Library 1949, 28.
6. Randolph, Vance. *Ozark Magic and Folklore.* New York: Dover Publications, Inc. 1964, 260
7. Opler, Morris Edward. *An Apache Life-Way: The Economic, Social, and Religious Institutions of the Chiricahua Indians.* Chicago: The University of Chicago Press 1941, 214.
8. Ibid 237.
9. Andrews, Tamra. *A Dictionary of Nature Myths.* Oxford: Oxford University Press 1998, 52.

*The Bat as "the bird of the Devil." A sculpture on the Chester Cathedral, Chester, England. Formerly a Benedictine Monastery built in 1092, it has been the mother church of the Church of England Diocese of Chester since 1541.*

# CHAPTER 22. THE SPIDER

The spider, small and mysterious in its ways, is an ancient and important symbol and continues to represent the unknown and mystical aspects of our world and our spirituality.

As the spider is renowned for its weaving, it is a natural candidate as a symbol of the Great Mother goddess, the weaver of destiny, the weaver of creation who spins the web of life and creates the pattern of the world that binds all of humanity. This concept is present in Egyptian, Greek, Hindu, Buddhist, Oceanic, Sumero-Semitic, and Scandinavian mythology. As J.E. Cirlot points out, "spiders, in their ceaseless weaving and killing — building and destroying — symbolize the ceaseless alternation of forces on which the stability of the universe depends."[1]

In Oglala lore the spider, called *Inktomi*, is a culture hero that gave culture to man and enticed man from his subterranean world to the world of the open sky. Inktomi is a trap-door spider and it too "occasionally comes out of the earth carrying his scampering children on his back."[2] Inktomi, though, is a trickster, will attempt to mislead humankind back into its subterranean world, and continually tries to make fools of humankind.

In Cherokee mythology, the Water Spider uses her web-net to capture a small bit of burning coal and brings it back to the Cherokee so that they will always have fire. [3]

1. Cirlot, J.E. *A Dictionary of Symbols, 2nd Edition.* New York: Barnes & Noble Books 1995, 304.
2. Powers, William K. *Oglala Religion.* Lincoln: University of Nebraska Press 1975, 55.
3. Mooney, James. *Myths of the Cherokee.* New York: Dover Publications, Inc. 1995, 241-242. A reprint of the 1900 publication "Nineteenth Annual Report of the Bureau of American Ethnology, 1897-98.

In Mesoamerican tradition spiders are associated with the various earth goddesses, as they are in the Classical World. However, as with all sacred symbols, the spider has a dual identity. In Mesoamerican culture, spiders were associated with the Tzitzimime star demons that threatened to descend to the earth via a thread from its abdomen.[4] These demons were, according to Miller and Traube, "among the most feared supernatural beings of Late Postclassic Central Mexico...the star demons of darkness."[5] The Tzitzimime were believed to have the power to devour the sun.

South African tales say that the gods used spider webs to get to and from heaven. Apache lore also places the spider's web as a bridge connecting our world with the home of Summer. To the Apache, the spider web was also to be avoided. "The Chiricahua will not walk into a spider web," said one Apache informant. "They call the strands of the web sunbeams and say that, if you damage these, Sun will make a web inside you and kill you."[6]

The spider was important enough to Native Americans to be named as a totemic creature in certain Hopi clans and to be one of the huge figures that were created on the Nazca plain in Peru. The Nazca figure is 150 feet long and is perfectly executed. Some Nazca researchers have proposed that the spider figure is "a good match for the shape of Orion in the sky," and may have had some astronomical importance to the people that fashioned it from the stones.[7] A straight line placed through the center of the figure points directly towards the Orion constellation as it sets in the evening sky.

As previously noted, the Apache took pains not to walk into a spider's web or to kill a spider. As the Apache informant related to Morris Opler, "We are all taught not to kill spiders. The spider has power and can do harm if angered."[8] One of those powers is to cause disease. The prohibition against killing spiders is fairly widespread — all with the fear of luck turning bad or illness striking the individual. Ozark folklore also cautions against killing a spider. "Very few of the mountain people would intentionally kill a spider," wrote folklorist Vance Randolph, "since such an act is supposed to bring misfortune in its wake."[9]

Other Native people did intentionally kill spiders — but took precautions in doing so! Sir James Frazer wrote, "When a Teton Indian is on a journey and he meets a grey spider or a spider with yellow legs, he kills it, because some evil would befall him if he did not. But he is very careful not to let the spider know that he kills it, for if the spider knew, his soul would go and

---

4. Miller, Mary and Karl Taube. *An Illustrated Dictionary of the Gods and Symbols of Ancient Mexico and the Maya.* London: Thames and Hudson Ltd., 1993, 156.

5. Ibid., 176.

6. Opler, Morris Edward. *An Apache Life-Way: The Economic, Social, and Religious Institutions of the Chiricahua Indians.* Chicago: The University of Chicago Press 1941, 240.

7. Hadington, Evan. *Lines to the Mountain Gods: Nazca and the Mysteries of Peru.* New York: Random House 1987, 86.

8. Opler, op. cit., 240.

9. Randolph, Vance. *Ozark Magic and Folklore.* New York: Dover Publications Inc. 1964, 259.

tell the other spiders, and one of them would be sure to avenge the death of his relation. So in crushing the insect, the Indian says, 'O Grandfather Spider, the Thunder-beings kill you.' And the spider is crushed at once and believes what is told him." The killer is safe for, as Frazer wrote, 'what can grey or yellow-legged spiders do to the Thunder-beings?"[10]

Folklore from other lands and cultures actually calls for the use of spiders to treat illness, usually at the detriment of the spider. In Cornwall, spiders were used to treat whooping cough, asthma and fever. It is doubtful if many voluntarily used the prescribed method to treat whooping cough. The treatment consisted of filling a muslin bag with spiders, which was hung around the sufferer's neck to be worn night and day.[11] Spider webs were commonly used to stop bleeding; they were supposed to be effective for the treatment of asthma — the webs were rolled into a ball and then swallowed. I am doubtful if this was an effective remedy for someone already having difficulty breathing! Spider webs were also considered important in the treatment of cancer and canker sores in 18th century Canada.[12]

While the killing of a spider or walking through its web may result in bad things happening, interacting with spiders can bring good things as well. "Good luck will attend anyone upon whose face a spider falls from the ceiling" is one bit of superstition promising good things rather than bad where the spider is concerned.

The spider in Christian theology is symbolic of "the Devil ensnaring sinners; the miser bleeding the poor."[13] We should not be surprised as this is the common interpretation given by the Church for all symbols important to the far older, but dominated, pagan cultures.

10. Frazer, Sir James. *The Golden Bough: A study in magic and religion.* Hertfordshire: Wordsworth Editions Ltd. 1993, 524.

11. Radford, Edwin and Mona A. *Encyclopaedia of Superstitions.* New York: Philosophical Library 1949, 224.

12. Lacourcière, Luc. "A Survey of Folk Medicine in French Canada from Early Times to the Present," in *American Folk Medicine,* edited by Wayland D. Hand. Berkeley: University of California Press 1976, 206.

13. Cooper, J.C. *An Illustrated Encyclopaedia of Traditional Symbols.* London: Thames and Hudson Ltd. 1978, 156.

# CHAPTER 23. THE BEE

The bee, small as it is, has acquired a huge reputation in folklore and mythology. Unlike many of the other animal/insect spirit beings already discussed, the bee does not have a dual identity in regard to being "good" or "demonic," although swarms of bees denoted misfortune to the ancient Romans — anyone caught in such a swarm will hardly disagree with this assessment!

The Scots echoed the Roman fear of swarms of bees. Anne Ross noted in her book, *The Folklore of the Scottish Highlands*, "Ill omens were of many kinds, and could cause deep unease in people. It was considered unlucky if a stray swarm of bees were to settle on someone's property without being claimed by their owner."[1] Another bit of British folklore says, "Should the bees swarm on a dead hedge or tree, or on a dead bough of a living tree, a death will occur in the family."[2]

That bees were more associated with God in ancient Britain is indicated by the practice of the time of calling them "Birds of God." Supposedly bees were "in communion" with the Holy Spirit. In the 19th century, it was even said that bees "could be heard humming hymns on Christmas eve."[3] Followers of other religions referred to the bees as "Birds of the Muses."[4]

---

1. Ross, Anne. *The Folklore of the Scottish Highlands.* Gloucestershire: Tempus Publishing Ltd. 2000, 100.
2. Radford, Edwin and Mona A. *Encyclopaedia of Superstitions.* New York: Philosophical Library 1949, 30.
3. Simpson, Jacqueline and Steve Roud. *Oxford Dictionary of English Folklore.* Oxford: Oxford University Press 2000, 20.
4. Ransome, Hilda M. *The Sacred Bee in Ancient Times and Folklore.* Mineola: Dover Publications Inc. 2004, 47. A reprint of the 1937 edition published by George Allen & Unwin, London.

Bees have also been called "beings of fire" in the Middle East and were symbols of purity. Bees were regarded as the souls of humans in many lands from Siberia, Central Asia, India, the Middle East and Great Britain. Individual bees flying or walking around were thought to be the souls of those dreaming or of the recent dead. Gimbutas wrote, "These associations are recorded in history as well as in archaeological data and continue throughout European folklore."[5] According to English folklore, if one went to sleep and then the soul, in bee form, departed the body, the body would die if the bee were unable to find it again. The lesson was to never move a sleeping person from where they were slumbering.

The bees' association with the soul was commonly held not only by the Christians but also by the Egyptians, followers of Mithras, and by the Greeks. In fact, the Greeks consecrated bees to the moon and the symbolism wasn't lost of the worshippers of Mithras either as, according to Sir Arthur Evans, "no fitter emblem could be found for the spirits of men that swarmed forth... from the horned luminary of the heavens, the moon, their primal dwelling-place..."[6] The Radfords noted, "Plato's doctrine of the transmigration of souls holds that the souls of sober, quiet people, untinctured by philosophy come to life as bees."[7]

In Britain, a tradition of "Telling the Bees" was observed for many years. According to tradition, the bees residing in family bee hives "had to be treated as members of the household; in particular, they must be told about deaths, births, and marriages in the family."[8] If these courtesies were not made the bees would either swarm to another hive elsewhere or die. In some areas of England, the hives were turned as the coffin was removed from the house so that the hive could witness the procession and in Yorkshire, the bees were actually invited to the funeral. Interestingly enough, a very similar "Telling the Bees" custom was also observed in the Ozarks. Randolph wrote, "When a death occurs in the family, the hillfolk attach a bit of black cloth to each hive; if this is not done, the bees are likely to leave the place and carry their stored honey away to bee trees in the woods."[9]

Donald Mackenzie wrote in 1922, "The custom of placing crape on hives and 'telling the bees' when a death takes place...still survives in the south of England and in the north of Scotland."[10] It appears that the custom traveled the Atlantic and reappeared in the Ozarks, brought along in the waves of human migration during and before the 19th century. Similar customs were observed in France and Switzerland. In Normandy, "The hives were usually

---

5. Gimbutas, Marija. *The Civilization of the Goddess: The World of Old Europe.* San Francisco: HarperSanFrancisco 1991, 244.

6. As quoted by Ramsome, op. cit., 277.

7. Radford, op. cit. 32.

8. Simpson, Jacqueline and Steve Roud. *Oxford Dictionary of English Folklore.* Oxford: Oxford University Press 2000, 20.

9. Randolph, Vance. *Ozark Magic and Folklore.* New York: Dover Publications Inc. 1964, 45.

10. Mackenzie, Donald A. *Ancient Man in Britain.* London: Senate 1996, 103.

---

draped in black, but in La Vendée a black ribbon was only put on for the master or mistress."[11] Other customs included placing a piece of the deceased persons clothing, "the dirtiest which can be found," on each hive so that the bees will believe that the owner is still there and they will remain in their hives.

The bee took on a more spiritual symbolism in a much earlier time in history. Because of its honey-making characteristics, work ethic, and flower pollination, bees came to "serve as images of the miraculous interconnectedness of life."[12] Honey was one of the most valued commodities in the world and was used for such diverse things as embalming, sacrificing, ritual offerings, ritual washing, anointing, charms to ward off evil, consecration and healing.

The bee represents immortality, rebirth, regeneration, purity, the soul, chastity and virginity in both pagan and Christian symbolism. They are messengers between our physical world and the world of spirit as well as to the oak and thunder gods. Mythology records that Zeus was born in a cave sacred to bees who fed him honey. Baring and Cashford wrote, "this rite was linked to the Bee goddess" depicted on Minoan seals.[13] During the Neolithic period, bees became "an epiphany of the goddess herself...in Minoan Crete 4,000 years later the goddess and her priestesses, dressed as bees, are shown dancing together on a golden seal buried with the dead."[14] The priestesses of the Great mother Demeter at Elusius were also called "bees." Other representations of the Bee goddess have been found in pottery and other artwork dating back to 6500 BCE throughout the Mediterranean world. Mycenaean tombs were shaped as bee hives, as were pre-historic communal houses on Crete. "The beehive," writes Nicholas Saunders "became a Christian metaphor for the ordered, chaste and charitable life of monastic communities."[15] Many of the Christian meanings placed on the bee originated in much older times, among the Egyptians. The bee was the "giver of life," with an important association with birth, death and resurrection. Worker bees were said to be the tears of Ra.

Not only were bees symbolic of the goddesses Demeter, Diana, Cybele, and the Hindu deities Vishnu and Krishna, but Pan and Priapus were protectors and keepers of them as well. Pan was referred to as "the Saviour of the Bees and Keeper of the Hives."

Bees are also prophetic in nature. In India, it was believed that "a swarm of bees settling on or near a man meant that he would attain sovereignty."[16] "A common Hampshire saying some years ago," wrote the Radfords, "was

11. Ransome, op. cit. 235.
12. Baring, Anne and Jules Cashford. *The Myth of the Goddess: Evolution of an Image.* London; Arkana/Penguin Books 1991, 73.
13. Ibid., 317.
14. Ibid., 73.
15. Saunders, Nicholas J. *Animal Spirits.* London: Duncan Baird Publishers 1997, 126.
16. Ransome, op. cit. 52.

that bees are idle or unfortunate at their work whenever there is a war in prospect....Is it purely coincidence," they ask, "that there was a marked scarcity of honey at the time of the breaking out of world war in 1939?"[17] Indeed, there has been a mass die-off of bees today across the United States in recent years!

17. Radford, op. cit. 31.

# AFTERWORD

Mythology. Many think of it as simple children's tales with dragons, winged-horses, magical powers and superhuman trials won by superhuman men. However, it is far more than this. One scholar noted that contemporary Western man believes other cultures have myth and legend, while we have history and gospel. Mircea Eliade wrote, "Myth narrates a sacred history; it relates an event that took place in primordial Time, the fabled time of the 'beginnings.'...[M]yth is regarded as a sacred story, and hence a 'true history,' because it always deals with realities."[1]

Most of the material in this book is mythology. But, as Eliade wrote, mythology is "true history" in a symbolic sense that is more profound than our superficial grasp of individual day-to-day physical experiences. Whether we speak of Judeo-Christian stories of Creation, or of one family riding out a worldwide flood with two of every kind of animal, or of the dead coming back to life, or of other traditions' stories that seek to respond to the unfathomable questions of life, similar myths are present the world over and have been repeated for thousands of years. These stories are part of all religious traditions and beliefs, as every society has puzzled over the origins of the earth, of life, of the apparently cyclical nature of time, and the conundrum of an inevitable death that strikes at random.

We have seen in this book that werewolf legends are found from Polynesia to France to North and South America and Africa. Stories of Wild Men are also universally found around the world. Sightings of Mermaids (and the Loch Ness monster) are still reported. Tales of fairies and vampires are abundant.

Mythology may be seen to serve as a kind of social tool, instructing, entertaining, and uniting members of a community by creating shared beliefs

---

1. Eliade, Mircea. *Myth and Reality*. New York: Harper & Row, Publishers 1963, 5-6.

and a sense of shared heritage. Our religions, our ethics, our moral codes and our attitudes towards one another evolve and are passed along in part through myth.

Some scientists have remarked that such creatures as Big Foot cannot exist as it has never been caught, killed, or discovered dead in the woods. This may be true; however, I have spent a great deal of time in the forests and have never stumbled upon the skeleton of a bear or an elk or even a squirrel. The Indians themselves have an explanation as to why the Big Foot hasn't been caught or killed: "The reason white men are unable to approach them is because 'Sasquatch does not like the white man's smell'."[2] In addition, "new" forms of life continue to be "discovered," including two new species of monkeys in Tanzania found in September 2005 and the first film taken of a 26-foot squid by Japanese scientist. The giant squid, long thought to be a creation of superstition and folklore, behaved in an extremely aggressive manner and may well be a smaller version of a truly giant monster that actually sunk ships in the past — just like the stories tell us they did. What else is out there that we have not as yet found after all this time? Certainly, many of the mythic tales of giants and fairy, "monsters" and others are stories that were invented, while some are more evidently extended and expanded from observed reality. Where we each think the line should be drawn is a personal choice.

There are a few scholars, mostly anthropologists, that seem to have a more liberal mindset anyway, who do believe in the very real possibility of the reality of many of the beings in these myths. I have quoted John Messenger several times in this book for his ethnography of the people living on a small Irish island he called Inis Beag. Professor Messenger wrote his Inis Beag ethnography in the late 1960s and was able to break through some of the concrete that was so prevalent in academe during that time with his candor concerning the beliefs of the residents, as well as himself, in the fairy, mermaids and other spirits on the island. However, it was apparently at a price. The Indiana University professor wrote:

> From November of 1959 until June of 1963, my wife and I experienced, first in Inis Beag and then in our home in the United States, the antics of an unseen being who opened doors and windows, turned on lights and water faucets, and imbibed our Irish whiskey. Tongue-in-cheek, we placed the blame for these uncanny occurrences on an amiable solitary fairy, who had attached himself to us, but eventually I felt compelled to report our unique contact with the Celtic supernatural to the anthropological community — a gesture regarded as "poison oak in the scientific groves of academe.[3]

Needless to say, the exploration of myth offers all of us a fascinating and complex set of possibilities.

---

2. Wherry, Joseph H. *Indian Masks & Myths of the West.* New York: Bonanaza Books 1969, 114.

3. Messenger, John C. *Inis Beag: Isle of Ireland.* Case Studies in Cultural Anthropology. New York: Holt, Rinehart and Winston, Inc. 1969, 99.

# APPENDIX A: THE FAIRY

This table illustrates the differences and similarities of the various Fairy legends from around the world which have been included in this book. Fairy-like creatures such as the Water Baby, the *cheneques*, the *Nûññĕ'hĭ*, are all contained in this chart showing the country of origin, their preferred residences, whether they are ambivalent or hostile to man, their physical descriptions, powers, etc. The similarities of accounts from country to country, culture to culture and age to age raise challenging questions.

*Origins/Attitudes and Descriptions of the Fairy*

| Local Name | Location/Origin of Lore | Attitude | Description | Powers |
|---|---|---|---|---|
| *Nûññĕ'hĭ*, or the "immortals" | NE Georgia — Cherokee lore. Live on high peaks, mounds and at the head of the Nottely River. | Friendly. Would help lost people and also helped the Cherokee fight enemies. | Normal sized when desiring to be seen by humans. | Invisible unless desiring to be seen. Could appear to be like human Indians. |
| *Yûñwĭ Tsunsdi'*, or the "Little People" | Live in rocks and grottos under waterfalls. Cherokee territory. | Good, help find lost children. Will secretly do chores for humans. | No larger than children, well formed with hair to their feet | Can cast spells |
| Tsăwa'sĭ | Lives in grassy areas of hillsides in Cherokee lore. | Mischievous but also helpful to hunters | Tiny, very handsome with hair flowing to his feet. | Great powers of the game animals |
| Yûñwĭ Amai'yĭñĕ'hĭ, or "Water-dweller" | Live in the waters, Cherokee lore | Will help fisherman who pray to them | Unknown | Powers over fish |
| Rock & Water Babies | Live in the rocks, springs, water holes in California, Nevada and Mexico | Responsible for much of the rock art, spirit helpers, enhanced the power of the shaman | Small, dwarf-like males, long hair. Some described as infant like with short black hair. | |
| Pauwiha | Water spirits that live in springs and rivers near Mono Lake, California | Believed that rock art sites are their lair | Rarely seen but have long, shiny black or blond hair | |
| Unktehi | A water "goblin" that causes flooding, drowning and other water accidents in Lakota lore. Said to also cause foul water. | A malicious creature that lived in the water. Also referred to as the Spirit of Water. | | It is Unktehi who punishes those who fail to cross the bridge to the spirit world after death. |
| Sompallwe | Chile | An elemental lake spirit that can change into a tiny man | Dark skin and curly hair | More feared than revered, can shape shift |
| Menehune | Common throughout Polynesia | Fond of dancing and music, industrious | Fair skinned with light or reddish hair, never age | Traverse between world through a magical fountain. |
| Korrigan | Ireland, live in or near fountains | Can be helpful | | |
| Corannians | Wales | Cannibals | Dwarfs | Can hear any word that touches the wind |
| nokondisi & gwomai | In Gururumba territory, New Guinea. The nokondisi live in the upland forests and the gwomai live in reeds or boulders along rivers | Nature spirits who may be contracted with to do good work, normally ambivalent but are malevolent if their needs are not met | Appear as mist or smoke, very small | |
| Geo-Lud-Mo-SisEg | New Brunswick, Maliseet & Iroquois | Healers & Tricksters | "Little beings" | |
| Pīpīntu | Venezuela | Friendly | Dwarfs with long beards, bald | Very fast, dance, eat smoke |
| *Bannik* | Russia | Mean spirited | "Old men with hairy paws and long fingernails" | Seldom seen |

# APPENDIX B: THE WILD MEN

The following table gives a listing of the descriptions, habitats, characteristics and historical origins of the Wild Men. Drawn from both mythological and historical accounts this information will enable the reader to compare and contrast available information about these creatures.

| Local Name | Location/Origin of Lore | Attitude | Description | Powers |
|---|---|---|---|---|
| Moss-Folk, Moss-Women, Wood Wives | Europe, esp. Germany | Can be helpful | "Dwarfs, grey and old looking, hideously overgrown with moss, giving them a hairy appearance"[1] | Protect the forests and weave their moss through the trees, have healing knowledge |
| Wild People | Forested areas of Europe | | "gigantic proportions, clothed in moss or rough shaggy hair from head to toe"[2] | |
| Big Foot/Sasquatch | Forested and wild areas of North America | shy but dangerous | "Gigantic," 8-9 feet tall, long hairy arms, covered in hair, walks like a human | very fast and able to jump great distances (12-14 feet), powerful |
| Winstead Wild Man | Connecticut 1895-1970s | | 6+ feet tall, covered in dark hair, approx. 300 pounds | Very fast ("lightning speed") |
| Dwendis, "goblin" | Jungles of Belize | | 3'6" to 4'6" in height, covered in short brown hair | |
| Mashiramû, "Bush Spirit" & the Karau | Jungles of Columbia and Venezuela, known to the Yupa Indians | Very dangerous, referred to as a "devastating demon" | Both are covered in hair, the Bush Spirit's feet are said to be turned backwards, the Karau has very large teeth and cold hands | |
| Wild Woman | Forests of Oregon, known to the Tillamook Indians | Dangerous but may be helpful if she likes you | A large woman with long beautiful hair, wears lots of dentalia | Can cause people to sicken and die, or trees to fall on one, connected to the Spruce tree, can give supernatural gifts to help diagnose illnesses or to cure the ill or to make baskets |
| Wild Women | Germany, originally in 1753 at the village of Grödich | Kindly and beautiful | Beautiful with fine flowing hair | Helpful but protective, will steal children if they believe that they are being neglected |
| Wild Women/ Wild Men | Mountain forests of Russia | Helpful or dangerous. May tickle one to death but will also help in harvests or other housework if offerings left to them. Wild Men may cause illness or grant powers to cure illnesses. | "Handsome females, fine square heads, abundant tresses, hairy bodies".[3] Wild Men are "ugly giants" | Can become invisible by applying certain herbal remedies. |
| Almas, Wild Men | Mountainous regions of China and Mongolia, few seen since 1922 | Dangerous, said to kill and eat any human in their vicinity. | Robust and human-like with "long, thick locks, fiery red in color, body covered in hair"[4] | Very powerful, able to break large rocks with one blow and to pull trees up by the roots. |
| Yeti | Himalayas, first noted in 1820 by Englishman B.H. Hodgson | | "Hairy, tailless, humanlike creatures"[5] 5'6" to 6' or taller in height, covered with long reddish hair | |

# Bibliography

Aaland, Mikkel. "The Russian Bania: History of the Great Russian Bath." http://www. cyberbohemia.com/Pages/russianbaniahistory.htm 1998

Addy, Sidney Oldall. Household Tales with Other Traditional Remains Collected in the Counties of York, Lincoln, Derby, and Nottingham. London: 1895

Alexander, Marc. *A Companion to the Folklore, Myths & Customs of Britain.* Gloucestershire: Sutton Publishing Limited 2002

Almstedt, Ruth Farrell. *Diegueño Curing Practices.* San Diego Museum Papers Number 10. San Diego: Museum of Man 1977

Andersen, Johannes C. *Myths and Legends of the Polynesians.* Rutland: Charles E. Tuttle Company: Publishers 1969. A reprint of the 1928 edition published by George G. Harrap & Company Limited, London.

Andrews, Tamra. *A Dictionary of Nature Myths.* Oxford: Oxford University Press 1998

Anon. "Traditions and Tales of Upper Lusatia, No. 1: The Fairies' Sabbath" in *Blackwood's Edinburgh Magazine,* No. CCCXLIV, Vol. LV, June 1844

Anon. *The Spirit World.* Alexandria: Time-Life Books 1992

Arrowsmith, Nancy and George Moorse. *A Field Guide to the Little People.* London: Macmillan Company 1977

Atalie, Princess. *The Earth Speaks.* New York: Fleming H. Revell Company, 1940

Atwater, Caleb. *Description of the Antiquities Discovered in the State of Ohio and Other Western States.* Ohio: American Antiquarian Society 1820

Balikci, Asen. *The Netsilik Eskimo.* Garden City: The Natural History Press 1970

Baring, Anne and Jules Cashford. *The Myth of the Goddess: Evolution of an Image.* London: Arkana/Penguin Books 1991

Baring-Gould, S. *Curious Myths of the Middle Ages*. New York: John B. Alden Publishers 1885

Beck, Horace. *Folklore and the Sea*. Mystic: Mystic Seaport Museum Incorporated 1973

Beckham, Stephen Dow. "Coos, Lower Umpqua, and Siuslaw: Traditional Religious Practices" in *Native American Religious Practices and Uses, Siuslaw National Forest*. Eugene: Heritage Research Associates Report No. 7(3), September 20, 1982

Beckwith, Martha. *Hawaiian Mythology*. Honolulu: University of Hawaii Press 1970

Berrnal, Ignacio. *The Olmec World*. Berkeley: University of California Press 1969

Bernard, Penny. 'Mermaids, Snakes and the Spirits of the Water in South Africa: Implications for River Health." Paper given as part of a lecture series, Rhodes University, Grahamstown, South Africa 2000

Bernard, Penny. "Water Spirits: Indigenous People's Knowledge Progamme: The relevance of indigenous beliefs for river health and wetland conservation in southern Africa," in *South African Wetlands*, No. 11, November, 2000, pgs. 12-16

Biedermann, Hans. *Dictionary of Symbolism: Cultural Icons & The Meanings Behind Them*. New York: Meridian Books 1994

Black, Jeremy and Anthony Green. *gods, Demons and Symbols of Ancient Mesopotamia*. Austin: University of Texas Press 2000

Blackman, W. Haden. *The Field Guide to North American Monsters*. New York: Three Rivers Press 1998

Bonwick, James. *Irish Druids and Old Irish Religions*. New York: Barnes & Noble Books 1986. A reprint of the 1894 edition.

Bourke, John G. *Apache Medicine-Men*. New York: Dover Publications, Inc. 1993. A reprint of the1892 edition of *The Medicine-Men of the Apache* published in the Ninth Annual Report of the Bureau of Ethnology to the Secretary of the Smithsonian Institution 1887-88, Washington, pgs 443-603.

Bradley, Michael. *Guide to the World's Greatest Treasures*. New York: Barnes & Noble 2005

Brandon, Elizabeth. "Folk Medicine in French Louisiana" in *American Folk Medicine*. Edited by Wayland D. Hand. Berkeley: University of California Press 1976, pgs 215-234.

Brewster, Harry. *The River gods of Greece: Myths and Mountain Waters in the Hellenic World*. London: I.B. Tauris & Co. Ltd. 1997

Briggs, Katherine. *British Folktales*. New York: Pantheon Books 1977

Briggs, Robin. *Witches & Neighbors: The Social and Cultural Context of European Witchcraft*. New York: Viking 1996

Brown, Ras Michael. "West-Central African Nature Spirits in the South Carolina Lowcountry." Paper given at the Southeastern Regional Seminar in African Studies (SERAS) Fall Meeting 27-28 October 2000, University of Tennessee, Knoxville

Budge, E. A. Wallis. *Babylonian Life and History.* New York: Barnes & Noble Books 2005. A reprint of the 1883 publication.

Budge, Sir E.A. Wallis. *Egyptian Magic.* New York: Dover Publications Inc. 1971

Buechler, Hans S. and Judith-Maria Buechler. *The Bolivian Aymara.* Case Studies in Cultural Anthropology. New York: Holt, Rinehart and Winston, Inc. 1971

Campbell, John Gregorson. *The Gaelic Otherworld,* edited by Ronald Black. Edinburgh: Birlinn Limited 2005

Campbell, Joseph. *The Hero With a Thousand Faces.* New York: MJF Books 1949

Campbell, Joseph. *The Masks of God: Primitive Mythology.* New York: The Viking Press 1959

Campbell, Joseph. *Creative Mythology: The Masks of God* Volume IV. London: Secker & Warburg 1968

Carrington, Dorothy. *The Dream Hunters of Corsica.* London: Phoenix 1995

Carrington, Richard. *Mermaids and Mastodons: A Book of Natural & Unnatural History.* New York: Rinehart & Company, Inc. 1957

Carrington, Richard. "The Natural History of the Mermaid," in *Horizon,* January, 1960, Vol. II, Number 3, pgs 129-136

Catherine, David. "The Green Fingerprint: Exploring a critical signature in the quest for the authentic Self." Unpublished paper copyright 2004 by Ufudu Medicinal Arts, South Africa

Cave, C.J.P. *Medieval Carvings in Exeter Cathedral.* London: Penguin Books 1953

Chagnon, Napoleon A. *Yanomamö: The Fierce People.* New York: Holt, Rinehart and Winston, Inc. Case Studies in Cultural Anthropology, 1968

Cirlot, J.E. *A Dictionary of Symbols, 2nd Edition.* New York: Barnes & Noble Books 1995

Clark, Ella E. *Indian Legends of the Pacific Northwest.* Berkeley: University of California Press 1953

Clark, Ella E., editor. "George Gibbs' Account of Indian Mythology of Oregon and Washington Territories" in *Oregon Historical Quarterly* Vol. LVI, Number 4, December 1955, 293-325

Cole, Mabel Cook and Fay-Cooper Cole. *The Story of Primitive Man: His Earliest Appearance and Development.* Chicago: University of Knowledge, Inc. 1938

Coleman, Loren. *Bigfoot! The True Story of Apes in America.* New York: Paraview Pocket Books 2003

Cooper, J.C. *An Illustrated Encyclopaedia of Traditional Symbols.* London : Thames and Hudson 1978

Cooper, John M. *Analytical and Critical Bibliography of the Tribes of Tierra Del Fuego and Adjacent Territory.* Bureau of American Ethnology Bulletin 63. Washington: Smithsonian Institution 1917

Cotterell, Arthur. The *Encyclopedia of Mythology: Classical, Celtic, Greek.* London: Hermes House 2005

Cremo, Michael A. and Richard L. Thompson. *The Hidden History of the Human Race: Forbidden Archaeology.* Los Angeles: Bhaktivedanta Book Publishing, Inc. 1996

D'Alviella, Count Goblet. *The Migration of Symbols.* New York: University Books 1956

Davidson, H.R. Ellis. *gods and Myths of the Viking Age.* New York: Bell Publishing Company 1981

Davidson, H.R. Ellis. *Myths and Symbols in Pagan Europe: Early Scandinavian and Celtic Religions.* Syracuse: Syracuse University Press 1988

Demetrio y Radaza, Francisco. *Dictionary of Philippine Folk Beliefs and Customs,* 4 vols. Philippines, 1970

Doel, Fran & Geoff. *The Green Man in Britain.* Gloucestershire: Tempus Publishing Ltd. 2001

Doresse, Jean. *The Secret Books of the Egyptian Gnostics.* New York: MJF Books 1986

Driver, Harold E. *Indians of North America, 2nd edition.* Chicago: University of Chicago Press 1969

Drury, C.M., ed. Nine Years with the Spokane Indians: The Diary, 1838-1848, of Elkanah Walker. Glendale: Arthur H. Clark 1976

Eliade, Mircea. *Shamanism: Archaic Techniques of Ecstasy.* Princeton University Press 1964

Erickson, Vincent O. "Maliseet-Passamaquoddy" in *Handbook of North American Indians, Vol.15: Northeast.* Edited by Bruce G. Trigger. Washington: Smithsonian Institution 1978, pgs 123-136

Evans, E. Estyn. *Irish Folkways.* Mineola: Dover Publications Inc. 2000. A reprint of the 1957 edition published by Routledge & Kegan Paul Ltd., London.

Evans, E.P. *Animal Symbolism in Ecclesiastical Architecture.* London: W. Heineman 1896

Evans-Wentz, W.Y. *The Fairy-Faith in Celtic Countries.* Mineola: Dover Publications Inc. 2002. A reprint of the 1911 edition published by Henry Frowde, London.

Fiske, John. *Myths and Myth-Makers: Old Tales and Superstitions Interpreted by Comparative Mythology.* Boston: Houghton, Mifflin and Company 1881

Floyd, E. Randall. *Great Southern Mysteries.* Little Rock: August House Publishers 1989

Franklin, Anna. *The Illustrated Encyclopaedia of Fairies.* London: Paper Tiger 2004

Frazer, James G. *The Golden Bough: The Roots of Religion and Folklore.* New York: Avenal Books 1981. A reprint of the two volume edition published in 1890 by Macmillan, London.

Frazer, Sir James. *The Golden Bough: A study in magic and religion.* Hertfordshire: Wordsworth Editions 1993

Gamst, Frederick C. *The Qemant: A Pagan-Hebraic Peasantry of Ethiopia.* Case Studies in Cultural Anthropology. New York: Holt, Rinehart and Winston 1969

Gimbutas, Marija. *The Civilization of the Goddess: The World of Old Europe.* San Francisco: HarperSanFrancisco 1991

Gimbutas, Marija. *The Language of the Goddess.* San Francisco: HarperSanFrancisco 1991

Gould, Charles. *Mythical Monsters.* London: Senate 1995

Gould, Rupert T. *Enigmas: Another Book of Unexplained Facts.* New Hyde Park: University Books 1965. A reprint of the 1945 edition.

Graham, Patrick. *Sketches Descriptive of the Picturesque Scenery of Perthshire.* Edinburgh 1810

Green, John. *Year of the Sasquatch: Encounters with Bigfoot from California to Canada,* Agassiz: Cheam Publishing Ltd. 1970

Green, Miranda. *The Gods of the Celts.* Gloucester: Alan Sutton 1986

Guiley, Rosemary Ellen. *The Encyclopedia of Witches & Witchcraft.* New York: Checkmark Books/Facts on File 1999

Hallam, Elizabeth, ed. *Gods and Goddesses.* New York: Macmillan 1996

Hardin, Terri, ed. *Legends & Lore of the American Indians.* New York: Barnes & Noble, Inc. 1993

H.G.T., "Piskies" in *Notes and Queries,* Vol. 2 (59), December 14, 1850, 475

Hoebel, E. Adamson. *The Cheyennes: Indians of the Great Plains.* New York: Holt, Rinehart and Winston, Case Studies in Cultural Anthropology 1960

Howells, William. *The Heathens: Primitive Man and His Religions.* New York: Doubleday Books 1962

Husain, Shahrukh. *The Goddess.* Alexandria: Time-Life Books 1997

Hutton, Ronald. *The Pagan Religions of the Ancient British Isles: Their Nature and Legacy.* Oxford: Blackwell Publishers Ltd., 1991

Hyde, Douglas. "Taking of Evidence in Ireland" in *The Fairy-Faith in Celtic Countries.* Mineola: Dover Publications Inc. 2002. A reprint of the 1911 edition published by Henry Frowde, London.

Inman, Thomas. *Ancient Pagan and Modern Christian Symbolism.* New York: Cosimo Classics 2005. A reprint of the 1869 edition.

Inwards, Richard. *Weather Lore.* London: Elliot Stock 1893.

Jacobs, Elizabeth D. *The Nehalem Tillamook: An Ethnography.* Corvallis: Oregon State University Press 2003

Jones, Louis C. "The Little People" in *New York Folklore Quarterly,* #18 (1962), pgs 243-264

Jordan, Katy. *The Haunted Landscape: Folklore, ghosts & legends of Wiltshire.* Wiltshire: Ex Libris Press 2000

Kahn, Max. "Vulgar Specifics and Therapeutic Superstitions" in *Popular Science Monthly,* #83 (1913), pgs 81-96

Kasner, Leone Letson. *Spirit Symbols in Native American Art.* Philomath: Ayers Mountain Press 1992

Keightley, Thomas. *The World Guide to Gnomes, Fairies, Elves, and Other Little People.* New York: Gramercy Books 1978. A reprint of the 1878 edition titled *Fairy Mythology* published by G. Bell, London.

Kerrigan, Michael. "The Faces of the Changeling" in *Forests of the Vampire: Slavic Myth.* New York: Barnes & Noble Books 1999, pgs 120-123

Kieckhefer, Richard. *Magic in the Middle Ages.* Cambridge: Cambridge University Press 1989

Kirk, G.S. *Myth: Its Meaning & Functions in Ancient & Other Cultures.* London: Cambridge University Press 1970

Kluckhohn, Clyde and Dorothea Leighton. *The Navaho.* Garden City: Anchor Books/ The American Museum of Natural History 1962

Knowlson, T. Sharper. *The Origins of Popular Superstitions and Customs.* London: Senate 1994. A reprint of the 1930 edition published by T. Werner Laurie Ltd., London.

Krickeberg, Walter & et al. *Pre-Columbian American Religions.* New York: Holt, Rinehart and Winston 1968

Kroeber, A. L. *The Seri.* Southwest Museum Papers Number Six. Los Angeles: Southwest Museum, April 1931

Lacourcière, Luc, "A Survey of Folk Medicine in French Canada from Early Times to the Present," in *American Folk Medicine*, edited by Wayland D. Hand. Berkeley: University of California Press 1976, pgs. 203-214.

Leakey, Richard E. *Origins.* New York: E.P. Dutton 1977

Lee, Gaylen D. *Walking where we lived: Memoirs of a Mono Indian Family.* Norman: University of Oklahoma Press 1998

Leisegang, Hans. "The Mystery of the Serpent" in *Pagan and Christian Mysteries: Papers from the Eranos Yearbook*, edited by Joseph Campbell. New York: The Bollingen Foundation/Harper & Row Publishers 1955, pgs 3-69

Lintrop, Aado. "On the Udmurt Water Spirit and the Formation of the Concept 'Holy" Among Permian Peoples" in *Folklore*, Vol. 26, April 2004, pgs 7-26. Published by the Folk Belief & Media Group of Estonian Literary Museum, Tartu

Long, E. Croft. "The Placenta in Lore and Legend," in *Bulletin of the Medical Library Association #51* (1963), pgs 233-241

MacCulloch, J.A. *The Religion of the Ancient Celts.* Mineola: Dover Publications, Inc. 2003. A reprint of the 1911 edition published by T &T Clark, Edinburgh.

Mack, Carol K. and Dinah Mack. *A Field Guide to Demons, Fairies, Fallen Angels, and Other Subversive Spirits.* New York: Owl Books 1998

Mackenzie, Donald A. *India Myths & Legends.* London: Studio Editions 1993

Mackenzie, Donald A. *Myths and Legends Crete & Pre-Hellenic.* London: Senate 1995. A reprint of the 1917 edition published as *Crete & Pre-Hellenic Europe* by The Gresham Publishing Company, London.

Mandeville, Sir John. *The Travels of Sir John Mandeville.* Translated by C.W.R.D. Moseley. London: Penguin Books 1983

Manes, Christopher. *Other Creations: Rediscovering the Spirituality of Animals.* New York: Doubleday 1997

Maringer, Johannes. *The Gods of Prehistoric Man: History of Religion.* London: Phoenix Press 2002

Markale, Jean. *The Great Goddess: Reverence of the Devine Feminine From the Paleolithic to the Present.* Rochester: Inner Traditions 1999

Matthews, John. *The Quest for the Green Man.* Wheaton; Quest Books 2001

Mbiti, John S. *African Religions and Philosophy.* Garden City: Anchor Books 1970

Mercatante, Anthony S. *Good and Evil in Myth & Legend.* New York: Barnes & Noble 1978

Merriam, C. Hart. Editor. *The Dawn of the World: Myths and Tales of the Miwok Indians of California.* Lincoln: University of Nebraska Press 1993

Merrifield, Ralph. *The Archaeology of Ritual and Magic.* New York: New Amsterdam Books 1987

Messenger, John C. *Inis Beag: Isle of Ireland.* Case Studies in Cultural Anthropology. New York: Holt, Rinehart and Winston 1969

Miller, Mary and Karl Taube. *An Illustrated Dictionary of the Gods and Symbols of Ancient Mexico and the Maya.* London: Thames and Hudson 1993

Mohen, Jean-Pierre. *Prehistoric Art: The Mythical Birth of Humanity.* Paris: Pierre Terrail/Telleri 2002

Mooney, James. *Myths of the Cherokee.* New York: Dover Publications, Inc. 1995. A reprint of the 1900 publication, "Nineteenth Annual Report of the Bureau of American Ethnology, 1897-98

Mooney, James. *The Ghost-Dance Religion and the Sioux Outbreak of 1890.* Chicago: The University of Chicago Press 1965. A reprint of the 1896 edition published by the Smithsonian Institution, *Fourteenth Annual Report of the Bureau of Ethnology to the Secretary of the Smithsonian Institution, 1892-93.*

Morgan, Elaine. *The Descent of Women.* New York: Bantam Books, Inc. 1973

Morwood, Mike & et al. "The People Time Forgot" in *National Geographic,* April 2005, pgs. 2-15

Nash, Tom & Twilo Scofield. *The Well-Traveled Casket: Oregon Folklore.* Eugene: Meadowlark Press 1999, 100

Newman, Philip L. *Knowing the Gururumba.* New York: Holt, Rinehart and Winston Case Studies in Cultural Anthropology 1965

O'Connell, Mark and Raje Airey. *The Complete Encyclopedia of Signs & Symbols.* London: Hermes House 2005

O'Grady, Joan. *The Prince of Darkness: The Devil in History, Religion and the Human Psyche.* New York: Barnes & Noble Books 1989

Ogden, Daniel. *Magic, Witchcraft, and Ghosts in the Greek and Roman Worlds.* Oxford: Oxford University Press 2002

Onion, Amanda. "Scientists Find Ancient Hobbit-Sized People." ABC News October 27, 2004. www.abcnews.go.Technology

Opler, Morris Edward. *An Apache Life-Way: The Economic, Social, and Religious Institutions of the Chiricahua Indians.* Chicago: The University of Chicago Press 1941

Osoba, Funmi. *Benin Folklore: A Collection of Classic Folktales and Legends.* London: Hadada Books 1993

Parrinder, Geoffry. "The Witch as Victim" in *The Witch in History,* edited by Venetia Newall. New York: Barnes & Noble 1996, pgs 125-138.

Paul, Pat. "Little People: Geow-Lud-Mo-Sis-Eg." ramseyc@nbnet.nb.ca

Pennick, Nigel. *Celtic Sacred Landscapes.* London: Thames and Hudson 1996

Phillips, Charles. "The Great Preserver" in *The Eternal Cycle: Indian Myth.* New York: Barnes & Noble Books 2005

Philips, David E. *Legendary Connecticut.* Willimantic: Curbstone Press 1992

Philpot, J.H. *The Sacred Tree in Religion and Myth.* Mineola: Dover Publications 2004. A reprint of the 1897 edition published by Macmillan and Co. Ltd., London and New York.

Porteous, Alexander. *The Lore of the Forest.* London: Senate 1996. A Reprint of the 1928 edition published by George Allen & Unwin Ltd., London.

Powers, William K. *Oglala Religion.* Lincoln: University of Nebraska Press 1982

Puckett, Newbell Niles. *Popular Beliefs and Superstitions: A Compendium of American Folklore from the Ohio Collection of Newbell Niles Puckett.* Edited by Wayland D. Hand. Boston: 1981

Radford, Edwin and Mona A. *Encyclopaedia of Superstitions.* New York: The Philosophical Library 1949

Radin, Paul. *The Trickster: A Study in American Indian Mythology.* New York: Schocken Books 1972

Randolph, Vance. *Ozark Magic and Folklore.* New York: Dover Publications, Inc.1964. A reprint of the 1947 edition of *Ozark Superstitions,* published by Columbia University Press.

Rands, Robert L. "Some Manifestations of Water in Mesoamerican Art," *Anthropological Papers,* No. 48, Bureau of American Ethnology Bulletin 157. Washington: Smithsonian Institution 1955, pgs 265-393

Ransome, Hilda M. *The Sacred Bee in Ancient Times and Folklore.* Mineola: Dover Publications, Inc. 2004. A reprint of the 1937 edition published by George Allen & Unwin, London.

Rappoport, Angelo. *The Sea: Myths and Legends.* London: Senate 1995. A reprint of the 1928 edition published by Stanley Paul & Company, London. Originally titled *Superstitions of Sailors.*

Rhys, John. *Celtic Folklore: Welsh and Manx.* New York: Gordon Press 1974. A reprint of the 1901 edition published in Oxford.

St. Leger-Gordon, Ruth E. *The Witchcraft and Folklore of Dartmoor.* New York: Bell Publishing Company 1972

St. Pierre, Mark and Tilda Long Soldier. *Walking in the Sacred Manner.* New York: Touchstone Books 1995

Sahi, Jyoti. *The Child and the Serpent: Reflections on Popular Indian Symbols.* London: Arkana/Penguin Books 1980

Santoso, Dewi and M. Taufiqurrahman. "Archaeologists divided over 'Homo floresiensis" in *The Jakarta Post*, October 30, 2004

Sarangerel (Julie Ann Stewart). *Riding Windhorses: A Journey into the Heart of Mongolian Shamanism.* Rochester: Destiny Books 2000

Saunders, Nicholas J. *Animal Spirits.* London: Duncan Baird Publishers 1997

Schoolcraft, Henry Rowe. *History of the Indian Tribes of the United States: Their Present Condition and Prospects, and a Sketch of their Ancient Status.* Philadelphia: J. B. Lippincott & Co. 1857

Schwartz, Howard. *Lilith's Cave: Jewish Tales of the Supernatural.* New York: Oxford University Press 1988

Service, Elman R. *Profiles in Ethnography.* New York: Harper & Row, Publishers 1963

Shackley, Myra. *Still Living? Yeti, Sasquatch and the Neanderthal Enigma.* New York: Thames and Hudson 1983

Siegel, Brian. "Water Spirits and Mermaids: The Copperbelt Case." Paper presented at the Spring 2000 Southeastern Regional Seminar in African Studies (SERSAS), Western Carolina University, Cullowhee, North Carolina April 14-15, 2000

Silverberg, Robert. *Mound Builders of Ancient America: The Archaeology of a Myth.* Greenwich: New York Graphic Society Ltd. 1968

Simmons, Marc. *Witchcraft in the Southwest: Spanish & Indian Supernaturalism on the Rio Grande.* Lincoln: University of Nebraska Press 1974

Simpson, Jacqueline and Steve Roud. *Oxford Dictionary of English Folklore.* Oxford: Oxford University Press 2000

Skinner, Fred Gladstone. *Myths and Legends of the Ancient Near East.* New York: Barnes & Noble Books 1970

Smith, Charles Hamilton. *The Natural History of the Human Species.* Edinburgh: W.H. Lizars 1848

Smith, William Ramsay. *Aborigine Myths and Legends.* London: Senate 1996. A reprint of the 1930 edition, *Myths & Legends of the Australian Aborigines* published by George G. Harrap, London.

Spence, Lewis. *North American Indians Myths & Legends.* London: Senate 1994. A reprint of *North American Indians* published 1914 by George G. Harrap & Company Ltd.

Spence, Lewis. *Ancient Egyptian Myths and Legends.* New York: Dover Publications, Inc. 1990. A reprint of the 1915 edition published as *Myths & Legends of Ancient Egypt,* published by George G. Harrap & Company, London.

Spence, Lewis. *Legends and Romances of Brittany.* Mineola: Dover Publications Inc. 1997. A reprint of the Frederick A. Stokes Company edition, New York, n.d

Spencer, D.L. "Notes on the Maidu Indians of Butte County" in *Journal of American Folklore,* Vol. 21, 1908, pgs 242-245

Spier, Leslie. *Yuman Tribes of the Gila River.* New York: Dover Publications, Inc. 1978. A reprint of the 1933 edition published by the University of Chicago Press.

Stone, Brian. "The Common Enemy of Man," in *Sir Gawain and the Green Knight,* trans. by Brian Stone. London: Penguin Books 1974

Stone, Merlin. *When God Was A Woman.* New York: Barnes & Noble Books 1993

Storaker, Joh. Th. "Sygdom og Forgjo/relse i den Norske Folketro," in *Norske Folkemin-nelag* #20, Oslo 1932

Sturluson, Snorri. *Edda.* London: J.M. Dent 1987

Summers, Montague. *The Werewolf in Lore and Legend.* Mineola: Dover Publications, Inc. 2003. A reprint of the 1933 edition published by Kegan Paul, Trench, Trubner & Co., Ltd., London

Swan, Harry Percival. *Highlights of the Donegal Highlands.* Belfast: H.R. Carter Publications LTD. 1955

Thompson, C.J.S. *The Hand of Destiny: Folklore and Superstitions for Everyday Life.* New York: Bell Publishing Company 1989. A reprint of the 1932 edition published by Rider & Company, London.

Thompson, Dr. C.J.S. *Mystery and Lore of Monsters.* New York: Barnes& Noble 1994

Thomsen, Marie-Louise. "Witchcraft and Magic in Ancient Mesopotamia" in *Witch-craft and Magic in Europe: Biblical and Pagan Societies.* Edited by Bengt Ankarloo and Stuart Clark. Philadelphia: University of Pennsylvania Press 2001, pgs 1-91

Titcomb, Margaret. *Dog and Man in the Ancient Pacific.* Honolulu: Bernice P. Bishop Museum Special Publication 59, 1969

Tresidder, Jack. *Symbols and Their Meanings.* London: Duncan Baird Publishers 2000

Unterman, Alan. *Dictionary of Jewish Lore & Legend.* New York: Thames and Hudson 1991

Varner, Gary R. *Sacred Wells: A Study in the History, Meaning, and Mythology of Holy Wells & Waters.* Baltimore: Publish America 2002

Varner, Gary R. *Water of Life Water of Death: The Folklore and Mythology of Sacred Waters.* Baltimore: Publish America 2004

Walker, Barbara G. *The Women's Encyclopedia of Myths and Secrets.* Edison: Castle Books 1983

Walker, James R. *Lakota Belief and Ritual.* Lincoln: University of Nebraska Press 1991

Webb, William S. and David L. DeJarnette. *An Archaeological Survey of Pickwick Basin in the Adjacent Portions of the States of Alabama, Mississippi and Tennessee.* Bureau of American Ethnology Bulletin 129. Washington: The Smithsonian Institution 1942

Werner, E.T.C. *Myths and Legends of China.* New York: Dover Publications, Inc. 1994. A reprint of the 1922 edition published by George G. Harrap & Co., Ltd., London.

Westervelt, William D. *Myths and Legends of Hawaii.* Honolulu: Mutual Publishing 1987

Westervelt, William D. *Hawaiian Legends of Ghosts and Ghost Gods.* Honolulu: Mutual Publishing 1998. A reprint of an edition originally published in 1916.

Westwood, Jennifer. *Albion: A Guide to Legendary Britain.* London: Paladin Grafton Books 1985

Wherry, Joseph H. *Indian Masks & Myths of the West.* New York: Bonanza Books 1969

White, Beatrice. "Cain's Kin" in *The Witch in History,* ed. by Venetia Newall. New York: Barnes & Noble 1996, pgs 188-199

White, David Gordon. *Myths of the Dog-Man.* Chicago: The University of Chicago Press 1991

Whitley, David S. *A Guide to Rock Art Sites: Southern California and Southern Nevada.* Missoula: Mountain Press Publishing Company 1996

Wilbert, Johannes. *Yupa Folktales.* Latin American Studies Volume 24. Los Angeles: Latin American Center, University of California 1974

Wilkinson, Richard H. *The Complete Gods and Goddesses of Ancient Egypt.* New York: Thames & Hudson 2003

Wilde, Lady. *Irish Cures, Mystic Charms & Superstitions.* New York: Sterling Publishing Co. Inc. 1991

Zigmond, Maurice L. "The Supernatural World of the Kawaiisu" in Thomas C. Blackburn (ed.) *Flowers of The Wind: Papers on Ritual, Myth, And Symbolism in California and the Southwest.* Socorro: Ballena Press 1977

Zigmond, Maurice L. *Kawaiisu Mythology: An Oral Tradition of South-Central California.* Ballena Press Anthropological Papers No. 18. Menlo Park: Ballena Press 1980

Zimmer, Heinrich. Ed. by Joseph Campbell. *Myths and Symbols in Indian Art and Civilization.* Princeton: Princeton University Press-Bollinger Series VI, 1946

# INDEX

## T

## U

## V

## W

## Y